THE MACMILLAN COMPANY
NEW YORK · CHICAGO
DALLAS · ATLANTA · SAN FRANCISCO
LONDON · MANILA

IN CANADA
BRETT-MACMILLAN LTD.
GALT, ONTARIO

The Vocab

The Vocabulary of the Church

A Pronunciation Guide

by

RICHARD C. WHITE

NEW YORK
The Macmillan Company
1960

First Printing

The Macmillan Company, New York
Brett-Macmillan Ltd., Galt, Ontario

Printed in the United States of America

Library of Congress catalog card number: 60–11810

Deep appreciation is expressed to the faculty of The College of the Bible, Lexington, Kentucky, for its assistance in shaping this book. Particular acknowledgment must be made of the contributions of Professor Roscoe M. Pierson, Librarian, and Mrs. Roland Jones, typist.

Introduction

PURPOSE

It is the purpose of this dictionary to provide a guide to the pronunciation of the language of the Church. There are many excellent dictionaries of religion which give the reader definition and interpretation of biblical and theological words, and others which give biographical information on the men whose names are important to the Church. Unfortunately, few of these have pronunciation guides, and those which do are likely either to be specialized to one area of study or to be out of date in content or pronunciation. Therefore, when the pastor or church school teacher or theological student desires to discover the pronunciation of a given word, he may have to search in a number of reference works to find it. And if the library at his disposal is modest, it is not unlikely that he may fail to find it at all. Few pastors' studies are equipped with *Webster's International Critical Dictionary* or the *Century Cyclopedia of Names.*

It is the aim of this dictionary, therefore, to collect the pronunciations available in many different reference works and present them in a single volume. Further, its aim is to edit these pronunciations in the light of current professional usage and to add to them many words of current importance (particularly proper names), which have not yet found their way into reference works that give pronunciation.

SCOPE

The basic rule in determining the content of this work has been inclusiveness; an exhaustive job of collection has been attempted. Specifically, the basic areas of content are as follows:

(1) All biblical person and place names are listed (including their variant forms in the Authorized Version, Revised Version, and Revised Standard Version).

(2) Other biblical words of importance to the vocabulary of the Church are included (particularly all transliterations of words from the biblical languages, and obsolete or obsolescent words found in the older English translations which puzzle the Bible reader).

(3) Person and place names important to the history, ecclesiology, and doctrine of the Church are included with all the thoroughness of standard reference works in these fields. In addition, many contemporary names have been included which are not in such reference works.

(4) The "jargon" of Christianity (as distinct from biblical words and person and place names) has been included liberally. As a subarea under this title, there has been included a selection of words from psychology, sociology, music, and philosophy. It is apparent that the Church employs much of the jargon of these fields as it ministers to the modern world; that which it uses with any regularity belongs in a volume entitled *The Vocabulary of the Church.*

To select is to risk mistake. Doubtless mistakes have been made; but it has been the aim of the selection of jargon from other fields to include only those words in rather wide use among church people who are not specialists in any of those other fields.

Limitations of Scope.   Although exhaustiveness has been the rule, some limitations have been set for the sake of keeping the dictionary as compact as possible. They are as follows:

(1) With the exception of the biblical entries, common American or Americanized names have not been included. Few pastors will want to know the pronunciation of "Jones" or "Davis"; therefore such names as are deemed commonly known in American English have not been included.

(2) Much of the jargon of the Church consists of words widely used (albeit with different meanings) all through the culture of America. Unless there were danger of confusion, or unless there existed a different pronunciation in religious usage, such common words were not included.

(3) Related technical language used by a segment of the Church or by other religious groups of interest to the Church has been listed selectively. Specifically, Latin terminology of interest basically to the Roman Church, and Hebrew terminology in use in that faith but of only nominal interest to Christianity, have been included spar-

ingly. The same is true for the jargon of the other world religions. Selection has been made here, as elsewhere, on the basis of use by Church people who are not specialists in the indicated fields.

STANDARD OF PRONUNCIATION

Since this work is to serve as a guide to the pronunciation of the vocabulary of the American Church, the standard of pronunciation is American religous usage. The dictionary has, in places, departed from *Webster's International Critical Dictionary* because that work reports international, not exclusively American, pronunciations. It has, in other places, departed from foreign language pronunciations for the same reason, that is, Americanized pronunciations are in general use. The dictionary attempts to present that usage which is accepted by churchmen, pastors, students, scholars, and lay members of the American Church.

Regional Variants. No attempt has been made to present the pronunciations of regional variations. The pronunciations found herein are those used in "General American English." That Southern or Eastern or Mountain variations are not reported here does not imply that those variant usages are incorrect. It does recognize that the majority usage in the United States is "General American," and that to include all regional variants would be to undertake a highly technical task far beyond the scope or intent of this dictionary.

Biblical Words. It is not the aim of this dictionary to furnish an accurate guide to the pronunciation of Hebrew and Greek words; rather, it presents the American English pronunciation of such Hebrew and Greek words as are to be found in English translations of the Bible. As a Hebrew word "Saul" would be pronounced something like "sha ool"; but as the word appears in our English Bibles, it is pronounced "sawl."

By virtue of hundreds of years of usage, reinforced constantly by pronouncing Bibles and reference works, such Anglicizing and Americanizing of biblical words has become too well established in the speech of church people to be shaken by the claim that it is not representative of the native language pronunciation.

Therefore, the student or scholar of biblical language may be dismayed by some of the pronunciations listed herein, particularly those for more obscure words of Hebrew or Greek origin which he does not frequently hear Anglicized. But it must be remembered that the lay reader of the Bible, the local pastor, the church school teacher have for scores of years used these words as they are presented in self-pronouncing Authorized and Revised Versions of the Bible and in popular reference works. It is well and good for the language student to be aware of native language pronunciation, and to use it as such at his discretion, but the vast membership of the English-speaking Church of the past centuries has Anglicized and Americanized biblical words. And self-pronouncing Bibles continue to perpetuate the practice. This dictionary presents those Americanized pronunciations which are in wide usage by church people. The language scholar will need no pronunciation guide when he desires to employ native language pronunciation for biblical words.

The dictionary departs from this principle at one point. From time to time, certain biblical words receive increased attention from contemporary writers and preachers. By virtue of this attention, the whole Church begins to become aware of a pronunciation for such words which approximates the native language pronunciation. These changes are slow to find their way into general dictionaries. For instance, the English transliteration of the Greek word *agape* is pronounced in Webster and older reference works "AG uh pi," but in modern usage, due to recent attention focused on the word, it is often "ah GAH pay" or "AH gah pay." All three pronunciations are listed for this word; and there are numerous other such occurrences.

Foreign Person and Place Names. The argument about whether to Anglicize or pronounce a proper name in its native language will survive this dictionary, and perhaps many others. Many Americans show some desire to retain native language pronunciations, even though this is often impossible because sounds are required which are not present in their speech.

For this dictionary, a decision has been made which probably deserves to be called arbitrary. The rule has been to present something approximating foreign language pronunciation in only two cases, as follows:

(1) For such words as are stable items of the American vocabulary in their native language form (or in some form approximating

it), that pronunciation is presented. For instance, although many Americans named Wagner pronounce their names "WAG nur," any relatively cultured American will call the great musician "VAHG nur." Such words are presented thus in a manner approximating their native language pronunciation.

(2) Some relatively obscure persons and places whose names have not been in wide enough use to have been Anglicized are presented in a form approximating their native language pronunciation (as one hears them used by scholars) rather than presenting some attempt by the author to Anglicize them. For instance, "Valence," a French city in which an important council was held, is so seldom heard in common parlance that it has not been Americanized and is pronounced "vah LONS," whereas "Valdez," a Spanish proper name, is often enough used in English that it has been Anglicized to "VAL dez," though it would be something like "vahl DAYS" in Spanish. In many such cases as the latter, both pronunciations have been presented.

To state the general rule in another way: Anglicized forms of proper names are presented in all cases for which such a form is in rather wide use in the American Church. In some cases where both Anglicized and foreign pronunciations are in use, both are listed. It should be emphasized, however, that no attempt has been made to pronounce names in their native languages simply because they are obviously of foreign rootage.

PRONUNCIATION SYSTEM

Probably the most accurate method of presenting the pronunciation of words is to present them in the International Phonetic Alphabet, narrowly transcribed. But relatively few people are equipped to use this excellent system. A system of diacritical marks, such as that used by Webster and others, might serve adequately for this dictionary. However, it is often said that the diacritical system is needlessly involved, since it may represent the same sound in several different ways, and requires the memorization of a rather involved system of markings.

In view of these factors, it has been found desirable by many authors of dictionaries, word lists, and newspaper columns to use a simplified spelling system. Such a system is used in this dictionary.

The spelling system used here is roughly phonetic. That is, with a few minor technical exceptions, a given sound in spoken English is always represented here by a single letter or combination of letters and never by any other. By the same token, a given letter used in this system always stands for the same sound in spoken English. Thus, the duplication of ways of representing a sound (which is found in the diacritical system) is avoided, and fewer letter symbols need be remembered in order to use the system with ease.

The system used in this dictionary is similar to that found in the *NBC Handbook of Pronunciation*, which is something of a standard volume for use in radio and television, and which has been well accepted by professional people in speech.

Explanation of the Symbols. The majority of the letters used for consonant sounds in American English represent only one sound so far as most of their use is concerned. These letters, which are relatively constant in phonetic value, are therefore used in this system to represent their usual sounds, as follows:

p	as in pity	*s*	as in sang
b	as in bee	*z*	as in zebra
t	as in tooth	*h*	as in how
d	as in dish	*m*	as in more
k	as in kitchen	*n*	as in no
g	as in go	*l*	as in let
f	as in full	*r*	as in run
v	as in vision	*y*	as in yet
j	as in jump	*w*	as in went

It will be noted that the letters *c*, *q*, and *x* are omitted; they do not have stable pronunciations which are distinct from the other letters. C can be either *s* or *k*; *q* accompanied by *u* is the same as *kw*; and *x* is usually pronounced *ks*.

The stable consonant sounds listed above do not exhaust the consonant sound vocabulary of English. In addition to those listed sounds, there are consonants spelled in less stable ways or spelled with more than one letter. A list of them, with the symbols used to represent them, follows:

th   is the voiceless, or whispered *th* sound (θ in the International Phonetic Alphabet), as used in the words *th*ick, a*th*wart, and ba*th*.

th̲   is the voiced, or sonant *th* sound (ð in IPA), as used in the words *th*en, ra*th*er, and ba*th*e.

sh   is the sound usually associated with these two letters (ʃ in IPA), as used in the words *sh*oe, bu*sh*el, and mu*sh*.

zh   is the voiced counterpart of the *sh* sound (ʒ in IPA), as used in the words azure and garage. It does not occur in the initial position in English words.

th   is the sound usually associated with these two letters (tʃ in IPA), as used in the words *ch*icken, but*ch*er, and cat*ch*.

ng   is the sound usually associated with these two letters in the -*ing* ending (ŋ in IPA), as used in the words si*ng*er and ri*ng*. It does not occur in the initial position in English words.

hw   is the sound usually associated with the letters *wh* (ʍ in IPA), as used in the words *wh*en and *wh*ile. It does not occur in the final position in English words.

The vowel and diphthong sounds of English are represented in the system by the symbols which follow:

ee   is the long vowel used in the word b*ee* (i in IPA).

i   is the short vowel used in the word p*i*ck. It is also used to represent the variants between ee and i, such as the varying pronunciations of the y ending in words such as pity, or the medial sounds such as the second vowel in the word visit (ɪ in IPA).

e   is the short vowel used in the word y*e*t (ɛ in IPA).

ay   is both the shorter vowel used in the word r*a*te (e in IPA), and the diphthong used in the word s*a*y (eɪ in IPA).

a   is the "flat *a*" sound used in the word h*a*t (æ in IPA).

oo   is the long vowel used in the word y*ou* (u in IPA).

u   is the short vowel used in the word p*u*t (ʊ in IPA).

o   is both the short vowel used in the word o*b*ey (o in IPA), and the diphthong used in the word l*o*w (oʊ in IPA).

aw   is the long vowel used in the word s*aw* (ɔ in IPA).

ah   is the "broad *a*" sound used in the word f*a*ther (ɑ in IPA).

ur   is both the long vowel used in the word t*ur*n (ɝ in IPA), and the short, inverted indeterminate vowel used in the word moth*er* (ɚ in IPA).

uh   is both the long, accented vowel used in the word th*u*mb (ʌ in IPA), and the short, unaccented, indeterminate vowel used in the word *a*bout (ə in IPA). These will be differentiated in that the unaccented will be in lower-case letters and the accented in capitals.

igh   is the diphthong used in the word s*igh* (aɪ in IPA).
ow   is the diphthong used in the word c*ow* (au in IPA).
oy   is the diphthong used in the word b*oy* (ɔɪ in IPA).

It will be noted by students of phonetics that no provision has been made for the sounds represented by the IPA symbols (ɒ) and (a), or for the variously named "short diphthongs" or "centering diphthongs" represented by the IPA symbols (ɪə, ɛə, uə, ɔə).

Since there are wide variations in the use of (ɒ), and in many sections of the country either (a) or (ɔ) is used in its stead, and since no distinctive way of representing the sound is at hand, it is usually represented in the entries by giving the reader a choice between *ah* and *aw*, that is, between (a) and (ɔ).

Since (a) is used in the speech of so few Americans except as a component part of the diphthongs (aɪ) and (au), and is generally dropped to (æ), it is represented here simply by *a*, that is by (æ). It is assumed that those schooled in its production as a single speech sound will also be schooled in the rules for its occurrence in sound combinations and will use it at their discretion according to that knowledge.

In order to keep the system as uncomplicated as possible, the "centering" or "short" diphthongs are represented by the symbols for their initial components followed by *r*, since this is roughly as they occur in General American English. Thus (ɪə) is *ir*; (ɛə) is *er*; (uə) is *oor* or *ur* (a seemingly unavoidable overlap with the inverted, indeterminate vowel occurs here); and (ɔə) is *or*.

Stress or Accent.   In this system primary stress is shown by capitalizing the letters in the syllable. Secondary and tertiary stress are shown by italicizing the letters in the syllable. Thus "commandment" is represented as "kuh MAND muhnt," and "anagram" is represented as "AN uh *gram*."

Order of Variant Pronunciations.   Only pronunciations in rather wide use have been included in the dictionary. Therefore, it is scarcely proper to indicate that one may be a preferred and another a second pronunciation. Though two or more pronunciations are listed after an entry, it should not be assumed that the one occurring first is preferred.

The Vocabulary of the Church

Aalar   AY uh lahr

Aaron   ER uhn

Aaronic   e RAHN ik

Aaronite   ER uhn ight

Ab   AHB, AB

Abacuc   AB uh kuhk

Abaddon   a BAD uhn, uh-

Abadias   *ab* uh DIGH uhs

Abagarus   a BAG uh ruhs, uh-

Abagtha   uh BAG thuh

Abalard   AB uh lahrd

Abanah   AB uh nuh

Abarim   AB uh rim

Abattachim   a BAT uh kim, uh-

Abauzit   a bo ZEET

Abba   AB uh

Abbadic   a ba DEE

Abbas   AB uhs

abbé   a BAY

abbess   AB uhs

abbey   AB i

Abbo   AB o

abbot   AB uht

abbreviator   uh BREE vi *ay* tur

Abda   AB duh

Abdas   AB duhs

Abdeel   AB di el

Abdi   AB digh

Abdias   ab DIGH uhs

Abdiel   AB di el

Abdon   AB dahn

Abecedarian   *ay* bee see DAR i uhn

à Becket   uh BEK it, -uht

Abednego   uh BED ni go

Abel   AY buhl

Abelard   AB uh lahrd

Abel-beth-maacah   *ay* buhl beth MAY uh kuh

Abel-cheramim   ay buhl KER uh mim

Abelite   AY buhl ight

Abel-machea   *ay* buhl MAY kee uh

Abel-maim   *ay* buhl MAY im

Abelmea   AY buhl *me* uh

Abel-meholah   *ay* buhl mi HO luh

Abel-mizraim   *ay* buhl MIZ ray im

Abel-shittim   *ay* buhl SHIT tim

Abenezra   *a* buhn EZ rah, -ruh

Abercrombie   AB ur *krahm* bi, -*kruhm* bi

Aberdeen   *ab* ur DEEN, AB ur deen

KEY: b*ee*, b*i*t, b*e*t, b*ay*, b*a*t, b*oo*t, b*u*tcher, b*o*ne, s*aw*, *ah*, t*ur*n, *uh* h*uh*, s*igh*, c*ow*, b*oy*, *th*in, *th* in *th*en, *sh*oe, *zh* in a*z*ure, *ch*op, si*ng*, *hw* in *wh*en.

1

Abernethy *ab* ur NEE thi,
-NETH i
abeyance uh BAY uhns
Abez AY bez, -buhz
Abgar AB gahr
Abgarus ab GAY ruhs, AB guh
ruhs
Abi AY bigh
Abia uh BIGH uh
Abiah uh BIGH uh
Abi-albon *ab* i AL bahn
Abiasaph uh BIGH uh saf
Abiathar uh BIGH uh thahr,
ab i AY thahr
Abib AY bib
Abida uh BIGH duh
Abidah uh BIGH duh
Abidan uh BIGH dan, -duhn,
AB i dan, -duhn
Abiel AY bi el, AB yel, a BIGH
el, uh-
Abiezer ab i EE zur, ay bi EE
zur
Abiezrite ab i EZ right, ay bi
EZ right
Abigail AB i gayl
Abigal AB i gal, -guhl
Abihail AB i hayl, -hay il
Abihu uh BIGH hyoo
Abihud uh BIGH huhd
Abijah uh BIGH juh
Abijam uh BIGH jam, -juhm
Abila AB i luh, -uh luh
Abilene *ab* i LEE nee, -ni, *ab*
uh-
Abimael uh BIM ay el, -i el

Abimelech uh BIM uh lek
Abinadab uh BIN uh dab
Abinoam uh BIN o uhm
Abiram uh BIGH ram, -ruhm
Abiron uh BIGH rahn, -ruhn
Abisei ab i SEE igh
Abishag AB i shag
Abishai uh BISH ay igh, AB i
shigh
Abishalom uh BISH uh lahm
Abishua uh BISH yoo uh
Abishur uh BIGH shur
Abissei uh BIS ee igh
Abisue uh BIS yoo ee
Abisum uh BIGH suhm, AB i
suhm
Abital uh BIGH tuhl, AB i tal,
-tuhl
Abitub uh BIGH tuhb, AB i
tuhb
Abiud uh BIGH uhd
abjuration *ab* ju RAY shuhn
ablution uhb LOO shuhn
Abner AB nur
abnormal ab NAWR ml
abomination uh *bahm* i NAY
shuhn
abortion uh BAWR shuhn
Abrabanel *a* vra va NEL
Abraham AY bruh *ham*
Abrahamic ay bruh HAM ik
Abrahamite AY bruh *ham* ight
Abrahamitic *ay* bruh ham IT ik
Abrahams AY bruh *hamz*
Abram AY bruhm
Abraxas uh BRAK suhs

KEY: bee, bit, bet, bay, bat, boot, butcher, bone, saw, ah, turn, uh huh, sigh,
cow, boy, thin, th in then, shoe, zh in azure, chop, sing, hw in when.

Abrech   AY brek, AB rek
Abronah   a BRO nuh, uh-
Absalom   AB suh lahm, -luhm
Absalon   AB suh lahn, -luhn
Absalon (Axel)   AP suh lawn
absinthium   ab SIN thi uhm
absolute   AB so lyoot, -loot
absolution   ab so LYOO shuhn,
   -LOO shuhn
abstemii   ab STEE mi igh
abstinence   AB stuh nuhns
abstinent   AB stuh nuhnt
Abubus   uh BYOO buhs
Abulfaraj   uh bul fa RAJ
Abuna   uh BOO nuh
Abyssinia   ab uh SIN i uh
Abyssinian   ab uh SIN i uhn
acacia   uh KAY shuh
Acacian   a KAY shuhn, uh-
Acacius   uh KAY shuhs
a cappella   AH kuh PEL uh
Acatan   AK uh tan, -tuhn
acatholic   ay KATH o lik, uh
   lik
Accaba   AK uh buh, ak AY buh
Accad   AK ad, -uhd
Accadian   uh KAY di uhn
Accaron   AK uh rahn
accelerando   ak sel ur AN do,
   ah chel uh RAHN do
accent   AK sent
acceptance   ak SEP tuhns
acceptant   ak SEP tuhnt
acceptilation   ak sep ti LAY
   shuhn
accession   ak SESH uhn

Accho   AK o
accident   AK suh duhnt
accidental   ak suh DEN t'l
accidie   AK si dee
acclimatization   uh kligh muh
   tuh ZAY shuhn, -tigh ZAY
   shuhn
Acco   AK o
accommodation   uh kahm uh
   DAY shuhn
accompaniment   uh KUHM
   puh ni muhnt, uh KUHMP
   ni-
Accos   AK ahs
Accoz   AK ahz
accubation   ak yoo BAY shuhn
acculturation   a KUHL chur ay
   shuhn
accursed   uh KUR suhd,
   -KURST
Aceldama   uh SEL duh muh
Acephali   uh SEF uh li
Achaia   uh KAY yuh, uh KIGH
   uh
Achaian   uh KAY yuhn, uh
   KIGH uhn
Achaicus   uh KAY i kuhs, -uh
   kuhs
Achan   AY kuhn
Achar   AY kahr
Achashdarpenim   ay kash dahr
   PEE nim
Achaz   AY kaz
Achbar   AK bahr
Achbor   AK bawr
Achiacharus   a kigh AK uh ruhs

KEY: bee, bit, bet, bay, bat, boot, butcher, bone, saw, ah, turn, uh huh, sigh,
cow, boy, thin, th in then, shoe, zh in azure, chop, sing, hw in when.

Achias   uh KIGH uhs
achievement   uh CHEEV
  muhnt
Achim   AY kim
Achior   AY ki awr
Achipha   AK i fuh, -uh fuh
Achish   AY kish
Achitob   AK i tahb, -uh tahb
Achmetha   AK me thah, -muh
  thuh
Acho   AK o
Achor   AY kawr
Achsa, Achsah   AK suh
Achsaph   AK saf
Achshaph   AK shaf
Achzib   AK zib
Acipha   AS i fuh, -uh fuh
Acitho, Acithoh   AS i tho,
  -uh tho
Acoemetae   uh SEM i tee
acolyte   AK o light
acosmism   ay KAHZ miz m
Acosta   ah KOS tah, uh KOS
  tuh
acoustic   uh KOOS tik
Acra   AK ruh, AY kruh
Acrabattene   *ak* ruh bat TEE
  nee
Acrabbim   ak RAB im, uhk-
acre   AH kur
acroamatic   *ak* ro uh MAT ik
acrostic   uh KRAWS tik
activism   AK tiv iz m
Acton   AK tuhn
Acua   uh KYOO uh, AK yoo uh
Acub   AY kuhb, AK uhb

Acud   AY kuhd
Ad   AD
Adad   AY dad
Adadah   AD uh duh, uh DAY
  duh
Adadrimmon   *ay* dad RIM
  ahn, -uhn
adagio   uh DAH jo, -ji o
Adah   AY duh
Adaiah   uh DAY yuh, uh
  DIGH uh
Adalbert   AD uhl burt
Adalia   uh DAY li uh, *ad* uh
  LIGH uh
Adam   AD uhm
Adamah   AD uh mah, -muh
adamant   AD uh *mant*
Adamantius   ad uh MAN tyuhs,
  -ti uhs
Adami   AD uh migh
Adami-Nekeb   *ad* uh migh NEE
  keb, -kuhb
Adamite   AD uhm ight
Adams   AD uhmz
Adamson   AD uhm suhn
Adan   AY dan, -duhn
adaptation   ad ap TAY shuhn
Adar   uh DAHR, AY dahr
Adarsa   uh DAHR suh
Adasa   AD uh suh
Adbeel   AD bi el, -beel
Addai   AD igh
Addan   AD uhn
Addar   AD ahr
adder   AD ur
Addi   AD igh

KEY: b*ee*, b*i*t, b*e*t, b*ay*, b*a*t, b*oo*t, b*u*tcher, b*o*ne, s*aw*, *ah*, t*ur*n, *uh* h*uh*, s*igh*,
c*ow*, b*oy*, *th*in, *th* in *th*en, *sh*oe, *zh* in a*zu*re, *ch*op, si*ng*, *hw* in *wh*en.

Addison   AD i sn, -uh sn
Addo   AD o
Addon   AD ahn
Addus   AD uhs
adeism   ay DEE iz m
Adelard   AD uh lahrd
Adelbert   AD uhl burt
Ader   AY dur
Adessenarii   ad es ee NAR i igh,
   -NER i igh
"Adeste Fideles"   ah DES tay
   fi DAY lays, ad ES tee   fi DEE
   leez
ad hoc   AD HAHK
Abiabene   ay di uh BEE nee
adiaphora   ad i AF uh ruh
adiaphorist   ad i AF uh rist,
   -ruhst
Adida   AD i duh, -uh duh
Adiel   AY di el, AD i el
Adin   AY din, -duhn
Adina   AD i nuh, uh DIGH
   nuh
Adino   AD i no, uh DIGH no
Adinu   AD i nyoo
Adinus   AD i nuhs, -uh nuhs
Adite   AD ight
Adithaim   ad i THAY im
adjuration   aj u RAY shuhn
adjustment   uh JUHST muhnt
Adlai   AD lay igh, ad LAY igh
Adler   AD lur, AHD lur
ad libitum   AD LIB uh tuhm
Admah   AD mah
Admatha   AD muh thuh, ad
   MAY thuh

Admin   AD min
admonition   ad mo NISH uhn,
   ad muh-
Adna   AD nuh
Adnah   AD nah
Ado   AD o, AH do
adolescence   ad uhl ES uhns
adolescent   ad uhl ES uhnt
Adonai   ad o NAY igh, uh DO
   nigh, AD o nigh, AHD-
Adonibezek   a do nigh BEE zek
Adonijah   ad o NIGH juh
Adonikam   ad o NIGH kuhm
Adoniram   ad o NIGH ruhm
Adonis   uh DO nis, uh DAHN
   is
adonist   uh DON ist, -uhst
Adoni-zedek   uh do nigh ZEE
   dek
adoptianism   uh DAHP shuhn
   iz m
adoptianist   uh DAHP shuhn
   ist, -uhst
Ador   AY dawr
Adora   uh DO ruh
Adoraim   ad o RAY im
Adoram   uh DO ram, -ruhm
adoration   ad o RAY shuhn
Adra   AY dra, -druh
Adrammelech   uh DRAM uh
   lek
Adramyttium   ad ruh MIT i
   uhm
Adria   AY dri uh
Adrian   AY dri uhn
Adrianist   AY dri uhn ist

KEY: bee, bit, bet, bay, bat, boot, butcher, bone, saw, ah, turn, uh huh, sigh,
cow, boy, thin, th in then, shoe, zh in azure, chop, sing, hw in when.

Adriel   AY dri el, -uhl
Aduel   uh DYOO el, -uhl
Adullam   uh DUHL uhm
Adullamite   uh DUHL uhm
 ight
adultery   uh DUHL tur i
Adummim   uh DUHM im
Advent   AD vent
Adventist   AD vent ist, -uhst
adversary   AD vur *ser* i
advocate   AD vo kuht, -kayt
advowson   ad VOW suhn,
 uhd-
adytum   AD i tuhm
Aëdias   ay i DIGH uhs, ay uh-
Aelfric   AL frik
Aelia   EE li uh
Aelred   AYL ruhd, EL-
Aeneas   ee NEE uhs, uh-
Aenon   EE nahn, -nuhn
aeolian   ee O li uhn
aeon   EE ahn
Aesora   EE saw ruh, -suh ruh
aesthetic   es THET ik
affection   uh FEK shuhn
affinity   uh FIN uh ti
affirmation   *af* ur MAY shuhn
affusion   uh FYOO zhuhn
a fortiori   ay *fawr* shi O ri
Agaba   AG uh buh
Agabus   AG uh buhs
Agade   ah GAH duh, AG uh
 dee
Agag   AY gag
Agagite   AG uh gight, AY gag
 ight

agape   AG uh pee, AH guh pay,
 ah GAH pay, uh-
Agapemone   *ag* uh PEM o nee,
 -uh nee
agapetus   *ag* uh PEE tuhs
Agar   AY gahr
Agarene   AG uh reen
agate   AG uht
Agatha   AG uh thuh
agathology   *ag* uhth AHL o ji,
 -uh ji
Agde   AG dee, AHG duh
Agee   AY gee, AY jee
Aggaba   uh GAY buh, AG uh
 buh
Aggaeus   uh GEE uhs
agglutination   uh *gloo* tuh NAY
 shuhn
aggregation   *ag* ri GAY shuhn,
 ag ruh-
Agia   AY gi uh
Agnellus   *ag* NEL uhs
Agnes   AG nis, -nuhs
Agnoetae   *ag* no EE tee
agnoiology   *ag* noy AHL o ji
agnostic   *ag* NAHS tik
agnosticism   *ag* NAHS tuh siz m
Agnus Dei   AG nuhs DEE igh,
 AHN yoos DAY ee
Agobard   AG o bahrd
Agonizant   AG o *niz* uhnt
agrammatus   uh GRAM uh tuhs
Agrapha   AG ruh fuh
Agricola   uh GRIK o luh, -uh
 luh
Agrippa   uh GRIP uh

KEY: b*ee*, b*i*t, b*e*t, b*ay*, b*a*t, b*oo*t, b*u*tcher, b*o*ne, s*aw*, *ah*, t*ur*n, *uh* h*uh*, s*igh*,
c*ow*, b*oy*, *th*in, *th* in *th*en, *sh*oe, *zh* in a*zu*re, *ch*op, si*ng*, *hw* in *wh*en.

Agrippinus *ag* ri PIGH nuhs
ague AY gyoo
Agur AY gur
Ahab AY hab
Aharah uh HER uh
Aharhel uh HAHR hel
Ahasai uh HAY sigh, uh HAS
  ay igh
Ahasbai uh HAS bigh, -bay igh
Ahasuerus uh *haz* yoo EE ruhs,
  uh *has-*
Ahava uh HAY vuh
Ahaz AY haz
Ahaziah *ay* huh ZIGH uh
Ahban AH ban, -buhn
Aher AY hur
Ahi AY high
Ahiah uh HIGH uh
Ahiam uh HIGH am, -uhm
Ahian uh HIGH an, -uhn
Ahiezer *ay* high EE zur
Ahihud uh HIGH huhd
Ahijah uh HIGH juh
Ahikam uh HIGH kam, -kuhm
Ahilud uh HIGH luhd
Ahimaaz uh HIM ay az, -uh az
Ahiman uh HIGH man, -muhn
Ahimelech uh HIM uh lek
Ahimoth uh HIGH mahth,
Ahinadab uh HIN uh dab
Ahinoam uh HIN o am, -uhm
Ahio uh HIGH o
Ahira uh HIGH ruh
Ahiram uh HIGH ram, -ruhm
Ahiramite uh HIGH ruhm ight
Ahisamach uh HIS uh mak

Ahishahar uh HISH uh hahr,
  uh HIGH-
Ahishar uh HIGH shahr
Ahithophel uh HITH o fel, -uh
  fel
Ahitob uh HIGH tahb
Ahitub uh HIGH tuhb
Ahlab AH lab
Ahlai AH ligh, -lay igh
Ahoah uh HO uh
Ahohite uh HO hight
Aholah uh HO luh
Aholiab uh HO li ab
Aholiah *a* ho LIGH uh
Aholibah uh HO li buh, -luh
  buh
Aholibamah uh *ho* li BAY muh
Ahumai uh HYOO migh, -may
  igh
Ahuzam uh HYOO zam
Ahuzzam uh HUHZ uhm
Ahuzzath uh HUHZ uhth
Ahzai AH zigh
Ai AY igh, IGH
Aiah *ay* IGH uh, AY yuh
Aiath *ay* IGH uhth, AY yath
Aidan AY dn
Aija *ay* IGH juh, IGH juh
Aijalon AY juh lahn
Aijeleth Shahar AY juh leth
  SHAY hahr
Aijeleth hash-Shahar AY juh
  leth hash SHAY hahr
Ailli, Ailly igh EE
Ailred AYL ruhd
Ain AH een, AY in, IGHN

KEY: b*ee*, b*i*t, b*e*t, b*ay*, b*a*t, b*oo*t, b*u*tcher, b*o*ne, s*aw*, *ah*, t*ur*n, *uh* h*uh*, s*igh*,
c*ow*, b*oy*, *th*in, *th* in *th*en, *sh*oe, *zh* in a*z*ure, *ch*op, si*ng*, *hw* in *wh*en.

Ain Karim   AH een kah
REEM, AY in KAR im
Ain Fashka   AY in FASH kuh,
AH een   FAHSH kuh
Ainsworth   AYNZ wurth
Airus   ay IGH ruhs
Aix-la-Chapelle   EKS lah sha
PEL
Ajah   AY juh
Ajalon   AJ uh lahn
Akan   AY kan, -kuhn
Akatan   AK uh tan
Akeldama   uh KEL duh muh
a Kempis   uh KEMP uhs, -is
Akhenaton   *ah* kuh NAH tn
Akhmim   ahk MEEM
Akhnaton   ahk NAH tn
Akiba   a KIGH vah
Akkad   AK uhd, AHK ahd
Akkadian   uh KAY di uhn, uh
KAH
Akkos   AK ahs, -uhs
Akkub   AK uhb
Akrabattine   *ak* ruh ba TIGH ni
Akrabbim   ak RAB im
alabarch   AL uh bahrk
alabaster   AL uh *bas* tur
Alain de Lille   a LAN duh
LEEL
Alameth   AL uh meth, -muhth,
uh LAY meth, -muhth
Alammelech   uh LAM uh lek
Alamoth   AL uh mawth, -moth
alb   ALB
Alba   AL buh
Alban   AHL buhn

Albanenses   *al* buh NEN seez
Alber   AL bur
Albert   AL burt
Alberti   ahl BER tee
Albertist   AL burt ist, -uhst
Albertus Magnus   al BUR tuhs
MAG nuhs
Albigenses   *al* buh JEN seez
Albright   AWL bright
Alcimus   AL si muhs
alcoholism   AL kuh *hawl* iz m
Alcuin   AL kwin
Alden   AWL duhn
Aldhelm   ALD helm, AWLD
helm
Aldrich   AWL drich
Aleander   al i AN der, -dur
Aleandro   *ah* luh AHN dro, *ah*
li-
Alema   AL i muh, -uh muh
Alembert   a lahm BER
Alemeth   AL i meth, -uh meth
aleph   AH luhf
Aleppo   uh LEP o
Alesius   uh LEE si uhs
Alexander   *al* eg ZAN dur
Alexander Nevski   -NEV ski,
-NEF ski
Alexander of Hales   -HAYLZ
Alexandra   *al* eg ZAN druh
Alexandria   *al* eg ZAN dri uh
Alexandrian   *al* eg ZAN dri uhn
Alexandrium   *al* eg ZAN dri
uhm
Alexian   uh LEK si uhn
Alexius   uh LEK si uhs

KEY: b*ee*, b*i*t, b*e*t, b*a*y, b*a*t, b*oo*t, b*u*tcher, b*o*ne, s*aw*, *ah*, t*ur*n, *uh* h*uh*, s*igh*,
c*ow*, b*oy*, *th*in, ŧħ in *th*en, *sh*oe, *zh* in a*z*ure, *ch*op, si*ng*, *hw* in *wh*en.

al fine   ahl FEE nay
Alfred   AL fred, -frid, -fruhd
algedonic   *al* jee DAHN ik
algorithm   AL go rith m
algum   AL guhm
Aliah   uh LIGH uh, AL i uh
Alian   AL i uhn, uh LIGH uhn
aliturgical   al i TUR ji kl
Allacci   ah LAHT chee
Allammelech   uh LAM i lek,
   -uh lek
Allan   AL in, -uhn
Allar   AL ahr
Allatius   uh LAY shi uhs
allegiance   uh LEE juhns
allegory   AL i *go* ri, -*gaw* ri
allegretto   *al* uh GRET o, *ahl*
   le GRAY to
allegro   uh LAY gro, uh LEG ro
Alleine   AL in
alleluia   *al* i LOO yuh, -LYOO
   yuh
Allemeth   AL ay meth, -uh
   meth, uh LAY meth
Allen   AL in, -uhn
allocution   *al* o KYOO zhuhn
Allom   AL ahm, -uhm
Allon   AL ahn, -uhn
Allon-bachuth   *al* uhn BAK
   uhth, -BAY kuhth
Almeida   ahl MAY duh
Almerician   *al* muh RISH uhn
Almeyda   ahl MAY duh
Almighty   awl MIGHT i
Almodad   al MO dad
Almon   AL mahn, -muhn

Almon-diblathaim   *al* mahn *dib*
   luh THAY im
almoner   AL muhn ur, AH
   muhn ur
alms   AHMZ
almuce   AL myoos
almug   AL muhg
Alnathan   AL na than, -nuh
   thuhn
aloe   AL o
Alogi   AL o jigh
Alogian   uh LO ji uhn
Alombrado   *ah* luhm BRAY do
Aloth   AY lahth
Aloysius Gonzaga   *al* o ISH uhs
   gon ZAH gah
alpha   AL fuh
Alphaeus   al FEE uhs
alphitomancy   al FIT o *man* si
Alphonso   al FAHN so, -zo
Alphonsus of Liguori   al FAHN
   suhs lee GWAW ree
Altaneus   *al* tuh NEE uhs
altar   AWL tur
Al-Tasheth   al TASH eth, -uhth
Al-Tashheth   al TASH heth
alto   AL to
altruism   AL troo iz m
Alumbrado   *ah* luhm BRAY do
Alush   AY luhsh
Alva   AL vuh, AHL vah
Alvah   AL vuh
Alvan   AL vuhn
Alvarez   AHL vah rayz, -rays,
   AL vuh rez
Amad   AY mad, -muhd

KEY: b*ee*, b*i*t, b*e*t, b*ay*, b*a*t, b*oo*t, b*u*tcher, b*o*ne, s*aw*, *ah*, t*ur*n, *uh* h*uh*, s*igh*,
c*ow*, b*oy*, *thin*, *th* in *then*, *sh*oe, *zh* in a*z*ure, *ch*op, si*ng*, *hw* in *wh*en.

Amadatha   uh MAD uh thuh
Amal   AY mal
Amalarius   am uh LAR i uhs,
   -LER i uhs
Amalek   AM uh lek
Amalekite   AM uh lek ight, uh
   MAL uh kight
amalgamation   uh *mal* guh
   MAY shuhn
Amalric   uh MAL rik
Amalrician   *am* uhl RISH uhn
Amam   AY mam, -muhm
Aman   AY man, -muhn
Amana   uh MAY nuh, uh MAH
   nuh, uh MAN uh
Amandus   uh MAN duhs
Amariah   *am* uh RIGH uh
Amarias   *am* uh RIGH uhs
Amasa   AM uh suh, uh MAY
   suh
Amasai   uh MAS ay igh, uh
   MAY sigh
Amashsai   uh MASH sigh
Amasiah   *am* uh SIGH uh
Amath   AY math, -muhth
Amatheis   *am* uh THEE is, -uhs
Amathis   AM uh this
Amaury   a MAW ri, ah mo
   REE
Amaziah   *am* uh ZIGH uh
ambo   AM bo
Ambrose   AM broz
Ambrosian   am BRO zi uhn,
   -zhuhn
Ambrosiaster   am *bro* zi AS tur
ambry   AM bri

ambulatory   AM byoo luh *to* ri,
   -taw ri
amen   AY MEN, AH MEN
amerce   uh MURS
Ames   AYMZ
Amharic   am HAR ik, -HER ik
Ami   AY migh, AH mee
Amiatine   AM i uh *tighn*
amice   AM is, -uhs
Aminadab   uh MIN uh dab
Amittai   uh MIT igh, -ay igh
Ammah   AM uh
Amman   AH mahn, uh MAN
Ammi   AM igh
Ammianus Marcellinus   *am* i
   AY nuhs   *marh* suh LIGH
   nuhs
Ammidioi   uh MID i oy
Ammidoi   AM i doy
Ammiel   AM i el
Ammihud   uh MIGH huhd,
   AM i huhd
Ammihur   uh MIGH hur
Amminadab   uh MIN uh dab
Amminadib   uh MIN uh dib
Ammisaddai   *am* i SAD igh, -ay
   igh
Ammishaddai   *am* i SHAD igh
Ammizabad   uh MIZ uh bad,
   uh MIGH zuh bad
Ammon   AM ahn, -uhn
Ammonite   AM ahn ight, -uhn
   ight
Ammonitess   AM ahn *ight* es,
   -is, AM uhn-
Ammonius   uh MO ni uhs

KEY: b*ee*, b*i*t, b*e*t, b*ay*, b*a*t, b*oo*t, b*u*tcher, b*o*ne, s*aw*, *ah*, t*ur*n, *uh* h*uh*, s*igh*,
c*ow*, b*oy*, *th*in, t*h* in t*h*en, *sh*oe, *zh* in a*zh*ure, *ch*op, si*ng*, *hw* in *wh*en.

Amnon   AM nahn, -nuhn
Amok   AY mahk
Amon   AY mahn
amoral   ay MAWR uhl
Amorite   AM o right, -uh right
Amos   AY mahs, -muhs
Amoz   AY mahz
Amphibalum   am FIB uh luhm
amphibalus   am FIB uh luhs
amphiboly   am FIB o li, -uh li
Amphilochius   *am* fi LO ki uhs
Amphipolis   am FIP o lis, -uh
    luhs
amphora   AM fuh ruh
Amplias   AM pli uhs
Ampliatus   am pli AY tuhs
ampulla   am PUHL uh
Amram   AM ram
Amramite   AM ram ight, -ruhm
    ight
Amraphel   AM ruh fel, am
    RAY fel
Amsdorf   AHMZ dawrf
Amsterdam   AM stur *dam*
amulet   AM yuh let, -lit, -luht
Amurru   uh MUR oo
Amyot   a MYO
Amyraut   a mee RO
Amzi   AM zigh
Anab   AY nab
Anabaptist   *an* uh BAP tist,
    -tuhst
anachoret   uh NAK o ret
Anacletus   *an* uh KLEE tuhs
Anael   AN ay el, -i el
anagnostes   *an* ag NAHS teez

anagogic   *an* uh GAHJ ik
anagogical   *an* uh GAHJ i kl
Anah   AY nuh, AN uh
Anaharath   uh NAY huh rath
Anaiah   uh NIGH uh
Anak   AY nak
Anakim   AN uh kim
analogy   uh NAL o ji, -uh ji
Anamim   AN uh mim
Anammelech   uh NAM uh lek
anamnesis   *an* am NEE sis,
    -suhs
Anan   AY nan
Anani   uh NAY nigh
Ananiah   *an* uh NIGH uh
Ananias   *an* uh NIGH uhs
Ananiel   uh NAN i el, -uhl
anaphora   uh NAF o ruh, -uh
    ruh
anarchism   AN ur kiz m
Anastasia   *an* uh STAY zhuh
anastasis   uh NAS tuh sis, -suhs
Anastasius   *an* uh STAY zhuhs
Anath   AY nath
anathema   uh NATH i muh,
    -uh muh
anathema maranatha   -*mar* uh
    NATH uh, *mer*-
Anathoth   AN uh thawth,
    -thoth
Anathothite   AN uh thawth ight
Anatolius   *an* uh TOL i uhs,
    -yuhs
Anaxagoras   *an* aks AG uh ruhs
Anaximander   an AKS uh *man*
    dur

KEY: bee, bit, bet, bay, bat, boot, butcher, bone, saw, ah, turn, uh huh, sigh,
cow, boy, thin, th in then, shoe, zh in azure, chop, sing, hw in when.

Anaximenes *an* aks IM uh
 neez
anchorite ANG kur ight
Ancillon ahn see YAWN
Ancyra an SIGH ruh
andante an DAN ti, ahn
 DAHN ti, -tay
andantino *ahn* dahn TEE no
Anderson AN dur suhn
Andrada ahn DRAH duh
Andrea ahn DRAY uh
Andreas ahn DRAY uhs
Andrew AN droo
Andrewes, Andrews AN drooz
Andronicus *an* dro NIGH kuhs,
 an druh-
Anem AY nem, -nuhm
Aner AY nur
anergy AN ur ji
Anethothite AN i thawth ight,
 AN uh-
Anetothite AN i tawth ight, *an*
 i TAWTH ight, *an* uh-
angel AYN juhl
Angela Merici AHN juh luh
 muh REE chee
Angela of Foligno -fo LEEN
 yo
angelic an JEL ik
angelical an JEL ik l
Angelico ahn JE li ko
Angelites AYN juhl ights
angelus AN juh luhs
Anglican ANG gli kuhn
Anglo ANG glo
Aniam uh NIGH uhm

Anim AY nim
animato *ahn* i MAH to
Animism AN uh miz m
anise AN is, -uhs
ankh ANGK, AHNGK
Annaas AN ay uhs
Annas AN uhs
Annates AN ayts
Anne AN
Annesley ANZ li
annihilation uh *nigh* uh LAY
 shuhn, uh *nigh* huh-
annis AN is, -uhs
anno AN o, AHN o
anno Domini AN o DAHM
 uh nee
annulus AN yoo luhs
annunciation uh *nuhn* si AY
 shuhn
annus AN uhs
Annuus AN yoo uhs
anoetic *an* o ET ik
anoint uh NOYNT
Anomoean *an* o MEE uhn
anorexia *an* o REK si uh
Anos AY nahs
ansarian an SAHR i uhn
Anschar ANS kahr
Anschauung AHN show ung
Anselm AN selm
Ansgar ANS gahr
ante AN tee
antediluvian *an* tee di LYOO
 vi uhn, -LOO vi uhn
antelapsarianism *an* tee lap
 SAR i uhn iz m

KEY: bee, bit, bet, bay, bat, boot, butcher, bone, saw, ah, turn, uh huh, sigh,
cow, boy, thin, th in then, shoe, zh in azure, chop, sing, hw in when.

antependium   an tee PEN di
   uhm
Anthedon   an THEE dahn,
   -duhn
anthem   AN thuhm
Anthony   AN tho ni, -thuh ni,
   -to ni
Anthothijah   *an* tho THIGH
   juh, *an* thuh-
anthropolatry   *an* thro PAHL
   uh tri
anthropology   *an* thro PAHL o
   ji, -uh ji
anthropomorphic   *an* thro po
   MAWR fik
anthropopathism   *an* thro po
   PATH iz m
anthroposophy   *an* thro PAHS o
   fi, -uh fi
anti-   AN ti
Antibaptist   *an* ti BAP tist,
   tuhst
Antiburgher   *an* ti BUR gur
antichrist   AN ti krighst
Anticlericalism   *an* ti KLER i
   kuhl iz m
antilegomena   *an* ti lee GAHM
   i nuh, -uh nuh
Anti-libanus   *an* ti LIB uh nuhs
antilogism   an TIL o jiz m, -uh
   jiz m
Antimarian   *an* ti MAR i uhn,
   -MER i uhn
antimensium   *an* ti MEN si
   uhm
antinomian   *an* ti NO mi uhn

antinomy   an TIN o mi, -uh mi
Antioch   AN ti ahk
Antiochian   *an* ti O ki uhn
Antiochis   an TIGH o kis, -uh
   kuhs
Antiochus   an TIGH o kuhs,
   -uh kuhs
Antiochus Epiphanes   -uh PIF
   uh neez
Antipas   AN ti pas, -tuh puhs
Antipater   an TIP uh tur
Antipatris   an TIP uh tris,
   -truhs
antiphon   AN ti fahn
antiphonal   an TIF o nl, -uh nl
antipope   AN ti pop
anti-Sabbatarian   *an* ti *sab* uh
   TAR i uhn
antithesis   an TITH i sis, -uh
   suhs
Antoine   an TWAHN
Antonelli   *ahn* to NEL li
Antoninus   *an* to NIGH nuhs
Antonio   an TO nyo, -ni o
Antonius   an TO ni uhs
Antony   AN to ni, -tuh ni
anxiety   ang ZIGH uh ti
Apame   uh PAY mi, AP uh mee,
   -mi
a parte ante   ay PAHR tee
   AN tee
a parte post   ay PAHR tee
   POST
apathy   AP uh thi
Apel   AH pel
Apelles   uh PEL eez

KEY: b*ee*, b*i*t, b*e*t, b*ay*, b*a*t, b*oo*t, b*u*tcher, b*o*ne, s*aw*, *ah*, t*ur*n, *uh* h*uh*, s*igh*,
c*ow*, b*oy*, *th*in, *th* in *th*en, *sh*oe, *zh* in a*z*ure, *ch*op, si*ng*, *hw* in *wh*en.

Apharsachite uh FAHR sak
ight, -suh kight
Apharsathchite af ahr SATH
kight
Apharsite uh FAHR sight
aphasia uh FAY zhuh, -zi uh
Aphek AY fek
Aphekah uh FEE kuh
Apherema uh FER i muh, -uh
muh
Apherra uh FER uh
Aphiah uh FIGH uh
Aphik AY fik
Aphrah AF ruh
Aphses, Aphsez AF seez
Apiarius ay pi ER i uhs
Apiru AHP i roo
Apis AY pis, -puhs
apocalypse uh PAHK uh lips
apocalyptic uh pahk uh LIP tik
apocatastasis ap o kuh TAS tuh
sis, -suhs
apocrisiarius ap o kris i AY ri
uhs
Apocrypha uh PAHK ri fuh,
-ruh fuh
apodeipnon ap o DIGHP nahn
apodictic ap o DIK tik
Apollinarian uh pahl i NER i
uhn
Apollinaris uh pahl i NER uhs
Apollinarius uh pahl i NER i
uhs
Apollonia ap o LO ni uh, ap uh-
Apollonius ap o LO ni uhs, ap
uh-

Apollophanes ap o LAHF uh
neez, uh pahl o FAY neez
Apollos uh PAHL os, -uhs
Apollyon uh PAHL yuhn, uh
PAHL i uhn
apologetics uh pahl uh JET iks
apologist uh PAHL o jist, -uh
jist
apology uh PAHL o ji, -uh ji
apolysis uh PAHL uh sis, -suhs
apolytikion ap o li TIK i ahn
apophthegm AP o theem
apostasy uh PAHS tuh si
apostate uh PAHS tayt
a posteriori ay pahs tee ri O
righ, -ri, ah pos-
apostle uh PAHS l
apostolic ap ahs TAHL ik,
ap uhs-
Apostolici ap uhs TAHL i sigh,
-uh sigh
apostolicity uh pahs to LIS uh
ti
apotheosis uh pahth ee O sis,
-suhs
Appaim AP ay im, -i im
apparition ap uh RISH uhn
apparitor uh PAR i tur, uh
PER-
appellant uh PEL uhnt
apperception ap ur SEP shuhn
Apphia AF i uh, AP fi uh
Apphus AF uhs, AP fuhs
Appii Forum AP i igh FO
ruhm
Appleton AP l tuhn, -tn

KEY: bee, bit, bet, bay, bat, boot, butcher, bone, saw, ah, turn, uh huh, sigh,
cow, boy, thin, th in then, shoe, zh in azure, chop, sing, hw in when.

approbation   *ap* ro BAY shuhn

a priori   *ay* pri O righ, *ah* pri
O ree

apse   APS

aptitude   AP tuh tood, -tyood

Apsu   AHP soo

Aquarii   uh KWAR i igh, uh
KWER-

Aquaviva   *ahk* wuh VEE vuh

Aquila   AK wi luh, -wuh luh,
uh KWIL uh

Aquinas   uh KWIGH nuhs

Ar   AHR

Ara   AY ruh

Arab (city of Judah)   AY rab

Arab   AR uhb, ER-

Arabah   AR uh buh, ER-

Arabattine   *ar* uh ba TIGH nee,
er-

Arabia   uh RAY bi uh

Arabian   uh RAY bi uhn

Arabic   AR uh bik, ER-

Araboth   AR uh bahth, ER-

Arad   AY rad

Aradus   AR uh duhs, ER-

Arah   AY ruh

Aram   AY ram, AR uhm, ER-

Aramaean   *ar* uh MEE uhn,
er-

Aramaic   *ar* uh MAY ik, er-

Aram-Dammesek   *ay* ram DAM
uh sek, *ay* ruhm-

Aramean   *ar* uh MEE uhn, er-

Aramite   AR uh might, ER-

Aramitess   AR uh might es, ER-,
-is

Aram-maacah   *ay* ram MAY uh
kuh, *ay* ruhm-

Aram-naharaim   *ay* ram nay huh
RAY im, *ay* ruhm-

Aram-Rehob   *ay* ram REE hahb,
ay ruhm-

Aram-Zobah   *ay* ram ZO bah,
-buh, *ay* ruhm-

Aran   AY ran, -ruhn, AR uhn

Ararat   AR uh rat, ER-

Ararath   AR uh rath, ER-

Arathes   uh RAY theez

Araunah   uh RAW nuh

Arba   AHR buh

Arbatta   *ahr* BAT uh

Arbattis   *ahr* BAT is, -uhs

Arbela   *ahr* BEE luh

Arbite   AHR bight

Arbonai   *ahr* BO nay igh, -ni igh

Arbuthnot, Arbuthnott   *ahr*
BUHTH nuht, AHR buhth
naht

arcade   *ahr* KAYD

arch   AHRCH

archaeology   *ahr* kee AHL o ji,
-uh ji

archangel   AHRK AYN jl

archbishop   AHRCH BISH
uhp

archchaplain   AHRCH CHAP
ln

archdeacon   AHRCH DEE kn

archdiocese   AHRCH DIGH o
sees, -uh sis, -suhs

Archelaus   *ahr* ki LAY uhs

arches   AHR chuhz

KEY: b*ee*, b*i*t, b*e*t, b*a*y, b*a*t, b*oo*t, b*u*tcher, b*o*ne, s*aw*, *ah*, t*ur*n, *uh* h*uh*, s*igh*,
c*ow*, b*oy*, *th*in, *th* in *th*en, *sh*oe, *zh* in a*z*ure, *ch*op, si*ng*, *hw* in *wh*en.

Archevite   AHR ki vight, -kuh
  vight
Archi   AHR kigh
archimandrite   *ahr* ki MAN
  dright, *ahr* kuh-
Archippus   ahr KIP uhs
Archite   AHR kight
architecture   AHR kuh *tek* chur
architrave   AHR ki trayv, -kuh
  trayv
archpresbyter   AHRCH PREZ
  bit ur
archpriest   AHRCH PREEST
arcosolium   *ahr* ko SO li uhm
Ard   AHRD
Ardat   AHRD at
Ardath   AHR dath
Ardite   AHRD ight
Ardon   AHR dahn
Areli   uh REE ligh
Arelite   uh REE light
Areopagite   *ar* i AHP uh jight,
  -gight, *er-*
Areopagus   *ar* i AHP uh guhs,
  er-
Areopolis   *ar* i AHP uh lis, -luhs,
  er-
Ares   AY reez, ER eez
Aretas   AR uh tas, -tuhs, ER-
Argenteus   ahr JEN tee uhs
Argob   AHR gahb
argot   AHR go, -guht
Argyle   AHR gighl
Arian   AR i uhn, ER-
aria   AH ri uh, ER-
Arianism   AR i uhn iz m, ER-

Ariarathes   *ar* i uh RAY theez,
  er-
Arias Montanus   AR i uhs
  MON tuh nuhs, ER-
Aridai   uh RID ay igh, -i igh,
  AR i digh, ER-
Aridatha   uh RID uh thuh, ar i
  DAY thuh, er-
Arieh   uh RIGH uh, AR i e, ER-
Ariel   ER i el, -uhl
arietta   ar i ET uh, -tuh
Arimathaea   *ar* i muh THEE
  uh, *er-*
Arioch   AR i ahk, ER-
arioso   ah RYO so
Arisai   uh RIS ay igh, -i igh, AR
  i sigh, ER-
Aristarchus   *ar* is TAHR kuhs,
  er-
Aristeas   uh RIS ti ahs, *ar* is
  TEE uhs
Aristides   *ar* is TIGH deez, *er-*
Aristobulus   uh *ris* to BYOO
  luhs
Aristotelianism   *ar* is to TEE li
  uhn iz m
Aristotle   AR uh stah tl, ER-
Arius (of Alexandria)   AR i uhs,
  ER-
Arius (of Sparta)   uh RIGH
  uhs, AY ri uhs
ark   AHRK
Arkite   AHR kight
Arles   AHRLZ, AHRL
Armageddon   *ahr* muh GED
  uhn, -n

KEY: b*ee*, b*i*t, b*e*t, b*ay*, b*a*t, b*oo*t, b*u*tcher, b*o*ne, s*aw*, *ah*, t*ur*n, *uh* h*uh*, s*igh*,
c*ow*, b*oy*, *th*in, *th* in *th*en, *sh*oe, *zh* in a*zh*ure, *ch*op, si*ng*, *hw* in *wh*en.

Armagh AHR mah

Armenia ahr MEE ni uh

Armenian ahr MEE ni uhn

Armill AHR mil

Arminianism ahr MIN i uhn iz m

Arminius ahr MIN i uhs

Armoni er MO nigh, ar-

Armstrong AHRM strawng

Arna AHR nuh

Arnan AHR nan

Arnaud ahr NO

Arnauld ahr NO

Arnd, Arndt AHRNT

Arni AHR nigh

Arno AHR no

Arnobius ahr NO bi uhs

Arnold AHR nuhld

Arnold of Brescia -BRAY shuh

Arnold of Villanova -vil uh NO vuh

Arnon AHR nahn

Arnulf AHR nuhlf

Arod AY rahd, ER ahd

Arodite AR uh dight, ER-

Aroer uh RO ur

Aroerite uh RO ur ight

Arom AY rahm, ER ahm

Arpachshad ahr PAK shad

Arpad AHR pad

Arpakhshad ahr PAK shad

arpeggio ahr PEJ i o, -PE jo

Arphad AHR fad

Arphaxad ahr FAK sad, -suhd,

Arriaga ahr RYAH guh

arrow AR o, ER o

Arrowsmith AR o smith, ER-

Arsaces AHR suh seez, ahr SAY seez

Arsareth AHR suh reth, -ruhth

Arhenius ahr SEE ni uhs

Arsiphurith *ahr* si FYOO rith, *ahr* suh FYOO ruhth

Artaxerxes *ahr* tag ZURK seez, *ahr* tak SURK seez, *ahr* tuh ZURK seez

Artemas AHR ti muhs, -tuh muhs

Artemis AHR tuh mis, -muhs

article AHR ti kl

artifact AHR ti *fakt*, -tuh *fakt*

artificer ahr TIF uh sur

Artotyrite *ahr* to TIGH right

Arubboth uh RUHB ahth, -uhth

Aruboth uh ROO both, -bahth

Aruma uh ROO muh

Arundel AR uhn d'l, ER-

Arvad AHR vad

Arvadite AHR vuhd ight

Arza AHR zuh

Arzan AHR zan, zuhn

Arzareth AHR zuh reth

Asa AY suh

Asadias *as* uh DIGH uhs

Asaeas uh SEE uhs

Asael AS ay el, -i el, AY say el, si el

Asahel AS uh hel, AY suh hel

Asahiah *as* uh HIGH uh

Asaiah uh SAY yuh, uh SIGH uh

KEY: bee, bit, bet, bay, bat, boot, butcher, bone, saw, ah, turn, uh huh, sigh, cow, boy, thin, th in then, shoe, zh in azure, chop, sing, hw in when.

Asana   AS uh nuh
Asaph   AS uhf, AY suhf, AY saf
Asara   AS uh ruh
Asarael   uh SAY ray el, -ri el
Asaramel   uh SAR uh mel, uh SER-
Asareel   uh SAY ri el, AS uh reel
Asarel   AS uh rel
Asarelah   *as* uh REE luh
Asbacaphath   as BAK uh fath
Asbasareth   as BAS uh reth, -ruhth
Asbazareth   as BAZ uh reth, -ruhth
Asbury   AZ ber i, -bur i, -bri
Ascalon   AS kuh lahn
ascendance   uh SEN duhns
ascension   uh SEN shuhn
ascent   uh SENT
ascetic   uh SET ik
asceticism   uh SET uh siz m
Aschenaz   ASH i naz, -uh naz
Ascough   AS kyoo
Ascue   AS kyoo
Aseas   uh SEE uhs
Asebebia   uh *seb* uh BIGH uh
Asebebias   uh *seb* uh BIGH uhs
Asebias   *as* i BIGH uhs, *as* uh-
aseity   uh SEE uh ti
Asenath   AS i nath, -uh nath
Aser   AY sur
Aserer   AS uh rur, uh SEE rur
Asgill   AZ gil
Ashan   AY shuhn, ASH uhn
Asharelah   *ash* uh REE luh
Ashbea   ASH bi uh, ash BEE uh

Ashbel   ASH bel
Ashbelite   ASH bel ight, -buh light
Ashdod   ASH dahd
Ashdodite   ASH dahd ight
Ashdothite   ASH dahth ight
Ashdoth-pisgah   ASH dahth PIZ guh
Ashdowne   ASH down, -duhn
Ashe   ASH
Asher   ASH ur
Asherah   uh SHEE ruh, -SHER uh
Asherite   ASH ur ight
ashes   ASH iz, -uhz
Ashhur   ASH ur, AH shoor
Ashima   uh SHIGH muh, ASH i muh, -uh muh
Ashkelon   ASH ki lahn, -kuh lahn
Ashkelonite   ASH kuh *lahn* ight
Ashkenaz   ASH ki naz, -kuh naz, ash KEE naz
ashlar   ASH lur
Ashmead   ASH meed
Ashmun   ASH muhn
Ashnah   ASH nuh
Ashpenaz   ASH pi naz, -puh naz
Ashriel   ASH ri el, -uhl
Ashtaroth   ASH tuh rahth, -rawth, -roth
Ashterathite   ASH tuh rath ight, ash TEE ruh thight
Ashteroth-karniam   *ash* tuh rahth kahr NAY im

KEY: b*ee*, b*i*t, b*e*t, b*ay*, b*a*t, b*oo*t, b*u*tcher, b*o*ne, s*aw*, *ah*, t*ur*n, *uh* h*uh*, s*igh*, c*ow*, b*oy*, *th*in, **th** in *th*en, *sh*oe, *zh* in a*zu*re, *ch*op, si*ng*, *hw* in *wh*en.

Ashton   ASH tuhn
Ashtoreth   ASH to reth, -tuh reth
Ashur (Assyrian deity)   AH shoor
Ashur (Heb. name)   ASH ur
Ashurbanipal   ah shur BAH ni pahl
Ashurite   ASH ur ight
Ashvath   ASH vath
Ashwell   ASH wel, -wuhl
Asiarch   AY shi ahrk
Asibias   as i BIGH uhs, as uh-
Asiel   AY si el, AS i el
Asinaeus   *as* i NEE uhs
Asipha   AS i fuh, -uh fuh
Askelon   AS kuh lahn
Askew   AS kyoo
Asmodaeus   *az* mo DEE uhs, *as*-
Asmonean   *az* mo NEE uhn, *as*
Asnah   AS nuh
Asnapper   as NAP ur
Asochis   uh SO kis, -kuhs
Asom   AY suhm
Asor   AY sawr
Aspalathus   as PAL uh thuhs
Aspatha   as PAY thuh
Asperges   as PUR jeez
aspergillum   *as* pur JIL uhm
aspersion   uhs PUR shuhn, -zhuhn
Asphaltum   as FAL tuhm
Asphar   AS fahr

Aspharasus   as FAR uh suhs, as FER-
aspirant   uhs PIGH ruhnt, AS puh ruhnt
aspiration   *as* puh RAY shuhn
Asriel   AS ri el, -uhl
ass   AS
Assalimoth   uh SAL i mahth, -mawth, -moth
Assamias   *as* uh MIGH uhs
Assanias   as uh NIGH uhs
Assaphioth   uh SAY fi ahth, -awth, -oth
assarion   uh SAY ri ahn
Assemani   *ahs* uh MAH nee
assembly   uh SEM bli
assent   uh SENT
Asser   AS ur
Asshur   AHS shoor
Asshurim   uh SHOO rim
Assidaean   *as* i DEE uhn, *as* uh-
assimilation   uh *sim* uh LAY shuhn
Assir   AS ur
Assisi   uh SEE zee, see
Assos   AS aws, -ahs
Assuerus   *as* yoo EE ruhs
assumption   uh SUHMP shuhn
Assur   AS ur, -oor
assurance   uh SHUR uhns
Assurbanipal   ah soor BAH ni pahl
Assyria   uh SIR i uh
Assyrian   uh SIR i uhn
Astad   AS tad, -tuhd

KEY: b*ee*, b*i*t, b*e*t, b*a*y, b*a*t, b*oo*t, b*u*tcher, b*o*ne, s*aw*, *ah*, t*ur*n, *uh* h*uh*, s*igh*, c*ow*, b*oy*, *th*in, *th* in *th*en, *sh*oe, *zh* in a*z*ure, *ch*op, si*ng*, *hw* in *wh*en.

Astaroth   AS tuh rahth, -rawth,
-roth
Astarte   as TAHR tee, uhs-
Astath   AS tath, -tuhth
Asteriscus   as tur IS kuhs
Asterius   as TER i uhs, uhs-
Astorga   as TAWR guh, uhs-
Astruc   as TROOK
Astyages   as TIGH uh jees, uhs-
asuppim   a SUHP im, -uhm
Asur   AH soor
asylum   uh SIGH luhm
Asyncritus   uh SING kri tuhs,
-kruh tuhs
Atad   AY tad
atar   AT ahr, -ur
Atarah   AT uh rah
Atargatis   uh TAHR guh tis,
-tuhs
Ataroth   AT uh rahth, -rawth,
-roth
Ataroth-addar   at uh rahth AD
ahr
a tempo   ah TEM po
Ater   AY tur
Aterezaias   uh ter uh ZIGH
uhs
Atergatis   uh TER guh tis,
-tuhs
Ateta   uh TEE tuh
Athach   AY thak
Athaiah   uh THAY yuh, uh
THIGH uh
Athaliah   ath uh LIGH uh
Athanasian   ath uh NAY
zhuhn, -shuhn

Athanasius   ath uh NAY shi
uhs, -shuhs
Atharias   ath uh RIGH uhs
Atharim   ATH uh rim
atheism   AY thee iz m
Athenagoras   ath uh NAG o
ruhs, -uh ruhs
Athenian   a THEE ni uhn,
uh-
Athenobius   ath uh NO bi uhs
Athens   ATH inz, -uhnz
Athlai   ATH lay igh, -li igh,
-ligh
Athos   ATH ahs, AY thahs
Atipha   AT i fuh, -uh fuh
atomism   AT uhm iz m
atonality   ay to NAL uh ti
atone   uh TON
atonement   uh TON muhnt
atrium   A tri uhm, AH-
Atroth-beth-joab   at rahth beth
JO ab, at rawth-, at roth-
Atroth-shophan   AT rath SHO
fan
Attai   AT ay igh, -i igh, -igh
Attalia   at uh LIGH uh
Attalus   AT uh luhs
attention   uh TEN shuhn
Atterbury   AT ur ber i, -bur i
Attharates   uh THAR uh teez,
uh THER-
Attharias   a thuh RIGH uhs
Atticus   AT i kuhs
Attila   AT i luh, -uh luh
attitude   AT uh tyood, -tood
Atto   AT o

KEY: bee, bit, bet, bay, bat, boot, butcher, bone, saw, ah, turn, uh huh, sigh,
cow, boy, thin, th in then, shoe, zh in azure, chop, sing, hw in when.

attribute AT ri byoot (n.),
uh TRIB yoot (v.)
attrition uh TRISH uhn
Atwater AT waw tur, -wah tur
Auberlen AW bur luhn, OW-
Aubertin o bur TAN
Aubigné o bee NYAY
Auburn AW burn
Audean, Audian aw DEE uhn
audience AW di uhns
Audin o DAN, AW duhn
Augian AW gi uhn
augment AWG ment (n.), awg
MENT (v.)
Augsburg AWGZ burg
Augusta aw GUHS tuh, uh-
Augusti aw GUHS ti
Augustine AW guhs *teen*, aw
GUHS tin, -tuhn
Augustinian aw guhs TIN i uhn
Augustus aw GUHS tuhs, uh-
Aulén ow LAYN
aumbry AM bri
Aurandt o RANT
Aurelius aw REE li uhs, -REL
yuhs
aureole AW ree ol
auricular aw RIK yoo lur
Austin AWS tin, -tuhn
Autaeas aw TEE uhs
authoritarian aw *thawr* i TAR i
uhn, -TER i uhn
authorized AW thur ighzd
autism AW tiz m
autistic aw TIS tik
autocephali *aw* to SEF uh li

autocephalous *aw* to SEF uh
luhs
autonomic aw tuh NAHM ik,
-NOM ik
autonomy aw TAHN o mi, -uh
mi
Auvergne o VURN
Auxentius awk SEN ti uhs, awg
ZEN-
Ava AY vuh
Avancini *a* van SEE nee
Avaran AV uh ran
avarice AV uh ris, -ruhs
Ave Maria AH vay mah REE
ah, -uh
Aven AY vuhn
Avenarius *av* uh NER i uhs
avenger uh VEN jur
Avesta uh VES tuh
Avicenna *av* i SEN uh
Avignon a vee NYAWN
Avila ah VEE luh, uh VIL uh
Avim AV im
Avite AY vight
Avith AY vith, -vuhth
Avitus uh VIGH tuhs
Avva AV uh
Avvim AV im
axiological *ak* si o LOJ i kl
axiology ak si AHL o ji, -uh ji
axiom AK si uhm
axiomatic *ak* si uh MAT ik
Axtell AKS tel
Axum ahk SOOM
Aydelott AY duh *laht*
ayin AH yeen, -yin, IGH uhn

KEY: b*ee*, b*i*t, b*e*t, b*ay*, b*a*t, b*oo*t, b*u*tcher, b*o*ne, s*aw*, *ah*, t*ur*n, *uh* h*u*h, s*igh*,
c*ow*, b*oy*, *th*in, *th* in *th*en, *sh*oe, *zh* in a*zure*, *ch*op, si*ng*, *hw* in *wh*en.

Ayliffe   AY lif, IGH lif
Aylmer   AYL mur
Aymon   AY muhn, IGH muhn
Ayscoth   AS kahth
Ayscough   AS kyoo
Azael   AZ ay el, -i el
Azaelus   *az* ay EE luhs, *az* i-
Azal   AY zal
Azaliah   *az* uh LIGH uh
Azaniah   *az* uh NIGH uh
Azaphion   uh ZAY fi ahn
Azara   AZ uh ruh
Azarael   uh ZAH ray el, -ri el,
    az uh RAY el
Azaraias   *az* uh RAY yuhs
Azareel   uh ZAY ri el, AZ uh
    reel
Azarel   AZ uh rel
Azariah   *az* uh RIGH uh
Azarias   *az* uh RIGH uhs
Azaru   AZ uh roo
Azaz   AY zaz
Azazel   uh ZAY zel, AZ uh zel
Azaziah   *az* uh ZIGH uh
Azbasareth   az BAS uh reth,
    -ruhth
Azbazareth   az BAZ uh reth,
    -ruhth
Azbuk   AZ buhk
Azekah   uh ZEE kuh
Azel   AY zel, -zuhl
Azem   AY zem, -zuhm
Azephurith   *az* i FYOO rith, *az*
    uh-, -ruhth
Azetas   uh ZEE tuhs
Azgad   AZ gad

Azia   uh ZIGH uh
Aziei   uh ZIGH i igh
Aziel   AY zi el
Aziza   uh ZIGH zuh
Azmaveth   az MAY veth, AZ
    muh veth
Azmon   AZ mahn
Aznoth-tabor   AZ nahth TAY
    bawr, -bur
Azor   AY zawr
Azotus   uh ZO tuhs
Azriel   AZ ri el
Azrikam   AZ ri kam, az RIGH
    kuhm
Azubah   uh ZYOO buh
Azur   AY zur
Azuran   AZ yoo ran, a ZYOO
    ran, -ruhn
azymite   AZ i might
Azzah   AZ uh
Azzan   AZ an, -uhn
Azzur   AZ ur

Baader   BAH dur
Baal   BAY uhl
Baalah   BAY uh luh
Baalath   BAY uh lath
Baalath-beer   BAY uh luhth
    BEE ur
Baalbek   BAHL bek, *bahl* BEK
Baal Berith   *bay* uhl   BEE rith,
    -ruhth
Baale Judah   BAY uh lee JOO
    duh
Baal-gad   BAY uhl gad
Baal-Gur   BAY uhl GUR

KEY: b*ee*, b*i*t, b*e*t, b*ay*, b*a*t, b*oo*t, b*u*tcher, b*o*ne, s*aw*, *ah*, t*ur*n, *uh* h*uh*, s*igh*,
c*ow*, b*oy*, *th*in, *th* in *th*en, *sh*oe, *zh* in a*z*ure, *ch*op, si*ng*, *hw* in *wh*en.

Baal-hamon   *bay* uhl HAY
muhn
Baal-hanan   *bay* uhl HAY nan
Baal-hazor   *bay* uhl HAY zawr
Baal-hermon   *bay* uhl HUR
muhn
Baali   BAY uh ligh
Baalim   BAY uh lim
Baalis   BAY uh lis, -luhs
Baal-meon   *bay* uhl MEE ahn,
-uhn
Baal-peor   *bay* uhl PEE awr
Baal-perazim   *bay* uhl puh RAY
zim, -PER uh zim
Baalsamus   bay AL suh muhs
Baal-shalishah   *bay* uhl SHAL i
shuh, -uh shuh
Baal-tamar   *bay* uhl TAY
mahr
Baalzebub   *bay* uhl ZEE buhb
Baal-zephon   *bay* uhl ZEE fahn,
-fuhn
Baana   BAY uh nuh
Baanah   BAY uh nuh
Baani   BAY uh nigh
Baanias   bay uh NIGH uhs
Baanite   BAY uh night
Baara   BAY uh ruh
Baaseiah   *bay* uh SIGH uh,
-SEE uh
Baasha   BAY uh shuh
Baasiah   *bay* uh SIGH uh
Babel   BAY buhl, -b'l
Babi   BAY bigh
Babylas   BAB i luhs
Babylon   BAB i lahn, -uh luhn

Babylonia   *bab* i LON i uh, *bab*
uh-
Babylonian   *bab* uh LO ni uhn
Babylonish   bab uh LO nish
Baca   BAY kuh
baccalaureate   *bak* uh LAW ri
uht
Baccanarist   *bak* uh NAHR ist
Bacchides   BAK uh deez, buh
KIGH deez
Bacchurus   buh KYOO ruhs
Bacchus   BAK uhs
Bacenor   buh SEE nawr
Bach   BAHK
Backus   BAK uhs
Bacon   BAY k'n
Baden   BAH d'n
Bader   BAY dur, BAH dur
Baean   BEE uhn
Bago   BAY go
Bagoas   buh GO uhs
Bagoi   BAG o igh
Bagot   BAG uht
Baharum   buh HAY ruhm
Baharumite   buh HAY ruhm
ight
Bahrdt   BAHRT
Bahumus   buh HYOO muhs
Bahurim   buh HYOO rim
Bailey   BAY li
Baillie   BAY li
Bainbridge   BAYN brij
Bainton   BAYN t'n
Baird   BERD
Baiterus   bay IGH tur uhs
Baius   BAY uhs

KEY: b*ee*, b*i*t, b*e*t, b*ay*, b*a*t, b*oo*t, b*u*tcher, b*o*ne, s*aw*, *ah*, t*ur*n, *uh* h*uh*, s*igh*,
c*ow*, b*oy*, *th*in, *th* in *th*en, *sh*oe, *zh* in a*z*ure, *ch*op, si*ng*, *hw* in *wh*en.

Bajith   BAY jith, -juhth
Bakbakkar   bak BAK ur
Bakbuk   BAK buhk
Bakbukiah   *bak* byoo KIGH uh,
  bak buh-
bakemeats   BAYK *meets*
baker   BAY kur
Balaam   BAY lam, -luhm
Balac   BAY lak
Baladan   BAL uh dan
Balah   BAY luh
Balak   BAY lak
Balamo   BAL uh mo
Balamon   BAL uh mon
Balasamus   buh LAS uh muhs
baldachin, baldakin, baldaquin
  BAL duh kin
Baldwin   BAWLD win
Bale   BAYL
Balfour   BAL foor, -fawr
ballad   BAL uhd
Ballerini   bal uh REE nee
Ballou   buh LOO
balm   BAHM
Balnuus   bal NYOO uhs
balsam   BAWL suhm
Baltasar   *bal* tuh ZAHR, bal
  TAY zur
Balthasar, Balthazar   *bal* thuh
  ZAHR
Baluze   bal YOOZ
bamah   BAH mah, bah MAH
Bamoth   BAH moth, bah
  MOTH
Bampton   BAMP t'n
Banaias   *ban* ay IGH uhs

Bancroft   BAN krawft, BANG-
Bangs   BANGZ
Bangor (Seminary)   BANG
  gur
Bangor (Wales)   BANG gawr
Bangorian   bang GAWR i uhn
Bani   BAY nigh
Banias   ba NIGH uhs, buh-
Banid   BAY nid, -nuhd
Bannaia   buh NAY uh, -NIGH
  uh
Bannas   BAN uhs
Banneas   ban EE uhs, buh
  NEE-
banns   BANZ
Bannus   BAN uhs
Banuas   BAN yoo uhs
Baphomet   BAF o met
baptise   bap TIGHZ
baptism   BAP tiz 'm
baptist   BAP tist
baptize   bap TIGHZ
Bar   BAHR
Barabbas   buh RAB uhs, bahr
  AB-
Barachel   BAR uh kel, buh RAY
  k'l
Barachiah   *bar* uh KIGH uh
Barachias   *bar* uh KIGH uhs
Barak   BAR uhk, BAY rak
Baratier   bah rah TEER
Barbara   BAHR buh ruh
barbarian   bahr BAR i uhn
Barbarossa   *bahr* buh ROS uh
Barberini   *bahr* buh REE nee
Barchus   BAHR kuhs

KEY: b*ee*, b*i*t, b*e*t, b*a*y, b*a*t, b*oo*t, b*u*tcher, b*o*ne, s*aw*, *ah*, t*ur*n, *uh* h*uh*, s*igh*,
c*ow*, b*oy*, *th*in, *th* in *th*en, *sh*oe, *zh* in a*zh*ure, *ch*op, si*ng*, *hw* in *wh*en.

Barclay BAHR kli, -klay
Bar-Cochba, -Cocheba *bahr*
  KOK vah, -bah
Bardesanes *bahr* duh SAY
  neez
Bar-Hebraeus bahr hi BREE
  uhs
Barhumite bahr HYOO might
Bariah buh RIGH uh
baritone BAR i *ton*
Bar-Jesus *bahr* JEE zuhs
Bar-Jonah *bahr* JO nuh
Barkos BAHR kos
Barlaam BAHR lay uhm
Barlow BAHR lo
Barmen BAHR muhn
Barnabas BAHR nuh buhs
Barnabite BAHR nuh bight
Barnes BAHRNZ
barodis buh RO dis
Baron ba RAWN, -RON
Baronto buh RAWN yo
Baronius buh RON i uhs
baroque buh ROK
Barré ba RAY
Barrow BAR o
Barsabas BAHR suh buhs
Barsumi bahr SYOO muh, bahr
  SOO-
Barsumas bahr SYOO muhs,
  bahr SOO-
Bartacus BAHR tuh kuhs
Barth BAHRT
Barthelmy bahr tayl MEE
Bartholomew bahr THAHL uh
  myoo

Bartholomite bahr THAHL o
  might, -uh might
Bartimaeus *bahr* ti MEE uhs,
  bahr tuh-
Bartok BAHR tok, -tawk
Bartoli BAHR to li
Bartolommeo *bahr* to lo
  MAY o
Barton BAHR t'n
Baruch BAR uhk, BAY rook
Barzillai bahr ZIL ay igh, -ZIL
  igh
Basaloth BAS uh lawth, -loth
basalt buh SAWLT, BAY sawlt
Bascama BAS kuh muh
Bascom BAS k'm
Basel BAHZ 'l
Bascmath BAS uh math,
  -muhth
Bashan BAY shan, -shuhn
Bashan-havvoth-jair *bay* shuhn
  hay vahth JAY ir, -voth JAY ir
Bashemath BASH uh math
Basil BAZ 'l, BAS 'l, BAY z'l,
  BAY s'l
Basilian buh SIL i uhn
basilica buh SIL i kuh, buh
  ZIL-
Basilides *bas* i LIGH deez,
  baz-
Basilis BAS uh lis
basilisk BAS uh lisk, BAZ-
Basilius buh SIL i uhs, buh
  ZIL-
Basle BAHL, BAHZ 'l
Baslith BAS lith

KEY: b*ee*, b*it*, b*et*, b*ay*, b*at*, b*oot*, b*u*tcher, b*o*ne, s*aw*, *ah*, t*ur*n, *uh* h*uh*, s*igh*,
c*ow*, b*oy*, *th*in, ᵺ in *th*en, *sh*oe, *zh* in a*z*ure, *ch*op, si*ng*, *hw* in *wh*en.

Basmath   BAS math
bason   BAY suhn, -s'n
bas relief   *bah* ri LEEF
bass   BAYS
Bassa   BAS uh
Bassai   BAS ay igh, BAS igh
basso   BAS o
bassoon   buh SOON
Bastai   BAS tay igh, -tigh
bastard   BAS turd
Basthai   BAS thay igh, BAS
   thigh
bastinado   *bas* tin AY do
Batanaea   bat uh NEE uh
Bates   BAYTS
Bath   BATH
Bath Kol   baht KOL, bath
   KAWL, -KOL
Bath-rabbim   *bath* RAB im
Bath-sheba   bath SHEE buh,
   BATH shi buh
Bath-shua   BATH shoo uh, bath
   SHOO uh
Bath-zacharias   *bath zak* uh
   RIGH uhs
baton   buh TAHN, BAT 'n
Bauer   BOW ur, BOY ur
Baur   BOWR
Bausset   bo SAY
Bavvai   BAV ay igh, buh VAY
   igh
Baxter   BAKS tur
Bayer   BAY ur, BIGH ur
Bayeux   bay YOO
Bayith   BAY ith
Bayle   BEL

Bayly   BAY li
bazaar   buh ZAHR
Bazlith   BAZ lith
Bazluth   BAZ luhth
bdellium   DEL i uhm, -yuhm
Bead   BEED
beadle   BEE d'l
Bealiah   *bee* uh LIGH uh
Bealoth   BEE uh lahth, -loth
beatific   *bee* a TIF ik
beatification   bi *at* i fi KAY
   shuhn
beatify   bi AT i figh
beatitude   bee AT i tyood, -uh
   tood
Beaton, Beatoun   BEE tuhn
Beatrice   BEE uh tris, -truhs
Beattie   BAY ti
Beauchamp   BEE chuhm
Beaufort   BO furt
Beaulieu   BYOO li
Beaumont   BO mahnt
Bebai   BEE bay igh, BEB ay
   igh, bee BAY igh
Bec   BEK
Becher   BEE kur
Bechorath   bee KO rath, -ruhth
Becker   BEK ur
Becket   BEK it, -uht
Becon   BEE kuhn
Becorath   bee KO rath, -ruhth
Bectileth   BEK ti luhth
Bedad   BEE dad
Bedan   BEE dan
Bede   BEED
Bedeiah   bee DEE yuh

Bedlam   BED l'm
Bedouin   BED oo in, -een
Beecham   BEE chuhm
Beecher   BEECH ur
Beeliada   *bee* uh LIGH uh duh,
  bee LIGH-
Beelsarus   bee EL suh ruhs, *bee*
  uhl SAR uhs
Beeltethmus   *bee* el TETH
  muhs
Beelzebub   bee EL zee buhb
Beelzebul   bee EL zee bul,
  -buhl
Beer   BEE ur, BIR
Beera   bee EE ruh, BEE uh ruh
Beerah   bee EE ruh, BEE uh
  ruh
Beer-elim   *bee* ur EE lim, -luhm
Beeri   bee EE righ, BEER igh
Beer-lahai-roi   *bee* ur luh HIGH
  roy, bir luh-
Beeroth   bee EE rahth, BEER
  oth
Beeroth Bene-jaakan   bee EE
  rath BEE nee JAY uh kuhn
Beerothite   bee EE rahth ight,
  BEER oth ight
Beersheba   bee ur SHEE buh,
  beer SHEE buh, bee UR shee
  buh
Beeshterah   bee ESH ti ruh,
  -tuh ruh
Beethoven   BAY *to* vuhn
Beghard   BEG urd, bi GAHRD
begotten   bee GAHT 'n
Beguard   BEG urd, bi GAHRD

Beguine   BEG een, bay GEEN
behaviorism   bi HAYV yur iz
  'm
behemoth   bee HEE mahth,
  -muhth, BEE hi mahth,
  -moth
Behistun   *bay* his TOON
behoove   bee HOOV
Beirut   BAY root, bay ROOT
beka   BEE kah
bekah   BEE kah
Bekker   BEK ur
Bel   BEL
Bela   BEE luh
Belah   BEE luh, -lah
Belaite   BEE luh ight
bel canto   bel KAHN to
Belch   BELSH
Belemus   BEL i muhs, -uh
  muhs
Belgic   BEL jik
Bellal   BEE li uhl, BEL yuhl
Bellamy   BEL uh mi
Bellarmine   BEL ur min,
  -meen
Bellay   be LAY
Belloc   BEL ahk, -uhk
Belmaim   BEL may im
Belmen   BEL muhn
Belmon   BEL mahn, -muhn
belomancy   BEL o *man* si
Belshazzar   bel SHAZ ur
Belteshazzar   *bel* tuh SHAZ ur
Belus   BEE luhs
bema   BEE muh
Ben, Ben-   BEN

KEY: b*ee*, b*i*t, b*e*t, b*a*y, b*a*t, b*oo*t, b*u*tcher, b*o*ne, s*aw*, *ah*, t*ur*n, *uh* huh, s*igh*,
c*ow*, b*oy*, *th*in, *th* in *th*en, *sh*oe, *zh* in a*zh*ure, *ch*op, si*ng*, *hw* in *wh*en.

Ben-abinadab *ben* uh BIN uh
  dab
Benaiah bee NAY uh, bee
  NIGH uh
Ben-ammi *ben* AM igh
Ben-deker *ben* DEE kur
Beneberak *ben* i BEE rak
benedicite *ben* i DIS i tee,
  -DIGHS uh tee
Benedict BEN i dikt, -uh dikt
Benedictine *ben* i DIK teen,
  ben uh-, -tin, tighn
benediction *ben* i DIK shuhn,
  ben uh-
Benedictus *ben* i DIK toos,
  -tuhs
benefice BEN i fis, -uh fis
Benejaakan *bee* ni JAY uh
  kuhn
Bene-Kedem *ben* i KEE dem,
  -duhm
Benet BEN et, -uht
benevolence *ben* EV o luhns
Benezet *ben* i ZET
Ben-geber *ben* GEE bur
Bengel BENG guhl
Ben-hadad *ben* HAY dad
Ben-hail *ben* HAY il, -HAYL
Ben-hanan *ben* HAY nan
Ben-hesed *ben* HEE sed, -suhd
Ben-Hinnom *ben* HIN ahm,
  -uhm
Ben-Hur *ben* HUR
Beninu *bee* NIGH nyoo, BEN
  i-
Ben-Jaakan *ben* JAY uh kuhn

Benjamin BEN juh min,
  -muhn
Benjaminite BEN juh min ight,
  -muhn ight
Benjamite BEN juh might
Bennet BEN uht
Bennui buh NYOO igh, -i
Beno BEE no
Ben-oni *ben* O nigh
Ben Sirach *ben* SIGH rak
Benson BEN s'n
Bentham BEN thuhm
Bentley BENT li
Ben-zoheth *ben* ZO heth
Beon BEE ahn
Beor BEE awr
Bera BEE ruh
Beracah buh RAY kah
Berachah BER uh kah
Berachiah *ber* uh KIGH uh
Beraiah *ber* ay IGH uh, buh
  RIGH uh
Berakah buh RAH kah, buh
  rah KAH
berceuse bur SUZ
Berdyaev byir DYA yef, bur
  JIGH ef
Berea BEE ri uh, buh REE uh,
  BER i uh
Berean buh REE uhn
Berechiah *ber* uh KIGH uh
Bered BEE red
Berengar buh RENG gur
Berengarian *ber* uhn GAR i
  uhn
Berengarius *ber* uhn GAR i uhs

KEY: b*ee*, b*i*t, b*e*t, b*a*y, b*a*t, b*oo*t, b*u*tcher, b*o*ne, s*aw*, *ah*, t*ur*n, *uh* huh, s*igh*,
c*ow*, b*oy*, *th*in, t*h* in *th*en, *sh*oe, *zh* in a*z*ure, *ch*op, si*ng*, *hw* in *wh*en.

Berenger buh rahn ZHAY, buh RENG gur

Berenice *ber* uh NEE si

Bereshith bi ray SHEETH, -SHEET

Berggrav bur GRAHV

Bergius BER gi oos

Bergson berg SON, -SAWN

Beri BEE righ

Beriah bi RIGH uh, buh-

Beriite bi RIGH ight, buh-

Berite BEE right

Berith BEE rith

Berkeley BURK li, BAHRK li

Berkouwer BUR kow ur

Berlioz *ber* LYOZ, -LYO

Bern BURN

Bernadette bur nuh DET

Bernard bur NAHRD, -NAHR

Bernardine BUR nur deen, -din

Bernardino bur nahr DEEN o

Berne BURN

Bernice bur NEE si, BUR nuhs, bur NEES

Berodach-baladan bi ro dak BAL uh dan, buh-

Beroea bi REE uh, buh-

Beroth BEE rahth, -roth

Berothah bi RO thuh, buh-

Berothai bi RO thigh, buh-

Berothite BEE rahth ight, BEE roth ight

Berquin bur KAN

Bertocci bur TO chi

beryl BUR uhl, -il

Berytus BER i tuhs, bee RIGH tuhs

Berzelus bur ZEE luhs

Besai BEE sigh

besant bi ZANT

Besodeiah *bes* o DEE yuh, -DIGH uh, -DAY uh

besom BEE zuhm

Besor BEE sawr

Bessarion bi SAR i uhn

bestead bee STED

Betah BEE tuh

Betanc BET uh ni

Beten BEE tuhn

Beth BETH, BAYTH

Beth- BETH

Bethabara *beth* AB uh ruh

Beth-anab -AY nab

Beth-anath -AY nath, -nuhth

Beth-anoth -AY nahth

Bethany BETH uh ni

Beth-arabah AR uh buh

Beth-aram -AY ram

Beth-arbel -AHR bel

Beth-ashbea -ASH bi uh

Bethasmoth -AZ moth

Beth-aven -AY vuhn

Beth-azmaveth -az MAY veth, -vuhth

Beth-baal-meon -*bay* uhl MEE ahn

Beth-barah -BER uh

Bethbasi -BAY sigh

Beth-birei -BIR i igh

Beth-biri -BIR i

Beth-car -KAHR

KEY: bee, bit, bet, bay, bat, boot, butcher, bone, saw, ah, turn, uh huh, sigh, cow, boy, thin, th in then, shoe, zh in azure, chop, sing, hw in when.

Beth-dagon -DAY gahn
Beth-diblathaim -*dib* luh
　THAY im
Beth-eden -EE d'n
Beth-eked -EE ked, -kuhd
Bethel BETH el, -uhl
Bethelite BETH uhl ight
Beth-emek -EE mek
Bether BEE thur
Bethesda buh THEZ duh
Beth-ezel -EE z'l
Beth-gader -GAY dur
Beth-gamul -GAY m'l, -GAM 'l
Beth-gilgal -GIL gal
Beth-haccerem -HAK suh rem
Beth-haccherem -ha KEE
　ruhm
Beth-haggan -HAG uhn
Beth-hanan -HAY nan
Beth-haram -HAY ruhm
Beth-haran -HAY ruhn
Beth-hoglah -HAHG luh
Beth-horon -HO rahn, -HAWR
　uhn
Beth-jeshimoth -JESH i mahth,
　-moth
Beth-joab -JO ab
Beth-leaphrah -li AF ruh
Beth-lebaoth -li BAY ahth,
　-LEB ay ahth
Bethlehem BETH li uhm,
　-hem
Bethlehemite BETH li uhm
　ight, -hem ight
Beth-lomon -LO mahn
Beth-maacah -MAY uh kuh

Beth-marcaboth -MAHR kuh
　bahth, -both
Bethmaus *beth* MAY uhs
Beth-meon -MEE ahn
Beth-merhak -MUR hak
Beth-millo -MIL o
Beth-nimrah -NIM ruh
Beth-palet -PAY luht
Beth-pazzez -PAZ ez
Beth-pelet -PEE luht
Beth-peor -PEE awr
Bethphage BETH fuh jee
Beth-phelet -FEE luht
Beth-rapha -RAY fuh
Beth-rehob -REE hahb
Bethsaida *beth* SAY i duh
Beth-samos -SAY mahs
Beth-shan -SHAN
Beth-shean -SHEE an, -uhn
Beth-shemesh -SHEE mesh
Beth-shemite -SHEE might
Beth-shittah -SHIT uh
Bethsura -SHOO ruh
Beth-tappuah -TAP yu uh
Beth-togarmah -to GAHR muh
Bethuel be THYOO 'l
Bethul BETH uhl, BEE thuhl
Bethulia beth yu LIGH uh,
　bi THYOO li uh
Bethune be THYOON
Beth-zacharias -*zak* uh RIGH
　uhs
Beth-zatha -ZAY thuh
Beth-zur -ZUR
Betolion bi TO li ahn
Betolius be TO li uhs

KEY: b*ee*, b*i*t, b*e*t, b*a*y, b*a*t, b*oo*t, b*u*tcher, b*o*ne, s*aw*, *ah*, t*ur*n, *uh* h*uh*, s*igh*,
c*ow*, b*oy*, *thi*n, *th* in *th*en, *sh*oe, *zh* in a*zh*ure, *ch*op, si*ng*, *hw* in *wh*en.

Betomasthem *bet* o MAS
thuhm
Betomesthaim *bee* to MES
thay im
Betomestham *bet* o MES
thuhm
Betonim BET o nim
betray bi TRAY
betroth bi TRAWTH,
-TRAHTH, -troth
Beulah BYOO luh
Bevan BEV 'n
Beveridge BEV ur ij
Bewer BAY vur, -wur
bewitch bi WICH, bee-
bewray bi RAY
Beza BEE zuh
Bezaanannim bi *zay* uhn AN
im
Bezai BEE zay igh, bee ZAY
igh
Bezalel BEZ uh lel
Beze BAYZ
Bezek BEE zek
Bezer BEE zur
Bezeth BEE zeth
Bezetha bi ZEE thuh
Biatus BIGH uh tuhs
Bible BIGH b'l
Bibliander BIB li *an* dur
Biblical BIB li k'l
Biblicism BIB li siz 'm, BIB
luh-
Biblicist BIB luh sist, -suhst
bibliolatry *bib* li AHL uh tri
bibliomancy BIB li o *man* si

bibliophile BIB li o fighl
bibliotheca *bib* li o THEE kuh
Bichri BIK righ
Bichrite BIK right
Biddle BID 'l
Bidkar BID kahr
Biel BEEL
bier BIR, BEE ur
Bigtha BIG thuh
Bigthan BIG than, -thuhn
Bigthana big THAY nuh, BIG
thuh nuh
Bigvai BIG vay igh, -vigh
Bikathaven *bik* ath AY v'n
Bildad BIL dad
Bileam BIL ee uhm, BIGH li
uhm
Bilgah BIL ga, -guh
Bilgai BIL gay igh, bil GAY
igh
Bilhah BIL ha, -huh
Bilhan BIL han
bilocation *high* lo KAY shuhn
Bilshan BIL shan
Bimhal BIM hal
Binea BIN i uh
Binet bi NAY
Bingham BING uhm
binitarianism *bin* i TAR i
uhn iz 'm
Binnui BIN yoo igh, bin YOO
igh
biretta bi RET uh, bur-
Birgitta bir GIT uh
Birsha BIR shuh
Birzaith bir ZAY ith, bur-

KEY: b*ee*, b*i*t, b*e*t, b*ay*, b*a*t, b*oo*t, b*u*tcher, b*o*ne, s*aw*, *ah*, t*ur*n, *uh* h*uh*, s*igh*,
c*ow*, b*oy*, *th*in, th in *th*en, *sh*oe, zh in a*z*ure, *ch*op, si*ng*, hw in *wh*en.

Birzavith bir ZAY vith, bur-
Bishlam BISH lam
bishop BISH uhp
bishopric BISH uhp rik
Bisutun *bee* su TOON
Bithiah bi THIGH uh, BITH
i uh
Bithron BITH rahn
Bithynia bi THIN i uh
bitumen bi TYOO m'n, bi
TOO-, bigh-
Bizet bee ZAY
Biziothiah biz i OTH i uh, biz
YOTH yuh
Bizjothjah biz JOTH juh
Biztha BIZ thuh
Blackwell BLAK *wel*, -w'l
Blackwood BLAK *wud*
Blaikie BLAY ki
Blake BLAYK
Blandina blan DEEN uh, blan
DIGH nuh
Blanshard BLAN shurd
Blasius BLAY zi uhs
blaspheme blas FEEM
blasphemy BLAS fi mi, -fuh
mi
Blass BLAHS
Blastus BLAS tuhs
Bleek BLAYK
blessed BLES uhd, -id
Blondel blahn DEL
Blount BLUHNT
Boanerges *bo* uh NUR jeez
Boaz BO az
Boccas BAHK uhs

Bocheru BO kuh roo, BAHK i
roo
Bochim BO kim
Bodleian bahd LEE uhn,
BAHD li uhn
Bodley BAHD li
Boece bo EES
Boehm BAHM, BAYM
Boerner BUR nur, BER nur
Boethius bo EE thi uhs
Bogomile BAHG o mighl
Bogomilian *bahg* o MIL i uhn
Bohairic bo HIGH rik
Bohan BO han
Bohemian bo HEE mi uhn
Bolland BAHL uhnd
Bollandist BAHL uhn dist
Bologna bo LO nyuh
Bolsena bol SEN uh
Bonar BON ur
Bonaventura *bon* uh ven
TYOO ruh
Bonaventure *bon* uh VEN
tyur, -chur
bondage BAHN dij
bondmaid BAHND *mayd*
bondman BAHND m'n
bondservant BAHND *sur*
vuhnt
Bonhoeffer BAHN *hawf* ur
Boniface BAHN i fays, -uh fays
Bonn BAHN
Bonnell bah NEL
Bonner BAHN ur
Booth BOOTH
Booz BO ahz

KEY: b*ee*, b*i*t, b*e*t, b*ay*, b*a*t, b*oo*t, b*u*tcher, b*o*ne, s*aw*, *ah*, t*ur*n, *uh* h*uh*, s*igh*,
c*ow*, b*oy*, *th*in, *th* in *th*en, *sh*oe, *zh* in a*zu*re, *ch*op, si*ng*, *hw* in *wh*en.

Bor-ashan *bawr* ASH uhn
Borgia BAWR juh
Borgian BAWR ji uhn
Borith BO rith
Bornkamm BAWRN *kahm*
Borodin bawr o DEEN
Borromeo *bawr* o MAY o
Bosanquet BO z'n ket
Boscath BAHS kath
Bosco BAHS ko
Bosio BO zi o
Bosley BAHZ li
Bosor BO sawr
Bosora BAHS o ruh
Bossuet bah SWAY, -soo AY
Boswell BAHZ wel
Bosworth BAHZ wurth
Botolph, Botulph BAHT uhlf,
  BO tuhlf
Bourchier BOW chur
Bourdaloue boor duh LOO
Bourignan boo RIN yuhn
Bourignon boo ray NYAWN
Bower BOW ur
Bowie BO i
Bowles BOLZ
Bowne BOWN
Bowyer BO yur
Bozcath BAHZ kath
Bozez BO zez
Bozkath BAHZ kath
Bozrah BAHZ ruh
Brabourne BRAY burn
Bradford BRAD furd
Bradlaugh BRAD law
Bradley BRAD li

Bradwardine BRAD wur *deen*
Brahms BRAHMZ
Bramhall BRAM *hawl*
Brandenburg BRAN duhn
  burg
Brandt BRAHNT
Bray BRAY
brazen BRAY z'n
Breasted BRES tid, -tuhd
Breda BRAY dah
Brendan BREN d'n
Brentano bren TAH no
Brenz BRENTS
brethren BRETH ruhn
Brett BRET
breve BREV
breviary BREE vi ur i,
  BREV i
Bride (St.) BRIGH di
Bridget BRI jit, -juht
Brigid BRIJ id, BREE id
brigittine BRIG i tin, -teen
brimstone BRIM *ston*
brio BREE o
Brisé bree ZAY
Brookes BRUKS
Brown, Browne BROWN
bruit BROOT
Brunner BROON ur
Bruno BROO no
Buber BOOB ur
Bucer BOO tsur, BU-
Buchanan byoo KAN uhn, bu-
Buchman BUK muhn
Buchner BOOK nur
buckler BUHK lur

KEY: b*ee*, b*i*t, b*e*t, b*ay*, b*a*t, b*oo*t, b*u*tcher, b*o*ne, s*aw*, *ah*, t*ur*n, *uh* h*uh*, s*igh*,
c*ow*, b*oy*, *th*in, *th* in *th*en, *sh*oe, *zh* in a*zh*ure, *ch*op, si*ng*, *hw* in *wh*en.

Bugenhagen   BOO guhn *hah* guhn
Bukki   BUHK igh
Bukkiah   buh KIGH uh
Bul   BOOL, BUL
Bulgakov   BUL ga kawf, -kawv
Bulgarian   bul GAY ri uhn
Bulgaris   bul GAY ris, -ruhs
bull   BUL
Bullinger   BUL ing ur
bulrush   BUL *ruhsh*
Bultmann   BULT *mahn*
bulwark   BUL wurk
Bunah   BYOO nuh
Bunni   BUHN igh
Bunsen   BUN zuhn
Bunting   BUHN ting
Bunyan   BUHN yuhn
Burgher   BUR gur
Burgundian   bur GUHN di uhn
Buridan   BYOO ri duhn
Burkitt   BURK it, -uht
Burnet   BUR nuht, -nit
Burney   BUR ni
Burns   BURNZ
Burr   BUR
burse   burs
Burton   BUR t'n
Bushnell   BUSH nuhl, -nel
bustrophedon   *buhs* tro FEE d'n
Butler   BUHT lur
Butzer   BOO tsur, BU-
Buxtehude   *buks* tuh HOO duh
Buxton   BUHKS tuhn
Buxtorf   BUKS tawrf

Buz   BUHZ
Buzi   BYOO zigh
Buzite   BYOO zight
Byblus   BIB   luhs
Byles   BIGHLZ
Byrd   BURD
byssus   BIS uhs
Byzantine   bi ZAN tin, -tighn, bigh-, BIZ uhn tin, -tighn, -teen

cab   KAB
cabala   KAB uh luh, kuh BAH la
Cabbon   KAB uhn, -'n
Cabul   KAY b'l, -bul
cadastral   kuh DAS truhl
Caddis   KAD is, -uhs
cadence   KAY duhns
cadenza   kuh DENT suh, kuh DEN zuh
Cades   KAY deez
Cadesbarne   *kay* deez BAHR nee
Cadesh   KAY desh
cadhe   TSAH ~~thay~~
Cadmiel   KAD mi el
Caedmon   KAD muhn
Caesar   SEE zur
Caesarea   *ses* uh REE uh
Caesarea Philippi   -fi LIP igh
Caiaphas   KAY yuh fuhs, KIGH-
Cain   KAYN
Cainan   kay IGH nuhn, KAY nuhn

KEY: b*ee*, b*i*t, b*e*t, b*ay*, b*a*t, b*oo*t, b*u*tcher, b*o*ne, *saw*, *ah*, t*ur*n, *uh* huh, s*igh*, c*ow*, b*oy*, *thi*n, ~~th~~ in *then*, *shoe*, *zh* in a*zh*ure, *ch*op, si*ng*, *hw* in *wh*en.

Cainite   KAYN ight
Cajetan   KAJ i tan
Calah   KAY luh
Calamolalus   *kal* uh MAHL uh
   luhs
calamus   KAL uh muhs
Calamy   KAL uh mi
Calas   ka LAS
Calatrava   kah luh TRAH vuh
Calcol   KAL kahl
Caldwell   KAWLD wel, -wuhl
Caleb   KAY luhb
Caleb-ephratah   -EF ruh tuh
Caleb-ephrathah   -EF ruh thuh
Calebite   KAY luhb ight
calendar   KAL uhn dur
calf   KAF
Caligula   kuh LIG yoo luh
Calitas   KAL i tas
Calixtine   kuh LIKS tin, -tighn
Calixtus   kuh LIKS tuhs
Callirhoe   kuh LIR o ee
Callisthenes   kuh LIS thee neez
Calmet   kal ME
Calneh   KAL ne
Calno   KAL no
Calphi   KAL figh
Calvary   KAL vuh ri
Calvin   KAL vin, -vuhn
Calvinism   KAL vuhn iz 'm
Cambridge   KAYM brij
Cambyses   kam BIGH seez
camel   KAM 'l, -uhl
Camerarius   *kam* ur ER i uhs
Cameron   KAM ur uhn
Camisard   KAM i zahrd

Camon   KAY mahn, -muhn
Campanella   *kam* puh NEL uh
Campbell   KAM buhl, -uhl
Campbellite   KAM uhl ight,
   -buhl ight
camphire   KAM fighr
Cana   KAY nuh
Canaan   KAY nuhn, -nyuhn
Canaanite   KAY nuhn ight
Canaanitess   KAY nuhn *ight* is,
   -uhs
Canaanitish   KAY nuhn *ight* ish
Cananaean, Cananean   *kay* nuh
   NEE uhn
Candace   KAN duh see, kan
   DAY si
Candelmas   KAN d'l muhs
Canisius   ka NISH uhs, -NEE
   shuhs
canker   KANG kur
Canneh   KAN e
cannon   KAN uhn
Cano   KAH no
canon   KAN uhn
canonical   kuh NAHN i k'l
canonization   *kan* uhn i ZAY
   shuhn
cantata   kuhn TAH tuh
Canterbury   KAN tur *ber* i,
   -*bur* i
cantharus   KAN thuh ruhs
Canticles   KAN ti k'lz
cantor   KAN tawr, -tur
Canus   KAY nuhs
caperberry   KAY pur *ber* i
Capernaum   kuh PUR nay uhm

KEY: bee, bit, bet, bay, bat, boot, butcher, bone, saw, ah, turn, uh huh, sigh,
cow, boy, thin, th in then, shoe, zh in azure, chop, sing, hw in when.

caph KAHF, KAF
Capharsalama *kaf* ahr SAL uh
 muh
Caphenatha kuh FEN uh thuh
Caphira kuh FIGH ruh
Caphthorim KAF tho rim
Caphtor KAF tawr
Caphtorim KAF to rim
Capistrano *kah* pi STRAH no,
 kap i STRAN o
Capistranus *kah* pi STRAH
 noos, *kap* i STRAN uhs
Capito KAP i to, -uh to
capitularies kuh PIT choo *ler*
 iz
Cappadocia *kap* uh DO shi uh,
 -shuh
capriccio kah PREET cho
captive KAP tiv
captivity kap TIV uh ti
Capuchin KAP oo chin, kap oo
 SHEEN
Carabasion *kar* uh BAY zi ahn
Caracalla *kar* uh KAL uh
caravan KAR uh van, *kar* uh
 VAN
caravansary *kar* uh VAN suh ri
caravanserai *kar* uh VAN suh
 righ
carbuncle KAHR buhng k'l
Carcas KAHR kuhs
carcase, carcass KAHR kuhs
Carchamis KAHR kuh mis,
 -muhs
Carchemish KAHR kem ish,
 kahr KEEM ish

cardinal KAHR duh n'l
Carea, Careah kuh REE uh
Carem KAY ruhm
Carey KAR i, KER i
Cargill KAHR gil
Caria KAY ri uh
carillon KAR i lahn, kuh RIL
 yuhn
Carites KAR i teez
Carkas KAHR kuhs
Carlstadt KAHRL stat, -stad
Carmanian kahr MAY ni uhn
Carme KAHR mee
Carmel KAHR mel, -m'l
Carmelite KAHR muhl ight
Carmelitess KAHR muhl *ight*
 is, -uhs
Carmi KAHR migh
Carmite KAHR might
Carmonian kahr MO ni uhn
Carnaim KAHR nay im, kahr
 NAY im
carnal KAHR nuhl, -n'l
Carneades kahr NEE uh deez
carnelian kahr NEEL yuhn
Carnion KAHR ni ahn
carol KAR uhl, KER-
carousing kuh ROWZ ing
Carpocrates kahr PAHK ra teez
Carpocratian *kahr* po KRAY
 shuhn
Carpus KAHR puhs
Carpzov KAHRP tsawf
Carranza kuh RAN zuh, kuh
 RAHN zuh
carrion KAR i uhn, KER-

KEY: b*ee*, b*i*t, b*e*t, b*ay*, b*a*t, b*oo*t, b*u*tcher, b*o*ne, s*aw*, *ah*, t*ur*n, *uh* h*u*h, s*igh*,
c*ow*, b*oy*, *thi*n, *th* in *the*n, *sh*oe, *zh* in a*zh*ure, *ch*op, si*ng*, *hw* in *wh*en.

Carshena   KAHR shi nuh, kahr
   SHEE nuh
Cartesian   kahr TEE zhuhn
Carthage   KAHR thij
Carthusian   kahr THYOO
   zhuhn, -THOO zhuhn
cartouche   kahr TOOSH
Cartwright   KAHRT right
Casas   KAH suhs
Casaubon   kuh SAW buhn, ka
   zo BON
Casdim   KAZ dim
Casiphia   kuh SIF i uh
Casluhim   KAS lyoo him, -loo
   him, kas LYOO him, -LOO
   him
Casphon   KAS fahn
Casphor   KAS fawr
Caspin   KAS pin
Caspis   KAS pis
Cassel (city)   KAHS uhl, -'l
Cassel   KAS uhl, 'l
cassia   KASH i uh
Cassianus   kas i AY nuhs, -AH
   nuhs
Castalio   kas TAY li o
castanets   kas tuh NETS
caste   KAST
Castellio   kas TEL i o
Castor   KAS tur
casualism   KAZH yu uhl iz 'm
casuistry   KAZH yu is tri, KAZ-
catacomb   KAT uh kom
catechetic   kat i KET ik
catechism   KAT i kiz 'm
catechist   KAT i kist

catechumen   kat i KYOO muhn
Catena   kuh TEE nuh
Catharine   KATH uh rin,
   KATH rin
Catharist   KATH uh rist
catharsis   kuh THAHR sis
cathedral   kuh THEE druhl
Catholic   KATH o lik, -uh lik,
   KATH lik
Cathua   kuh THYOO uh
Cauda   KAW duh
caul   KAWL
causality   kaw ZAL i ti, -uh ti
causa sui   KAW zuh SOO igh
cease   SEES
cedar   SEE dur
Cedron   SEE druhn
Ceilan   SEE luhn
celebrate   SEL i brayt, -uh brayt
celestial   si LES chuhl
Celestine   si LES tin, SEL uhs
   tighn
celibacy   SEL i buh si
celibate   SEL i bayt
cella   SEL uh
Cellite   SEL ight
Celosyria   see lo SIR i uh, sel
   o-
Celsus   SEL suhs
Celtic   SEL tik
cemetery   SEM i ter i, -tri
Cenchrea   sen KREE uh, SEN
   kri uh
Cenchreae   SEN kri ee
Cendebaeus, Cendebeus   sen di
   BEE uhs

KEY: bee, bit, bet, bay, bat, boot, butcher, bone, saw, ah, turn, uh huh, sigh,
cow, boy, thin, th in then, shoe, zh in azure, chop, sing, hw in when.

censer   SEN sur
censure   SEN shur
census   SEN suhs
centurion   sen TYOO ri uhn
Cephas   SEE fuhs
Ceras   SEE ruhs
Cerdo   SUR do
ceremonial   *ser* i MO ni uhl
ceremony   SER i *mo* ni
Cerinthian   see RIN thi uhn
Cerinthus   si RIN thuhs
Cesarea   *ses* uh REE uh
Cetab   SEE tab
Chabris   KAY bris
Chadias   KAY di uhs
Chaereas   KEE ri uhs
chafe   CHAYF
chaff   CHAF
Chalcedon   KAL si dahn, kal
   SEE d'n
chalcedony   kal SED o ni, KAL
   si *do* ni
Chalcol   KAL kahl
chalcolithic   *kal* ko LITH ik
Chaldea   kal DEE uh
Chaldean   kal DEE uhn
Chaldee   kal DEE, KAL dee
chalice   CHAL is, -uhs
chalkstone   CHAWK STON
Chalmers   CHAH murz,
   CHAL murz
Chalons   shah LAWN, sha
   LON
Chalphi   KAL figh
chameleon   kuh MEE li uhn,
   kuh MEL yuhn

chamois   SHAM i
Champaign   sham PAYN
Chanaan   KAY nuhn, -nay uhn
Chanaanite   KAY nuhn ight
chancel   CHAN suhl, -s'l
chancellor   CHAN suh lur
Channing   CHAN ing
Chanok   KAH nahk, KAN ahk
chant   CHANT
Chanuneus   *kan* yu NEE uhs
chapel   CHAP 'l
Chaphenatha   kuh FEN uh
   thuh
chapiter   CHAP i tur
chaplain   CHAP lin, -luhn
Chapman   CHAP muhn
Charaathalar   *kar* i ATH uh
   lahr
Characa   KAR uh kuh
Charashim   KAR uh shim
Charasim   KAR uh sim
Charax   KAR aks
Charchamis   KAHR kuh mis
Charchemish   KAHR kee mish,
   kahr KEE mish
Charchus, Charcus   KAHR
   kuhs
Charea   KAY ri uh
charger   CHAHR jur
chariot   CHAR i uht
charisma   kuh RIZ muh
charismatic   *kar* iz MAT ik
charity   CHAR uh ti
Charme   KAHR mi
charmel   KAHR mel, -muhl
Charmis   KAHR mis

KEY: bee, bit, bet, bay, bat, boot, butcher, bone, saw, ah, turn, uh huh, sigh,
cow, boy, thin, th in then, shoe, zh in azure, chop, sing, hw in when.

charnel   CHAHR nuhl, -n'l
Charran   KAR uhn
Chaseba   KAS i buh
Chasidim   KAS i dim
chaste   CHAYST
chasten   CHAYS 'n
chastise   chas TIGHZ
chastisement   CHAS tiz muhnt
chastity   CHAS ti ti, -tuh ti
chasuble   CHAZ yoo b'l,
   CHAS-
Chavah   KAY vuh
Cheaps   KEE ahps
Chebar   KEE bahr
chebel   CHEB uhl, -'l
Chedorlaomer   ked awr lay O
   mur
Chelal   KEE lal
Chelcias   KEL shi uhs
Chellian   KEL i uhn
Chelluh   KEL yoo
Chellus   KEL uhs
Chelod   KEE lahd
Chelub   KEE luhb
Chelubai   ki LOO bigh
Cheluhi   KEL u high
Chemarim   KEM uh rim
Chemnitz   KEM nits
Chemosh   KEE mahsh
Chenaanah   ki NAY uh nah
Chenani   ki NAY nigh, KEN
   uh nigh
Chenaniah   ken uh NIGH uh
Cheops   KEE ahps
Chepharammoni   kee fahr AM
   o nigh

Chephar-haammonai, -haamoni
   kee fahr ha AM o nigh
Chephirah   ki FIGH ruh
Cheran   KEE ruhn
Chereas   KEE ri uhs
Cherethite   KER i thight
cherish   CHER ish
Cherith   KEE rith
cherub   CHER uhb
cherubic   chi ROO bik
cherubim   CHER yoo bim,
   CHER oo-, CHER uh-
Chesalon   KES uh lahn
Chesed   KEE sed, KES uhd
Chesil   KEE suhl
Chesulloth   ki SUL ahth, -oth,
   -uhth
cheth   KAYTH
Chettiim   ki TIGH im, KET i
   im
Cheverus   shuh vuh ROOS
Chezib   KEE zib
Chichester   CHICH uhs tur
Chidon   KIGH d'n
Chileab   KIL i ab, KIGH li ab
chiliarch   KIL i ahrk
chiliasm   KIL i az 'm
Chilion   KIL i ahn, KIGH li
   ahn
Chillingworth   CHIL ing wurth
Chilmad   KIL mad
chimer   CHIM ur, SHIM ur
chimere   chi MER, shi-
Chimham   KIM ham
Chinnereth   KIN i reth
Chinneroth   KIN i roth

KEY: bee, bit, bet, bay, bat, boot, butcher, bone, saw, ah, turn, uh huh, sigh,
cow, boy, thin, th in then, shoe, zh in azure, chop, sing, hw in when.

Chios   KEE ahs, KIGH ahs
Chi Rho   KIGH RO
chirographology   *kigh* ro graf
AHL o ji, -uh ji
Chisleu   KIS loo
Chislev   KIS lev
Chislon   KIS lahn, KIZ-
Chisloth-tabor   *kis* lahth TAY
bur, *kiz-*
Chitlish   KIT lish
Chittim   KIT im
Chiun   KIGH uhn
Chloe   KLO ee
Choba   KO buh
Chobai   KO bay igh, KAHB ay
igh
choenix   KEE niks
choir   KWIGHR
Chola   KO luh
choler   KAHL ur
Chopin   SHO pan
choral   KO ruhl, KAWR 'l
chorale   ko RAL, kaw-, ko
RAHL, kaw-
Chor-ashan   kawr ASH uhn
Chorazin   ko RAY zin
Chorbe   KAWR bee
chord   KAWRD
chorepiscopus   ko ri PIS kuh
puhs
chorus   KO ruhs, KAW ruhs
Chosamaeus   *kahs* uh MEE uhs
Chozeba   ko ZEE buh
Chrestus   KRES tuhs
chrism   KRIZ 'm
chrisom   KRIZ uhm

Christ   KRIGHST
christen   KRIS 'n
Christian   KRIS chuhn
Christianity   *kris* chi AN uh ti,
kris ti-
Christology   kris TAHL o ji, -uh
ji
Christopher   KRIS to fur, -tuh
fur
Christmas   KRIS muhs, KRIST
muhs
chromatic   kro MAT ik
Chronicles   KRAHN i k'lz
chronology   kro NAHL o ji, -uh
ji, krahn AHL-
chrysolite   KRIS o light
chrysoprase   KRIS o prayz
chrysoprasus   kri SAHP ruh
suhs
Chrysostom   KRIS uhs tuhm,
kri SAHS tuhm
Chub   KUHB, CHUHB
Chubb   CHUHB
Chun   KUHN, CHUHN
church   CHURCH
churl   CHURL
Chushan-rishathaim   KYOO
shan *rish* uh THAY im,
CHOO-
Chusi   KYOO sigh, CHOO
sigh
Chuza   KYOO zuh, CHOO zuh
ciborium   si BO ri uhm
Ciccar   SIK ahr
Cilicia   si LISH i uh, si LISH
uh

KEY: b*ee*, b*i*t, b*e*t, b*ay*, b*a*t, b*oo*t, b*u*tcher, b*o*ne, s*aw*, *ah*, t*ur*n, *uh* h*uh*, s*igh*,
c*ow*, b*oy*, *th*in, *th* in *then*, *sh*oe, *zh* in a*z*ure, *ch*op, si*ng*, *hw* in *when*.

cinnamon   SIN uh muhn
Cinnereth   SIN uh reth
Cinneroth   SIN uh rahth,
   -roth
Cippus   SIP uhs
Cirama   SIR uh muh, si RAY
   muh
Circumcellion   *sur* kuhm SEL
   yuhn
circumcise   SUR kuhm sighz
circumcision   sur kuhm SIZH
   uhn
Cis   SIS
Cisai   SIGH say igh
Cistercian   sis TUR shuhn,
   -shi uhn
cistern   SIS turn
Cistertian   sis TUR shuhn, -shi
   uhn
citadel   SIT uh del, -d'l
cithern   SITH urn
Citim   SIT im
Citims   SIT imz
citron   SIT ruhn
Clairvaux   kler VO
Clare   KLAR, KLER
Clarendon   KLAR uhn d'n
clarion   KLAR i uhn
Clark, Clarke,   KLAHRK
Clauda   KLAW duh
Claude   KLAWD
Claudia   KLAW di uh
Claudianus   *klaw* di AY nuhs
Claudius   KLAW di uhs
Claudius Lysias   -LIS i uhs
clavichord   KLAV i kawrd

cleave   KLEEV
clef   KLEF
cleft   KLEFT
clemency   KLEM uhn si
Clemens   KLEM uhnz
Clement   KLEM uhnt
Clementine   KLEM uhn tin,
   -tighn
Cleopas   KLEE o puhs
Cleopatra   *klee* o PAT ruh,
   -PAYT ruh, -PAHT ruh
Cleophas   KLEE o fuhs
Clerc, Le   luh KLAR, -KLER
clergy   KLUR ji
clerical   KLER i kuhl, -k'l
Clermont   KLER mahnt
Cletus   KLEE tuhs
Clitus   KLIGH tuhs
cloister   KLOY stur
Clopas   KLO puhs
cloven   KLO vuhn
Clovis   KLO vis, -vuhs
Cloyne   KLOYN
Clugny   KLOO ni
Clysma   KLIZ muh
Cnidus   NIGH duhs
coadjutor   ko AJ oo tur, *ko*
   a JOO tur
Cobb   KAHB
Cobham   KAHB uhm
Cocceius   ko SEE yuhs
Cochlaeus   ko KLEE uhs
cockatrice   KAHK uh tris,
   -trighs
cocker   KAHK ur
cockle   KAHK 'l

KEY: bee, bit, bet, bay, bat, boot, butcher, bone, saw, ah, turn, uh huh, sigh,
cow, boy, thin, ᵺ in then, shoe, zh in azure, chop, sing, hw in when.

coda   KO duh
code   COD
codex   KO deks
Coele-Syria   *see* lo SIR i uh, *sel o-*
Coelicolae   see LIK o lee
coenobite   SEE no bight, SEN o-
coffer   KAWF ur, KAHF ur
cogitation   *kahj* i TAY shuhn
cognition   kahg NISH uhn
coherence   ko HIR uhns
cohort   KO hawrt
Coke   KOK, KUK
Cola   KO luh
Colbert   KOL burt
Coleridge   KOL rij
Colet   KAHL it, -uht
Col-hozeh   kahl HO ze
Coligni   ko LEEN yi, ko LEE ni
Colius   KO li uhs
collation   ko LAY shuhn
collect   KAHL ekt
college   KAHL ij
collegial   ko LEE ji uhl
collegiant   ko LEE ji uhnt
collegiate   ko LEE ji uht, -jit
colligation   *kahl* i GAY shuhn
Collop   KAHL uhp
Collyridian   *kahl* i RID i uhn
Colman   KOL muhn
Cologne   ko LON
Colonna   ko LO nuh
coloratura   kuhl ur uh TYOO ruh, ko luh ruh TOO ruh

Colossae, Colosse   ko LAHS ee
Colossians   ko LAHSH uhnz, ko LAWSH uhnz
Columba   ko LUHM buh
Columbanus   *kahl* uhm BAY nuhs
comeliness   KUHM li nes, -nis, -nuhs
Comenius   ko MEE ni uhs
comforter   KUHM furt ur
commandment   kuh MAND muhnt
commend   kuh MEND
commendam   kuh MEN duhm
commentary   KAHM uhn *ter* i, -tur i
commination   *kahm* i NAY shuhn
commit   kuh MIT
Commodianus   ko *mo* di AY nuhs, kuh-
commodious   kuh MO di uhs
Commodus   KAHM o duhs, -uh duhs
commune   kuh MYOON
communicant   kuh MYOO ni kuhnt
communion   kuh MYOON yuhn
communism   KAHM yoo niz 'm
communitarian   kuh *myoon* i TER i uhn
community   kuh MYOO nuh ti
commutative   kuh MYOO tuh tiv, KAHM yoo *tay* tiv
compassion   kuhm PASH uhn

KEY: b*ee*, b*i*t, b*e*t, b*ay*, b*a*t, boot, b*u*tcher, b*o*ne, s*aw*, *ah*, t*ur*n, *uh* h*uh*, s*igh*, c*ow*, b*oy*, *th*in, *th* in *th*en, *sh*oe, *zh* in a*zh*ure, *ch*op, si*ng*, *hw* in w*h*en.

Compiègne   kawm PYAYN
completorium   *kahm* pli TO ri
uhm
Complin   KAHM plin
Compline   KAHM plighn, -plin
comprehend   *kahm* pri HEND
Comte   KOMT, KAWNT
Conaniah   *kahn* uh NIGH uh,
ko nuh-
concept   KAHN sept
conception   kuhn SEP shuhn
conceptualism   kuhn SEP tyoo
uhl iz 'm
concert   KAHN surt (n.), kuhn
SURT (v.)
concerto   kuhn CHER to
Concha   KAHNG kuh
concision   kuhn SIZH uhn
concitato   *kon* chee TAH to
conclave   KAHN klayv,
KAHNG-
concomitant   kahn KAHM i
tuhnt
concord   KAHNG kurd
concordance   kahn KAWR
duhns, kuhn
Concordat   kahn KAWR duht
concretion   kahn KREE shuhn
concubinage   kahn KYOO bi
nij
concubine   KAHNG kyoo
bighn
concupiscence   kahn KYOO pi
suhns, -s'ns
condescension   kahn di SEN
shuhn

Condillac   kawn di YAK
Cone   KON
coney   KO ni
conference   KAHN fur uhns
confess   kuhn FES
confession   kuhn FESH uhn
confessional   kuhn FESH uhn
'l
confessor   kuhn FES ur, KAHN
fes ur
confirmation   *kahn* fur MAY
shuhn
conformity   kuhn FAWR mi ti
confound   kahn FOWND,
kuhn-
Confucius   kuhn FYOO shuhs,
-shi uhs
congé d'élire   kawn *zhay* day
LEER
congregation   *kahng* gri GAY
shuhn
congregational   *kahng* gri GAY
shuhn 'l
Congregationalist   *kahng* gri
GAY shuhn 'l ist
congruity   kahn GROO uh ti,
kuhn-
Coniah   ko NIGH uh
conjugal   KAHN joo guhl
connotation   *kahn* o TAY
shuhn
Conon   KO nahn, -nuhn
Cononiah   *kahn* o NIGH uh,
ko no NIGH uh
Consalvi   kon SAHL vi
conscience   KAHN shuhns

KEY: bee, bit, bet, bay, bat, boot, butcher, bone, saw, ah, turn, uh huh, sigh,
cow, boy, thin, ŧħ in then, shoe, zh in azure, chop, sing, hw in when.

conscious   KAHN shuhs, -chuhs
consecrate   KAHN si krayt
consecration   *kahn* si KRAY shuhn
consentience   kuhn SEN shuhns, -shi uhns
consistory   kuhn SIS tuh ri
console   KAHN sol (n.), kuhn SOL (v.)
consort   kuhn SAWRT
Constantine   KAHN stuhn tighn, -teen
Constantinople   *kahn* stan ti NO p'l
constrain   kuhn STRAYN
consubstantial   *kahn* suhb STAN shuhl
consubstantiation   *kahn* suhb *stan* shi AY shuhn
consummation   *kahn* suh MAY shuhn
Contarini   *kon* tuh REE nee
contiguity   *kahn* ti GYOO i ti, -uh ti
continence   KAHN tuh nuhns
contingency   kuhn TIN juhn si
contralto   kahn TRAL to, kuhn-
contrapuntal   *kahn* truh PUHN t'l
contrite   KAHN tright
contrition   kuhn TRISH uhn
convent   KAHN vent
conventicle   kuhn VEN ti kuhl, -k'l
conventual   kuhn VEN tyoo uhl, -choo uhl

conversion   kuhn VUR zhuhn, -shuhn
convert   KAHN vurt (n.), kuhn VURT (v.)
conviction   kuhn VIK shuhn
convocation   *kahn* vo KAY shuhn
Conybeare   KON i ber, KUHN-
Cooper   KOO pur, KUP ur
Coornhert   KAWRN hurt
Coos   KO ahs
Copleston   KAHP 'lz tuhn
Copt   KAHPT
Coptic   KAHP tik
copula   KAHP yu luh
cor   KAWR
coral   KAWR uhl
Cor-ashan   kawr ASH uhn
corban   KAWR ban, -buhn
Corbe   KAWR bee
corbel   KAWR buhl
Corbie   kawr BEE
Cordelier   kawr duh LEER
Cordova   KAWR do va
coriander   ko ri AN dur, *kawr* i-
Corinth   KAWR inth
Corinthians   ko RIN thi uhnz
Corinthus   ko RIN thuhs
cormorant   KAWR muh ruhnt
Cornelius   kawr NEEL yuhs, kawr NEE li uhs
Cornhert   KAWRN hurt
coronation   *kawr* o NAY shuhn
corpus   KAWR puhs
corrupt   kuh RUHPT
corruption   kuh RUHP shuhn

KEY: bee, bit, bet, bay, bat, boot, butcher, bone, saw, ah, turn, uh huh, sigh, çow, boy, thin, th in then, shoe, zh in azure, chop, sing, hw in when.

Corvei, Corvey   KAWR vigh
Cos   KOS
Cosam   KO sam
cosmogony   kahz MAHG o ni,
   -uh ni
cosmology   kahz MAHL o ji,
   -uh ji
cotes   KOTS
Coulter   KOL tur
council   KOWN suhl, -s'l
counsel   KOWN suhl, -s'l
counsellor   KOWN suh lur
countenance   KOWN tuh
   nuhns
counterpoint   KOWN tur
   poynt
court   KORT, KAWRT
Cousin   koo ZAN, KUH z'n
covenant   KUHV uh nuhnt
Covenanter   KUHV uh nuhn
   tur, *kuhv* uh NAN tur
Coverdale   KUHV ur dayl
covert   KUHV urt
covet   KUHV uht, -it
covetous   KUHV uh tuhs
covetousness   KUHV uh tuhs
   nuhs
cowl   KOWL
Coz   KAHZ
Cozbi   KAHZ bigh
Cozeba   ko ZEE buh
cracknel   KRAK n'l
Cranmer   KRAN mur
Crates   KRAY teez
create   kree AYT
creation   kri AY shuhn

creator   kri AY tur
creature   KREE chur
creed   KREED
cremation   kri MAY shuhn
crescendo   kruh SHEN do,
   -SEN do
Crescens   KRES uhnz
Cretan   KREE t'n
Crete   KREET
Crispin   KRIS pin, -p'n
Crispus   KRIS puhs
criterion   krigh TIR i uhn
criticism   KRIT uh siz 'm
crocodile   KRAHK o dighl, -uh
   dighl
cromlech   KRAHM lek
crosier   KRO zhur
cross   KRAWS, KRAHS
crown   KROWN
crucible   KROO si b'l, -suh b'l
crucifix   KROO suh fiks
crucifixion   *kroo* suh FIK shuhn
crucify   KROO si figh, -suh figh
Cruden   KROO d'n
crusade   kroo SAYD
crusader   kroo SAY dur
cruse   KROOZ
Crusius   KROO zi uhs
crypt   KRIPT
Cub   KUHB
cubit   KYOO bit
cuckow   KUK oo
cud   KUHD
Cudworth   KUHD wurth
Cujacius   kyoo YAY shi uhs,
   koo-

KEY: bee, bit, bet, bay, bat, boot, butcher, bone, saw, ah, turn, uh huh, sigh,
cow, boy, thin, th in then, shoe, zh in azure, chop, sing, hw in when.

Culdee   KUHL dee
cult   KUHLT
culture   KUHL chur
cultus   KUHL tuhs
cumber   KUHM bur
Cumberland   KUHM bur luhnd
Cumi   KOO mi, KYOO migh
cumin   KUHM in
cummin   KUHM uhn
Cun   KUHN
cuneiform   kyoo NEE uh
   fawrm, KYOO nee uh *fawrm*
curate   KYOO rayt, -rit
curse   KURS
cursive   KUR siv
Curtius   KUR shi uhs
Cusa   KYOO zuh
Cush   KUHSH
Cushan   KYOO shan
Cushan-rishathaim   KYOO
   shan *rish* a THAY im
Cushi   KYOO shigh
Cushite   KUHSH ight
custom   KUHS tuhm
Cuth   KUHTH
Cutha, Cuthah   KYOO thuh
Cuthbert   KUHTH burt
Cuthean   kyoo THEE uhn
Cuthite   KUHTH ight
cutty stool   KUHT i STOOL
Cyamon   SIGH uh mahn
Cyaxares   sigh AKS uh reez
cymbal   SIM buhl, -b'l
cynic   SIN ik
cypress   SIGH pruhs
Cyprian   SIP ri uhn

Cyprus   SIGH pruhs
Cyrama   SIR uh muh, si RAY
   muh
Cyrenaic   *sigh* ri NAY ik,
   sir i-
Cyrene   sigh REE nee
Cyrenian   sigh REE ni uhn
Cyrenius   sigh REE ni uhs
Cyria   SIR i uh
Cyril   SIR uhl
Cyrus   SIGH ruhs

Dabareh   DAB uh re
Dabbasheth, Dabbesheth   DAB
   uh sheth
Daberath   DAB uh rath
Dabria   DAY bri uh, DAB ri uh
Dacobi   duh KO bigh
Da Costa   dah   KAWS tuh,
   dah   KAHS tuh
Dacubi   duh KYOO bigh
Daddaeus, Daddeus   da DEE
   uhs
daemon   DEE muhn
Dagobert   DAG o burt
Dagon   DAY gahn
Daillé   dah YAY
d'Ailly   digh EE
Daimbert   dam BER
Daisan,   DAY suhn, DAY i
   suhn
Dakubi   duh KYOO bigh
Dalaiah   dal ay IGH uh, duh
   LIGH uh
Dalberg   DAHL burg
d'Alembert   da lahm BER

daleth   DAH leth, -luhth
Dalmanutha   *dal* muh NYOO
thuh
Dalmatia   dal MAY shi uh,
-shuh
Dalmatic   dal MAT ik
Dalphon   DAL fahn
dal segno   dahl SAY nyo
Damaris   DAM uh ris, -ruhs
Damascene   DAM uh seen,
dam uh SEEN
Damascius   duh MASH i uhs
Damascus   duh MAS kuhs
Damaskios   duh MAS ki os, -ahs
Damasus   DAM uh suhs
Damian   DAY mi uhn
Damianist   DAY mi uhn ist
Damianus   *day* mi AY nuhs
Damien   dah MYAYN
damn   DAM
damnation   dam NAY shuhn
damp   DAMP
damper   DAMP ur
damsel   DAM zuhl
Dan   DAN
Dana   DAY nuh
dandle   DAN d'l
Daniel   DAN yuhl
Danite   DAN ight
Dan-jaan   *dan* JAY uhn
Dannah   DAN uh
Dante   DAN ti, DAHN ti
Daphne   DAF ni
Dara   DAR uh, DER uh
Darbyite   DAHR bi ight
Darda   DAHR duh

daric   DAR ik, DER ik
Darius   du RIGH uhs
Darkon   DAHR kahn
Darwin   DAHR win
Darwinism   DAHR win iz 'm
Dathan   DAY thuhn
Dathema   DATH i muh
datum   DAY tuhm
Daub   DOWP
d'Aubigné   do bee NYAY
Davenant   DAV uh nuhnt
Davenport   DAV uhn pawrt,
-port
David   DAY vid, -vuhd
daysman   DAYZ muhn
dayspring   DAY *spring*
deacon   DEE kuhn, -k'n
deaconess   DEE k'n is, -es
dean   DEEN
dearth   DURTH
Debir   DEE bur
Deborah   DEB o ruh, -uh ruh
De Bruys   duh broo EE
debt   DET
debtor   DET ur
Debussy   de BYOO si, de byoo
SEE
decadary   DEK uh *der* i, -dur i
decadence   di KAY duhns,
DEK uh duhns
decalogue   DEK uh lawg
decani   di KAY nigh
Decapolis   di KAP o lis, -uh
luhs
deceit   di SEET
decius   DEE shi uhs

declamando   *day* klah MAHN
do, *dek* luh MAN do
decollation   *dee* ko LAY shuhn
decree   di KREE
decrescendo   *day* kre SHEN do,
dee kre SEN do
decretal   di KREE tuhl, -t'l
decurione   di KYOO ri uhn
Dedan   DEE duhn
Dedanim   DED uh nim, di
DAY nim
Dedanite   DED uhn ight
dedicate   DED i kayt
dedication   *ded* i KAY shuhn
deduction   di DUHK shuhn
deer   DIR
de facto   *dee* FAK to
defame   di FAYM
defile   di FIGHL
degenerate   di JEN ur it, -uht
(adj.), di JEN ur ayt (v.)
degradation   *deg* ruh DAY
shuhn
Dehaite   di HAY ight
Dehavite   di HAY vight
dehort   di HAWRT
deification   *dee* uh fuh KAY
shuhn
Dei gratia   DEE igh GRAY
shi uh
deism   DEE iz 'm
Deissmann   DIGHS mahn
deity   DEE uh ti
Dekar   DEE kahr
Delaiah   di LAY yuh, di LIGH
uh

Delany   di LAY ni
delegate   DEL i *gayt* (v.), DEL
i guht (n.)
Delilah   di LIGH luh
delinquency   di LING kwuhn
si
de Lisle   duh LEEL
Delitzsch   DAY lich
Delos   DEE lahs
deluge   DEL yooj
delusion   di LYOO zhuhn, di
LOO zhuhn
de Maistre   duh MESTR', duh
MAYSTR'
Demas   DEE muhs
Demetrius   di MEE tri uhs
demission   di MISH uhn
Demiurge   DEM i urj
Demme   DEM i
Democritus   di MAHK ri tuhs
demograph   DEE mo graf
demography   di MAHG ruh
fi
demon   DEE muhn
demoniac   di MO ni ak
demonology   *dee* muhn AHL
o ji
Demophon   DEM o fahn
demotic   di MAHT ik
Dempster   DEMP stur
demythologize   *dee* mi THAHL
o jighz
denarius   di NAR i uhs, di
NER-
Denderah   DEN dur ah, -uh
Denis   DEN is, di NEE

KEY: bee, bit, bet, bay, bat, boot, butcher, bone, saw, ah, turn, uh huh, sigh,
cow, boy, thin, th in then, shoe, zh in azure, chop, sing, hw in when.

denomination di *nahm* i NAY
shuhn
denotation di no TAY shuhn
deny di NIGH
Denys DEN is, di NEE
deontology *dee* ahn TAHL o ji
Deosculatorium di *ahs* kyu
luh TO ri uhm, -TAWR i uhm
deposition *dep* o ZISH uhn
deprave di PRAYV
depravity di PRAV uh ti
De Profundis *dee* pro FUHN
dis
Derbe DUR bi
Dereism DEE ri iz 'm
Derham DUR uhm
derision di RIZH uhn
de' Rossi duh RAHS i
dervish DUR vish
descant DES kant, -kuhnt
Descartes day KAHRT
descry di SKRIGH
desolate DES o lit, -luht (adj.),
DES o layt (v.)
Dessau DES aw, -ay oo
destiny DES tuh ni
determinism di TUR min
iz 'm
Deuel DYOO el, -uhl, di YOO
el, -uhl
deutero- DYOO tur o, DOO-
Deuteronomy *dyoo* tur AHN
uh mi, *doo-*
devil DEV 'l
devotion di VO shuhn
devout di VOWT

De Wette di WET uh, di
VET uh
Dewey DYOO i, DOO i
diabolic *digh* uh BAHL ik
diabolism digh AB o liz 'm
diabolus digh AB o luhs
diaconicum *digh* uh KAHN i
kuhm
diaconikon *digh* uh KAHN i
kahn
diadem DIGH uh dem
Diadochus digh AD o kuhs,
-uh kuhs
dialectic *digh* uh LEK tik
dialectical *digh* uh LEK ti kuhl
dialogism di AL o jiz 'm
Diana digh AN uh
diapason *digh* uh PAY zuhn,
-suhn
Diaspora digh AS po ruh
diatessaron *digh* uh TES uh
rahn
diatonic *digh* uh TAHN ik
Dibelius di BAY li uhs, di
BAYL yuhs
Diblah DIB la, luh
Diblaim dib LAY im, DIB lay
im
Diblath DIB lath
Diblathaim dib luh THAY im
Dibon DIGH bahn
Dibon-gad *digh* bahn GAD
Dibri DIB righ
dichotomy digh KAHT o mi,
-uh mi
Dickins DIK inz, -uhnz

Dickinson   DIK in suhn
Didache   DID uh kee
didactic   digh DAK tik, di-
Diderot   dee DRO
didrachm   DIGH dram
didrachma   digh DRAK muh
Didymus   DID i muhs, -uh
muhs
Dieffenbacher   DEE fuhn *bahk*
ur
Dies Irae   DIGH ayz IGH ray
diet   DIGH uht
Dietrich   DEE trik
diffusion   di FYOO zhuhn
digamist   DIG uh mist, -muhst
digamy   DIG uh mi
Digby   DIG bi
digger   DIG ur
dike   DIGHK
Diklah   DIK lah
Dilean   DIL i uhn, DIGH li
uhn
Dillmann   DIL mahn
diminuendo   di *min* yoo EN
do
dimissory   DIM i so ri, -saw ri,
digh MIS o ri
Dimnah   DIM nuh
di molto   dee MOL to
Dimon   DIGH mahn
Dimonah   digh MO nuh
Dinah   DIGH nuh
Dinaite   DIGH nuh ight
Ding an sich   ding ahn ZIK
Dinhabah   DIN huh bah
Dinter   DIN tur

diocesan   digh AHS i suhn,
-zuhn
diocese   DIGH o sees, -sis
Dioclesian, Diocletian   *digh* o
KLEE shuhn
Diodati   *dee* o DAH ti
Diodorus   *digh* o DO ruhs,
-DAWR uhs
Diognetus   *digh* ahg NEE tuhs
Dionysia   *digh* o NISH i uh,
-NIS i uh, -NIZ i uh
Dionysius   *digh* o NISH i uhs,
-NIGH si uhs
Dionysus   *digh* o NIGH suhs
diorite   DIGH o right
Dioscorinthius   *digh* ahs kuh
RIN thi uhs
Dioscurus   *digh* o SKYOO ruhs
Dioscuri   *digh* ahs KYOO ri
Diotrephes   digh AHT ri feez
Diphath   DIGH fath, -fuhth
Dippel   DIP el, -'l
diptychs   DIP tiks
dirge   DURJ
diriment   DIR i muhnt, -uh
muhnt
discalced   dis KALST
disciple   di SIGH p'l
discipline   DIS uh plin, -pluhn
discomfit   dis KUHM fit, -fuht
discord   DIS kawrd
discrete   dis KREET, DIS kreet
discus   DIS kuhs
disfranchise   dis FRAN chighz
Dishan   DIGH shan, -shuhn
Dishon   DIGH shahn, -shuhn

KEY: b*ee*, b*i*t, b*e*t, b*ay*, b*a*t, b*oo*t, b*u*tcher, b*o*ne, s*aw*, *ah*, t*ur*n, *uh* h*uh*, s*igh*,
c*ow*, b*oy*, *th*in, *th* in *th*en, *sh*oe, *zh* in a*zh*ure, *ch*op, si*ng*, *hw* in *wh*en.

disintegration   dis *in* ti GRAY
shuhn
disjunctive   dis JUHNGK tiv
Dismas   DIS muhs
dispensation   *dis* pen SAY
shuhn
dispersion   dis PUR shuhn,
-zhuhn
disputation   *dis* pyoo TAY
shuhn
dissenter   di SEN tur
dissident   DIS uh duhnt
dissonance   DIS o nuhns, -uh
nuhns
dithcism   DIGH thee iz 'm
dittography   di TAHG ruh fi
diurnal   digh UR nuhl, -n'l
divers   DIGH vurz
Dives   DIGH veez
divination   *div* uh NAY shuhn
divine   di VIGHN
diviner   di VIGHN ur
divorce   di VORS, -VAWRS
Dix   DIKS
Dizahab   DIZ uh hab
Docetism   do SEE tiz 'm, DO
see-
Docetist   do SEE tist, DO see-
doctrinal   DAHK tri nuhl, dahk
TRIGH n'l
doctrine   DAHK trin, -truhn
Docus   DO kuhs
Dodai   DO digh, DO day igh
Dodanim   DAHD uh nim
Dodavah   DO duh vuh
Dodavahu   do DAV uh hyoo

Dodd   DAHD
Doddridge   DAHD rij
Dodo   DO do
Dodwell   DAHD wel, -wuhl
Doeg   DO eg
dogma   DAWG muh, DAHG
muh
dogmatic   dawg MAT ik, dahg-
dogmatism   DAWG muh tiz
'm, DAHG-
Dok   DOK
dolce   DOL chay
Döllinger   DUR ling ur, DEL
ing ur, DAHL in jur
dolmen   DAHL muhn
dom   DAHM
domestication   do *mes* ti KAY
shuhn
dominance   DAHM uh nuhns
domination   *dahm* uh NAY
shuhn
Dominic   DAHM i nik, -uh nik
Dominican   do MIN i kuhn
dominion   do MIN yuhn
dominis   DAHM i nees
Domitian   do MISH uhn
domus   DO muhs
Donatism   DAHN uh tiz 'm
Donatist   DAHN uh tist
donative   DAHN uh tiv, DON-
Donne   DUHN, DAHN
Donoso Cortés   do NO so
kawr TAYS
Dophkah   DAHF kuh
Dor   DAWR
Dora   DO ruh, DAW ruh

KEY: bee, bit, bet, bay, bat, boot, butcher, bone, saw, ah, turn, uh huh, sigh,
cow, boy, thin, th in then, shoe, zh in azure, chop, sing, hw in when.

Dorcas   DAWR kuhs
Doris   DAWR is, DO ris
Dorotheus   do RO thee uhs
Dorothy   DAWR o thi, -uh thi
Dort   DAWRT
Dorter   DAWR tur
Dorymenes   do RIM uh neez
Dosithean   do SITH i uhn
Dositheus   do SITH i uhs
Dostoevsky   *dahs* tuh YEF ski
dote   DOT
Dothaim   DO thay im
Dothan   DO thuhn
Douai   doo AY
Douai-Reims   doo *ay* REEMZ
Douay   doo AY
doubt   DOWT
Doukhobor   DYOO ko bawr,
   DOO-
dove   DUHV
doxa   DAHK suh
doxology   dahks AHL o ji, -uh
   ji
drachma   DRAK muh
Draconite   DRAK o night, -uh
   night
Dracontius   druh KON shi uhs,
   -ti uhs
dragon   DRAG uhn
dragonnade   drag uh NAYD
dram   DRAM
drama mimic   DRAH muh
   MIM ik
draught   DRAFT
dregs   DREGZ
driver   DRIGH vur

dromedary   DRAHM uh *der* i,
   DRUHM-
dropsy   DRAHP si
dross   DRAWS, DRAHS
drought   DROWT
druid   DROO id, -uhd
Drummond   DRUHM uhnd,
   -'nd
Druse   DROOZ
Drusilla   droo SIL uh
Drusius   DROO si uhs
dualism   DYOO uhl iz 'm,
   DOO-
Ducange   dyoo KAHNZH, doo
   KANJ
Duchobortzi   doo ko BAWR tsi
Du Halde   doo AHLD
Dukhobor   DYOO ko bawr,
   DOO-
Dukhobortsy   doo ko BAWR
   tsi
dulcet   DUHL sit
dulciana   *duhl* si AN uh
dulcimer   DUHL si mur
Dulcinist   DUHL suh nist
dulcinite   DUHL suh night
dulia   dyoo LIGH uh, doo-
Dumah   DYOO muh
dung   DUHNG
dunghill   DUHNG hil
Duns Scotus   *duhnz* SKO tuhs
Dunstan   DUHN stuhn
Duperron   doo pe RAWN
Dupin   doo PAN
du Plessis-Mornay   doo ple *see*
   mawr NAY

KEY: bee, bit, bet, bay, bat, boot, butcher, bone, saw, ah, turn, uh huh, sigh,
cow, boy, thin, th in then, shoe, zh in azure, chop, sing, hw in when.

Dura DYOO ruh
Dura-Europas DOO rah ev RO
  puhs
Durand doo RAWN, dyu
  RAND
Durandus dyu RAN duhs
dure DYOOR
Dürer DYOO rur
Dutens doo TAWN
duty DYOO ti, DOO ti
Duverger, Duvergier doo ver
  ZHAY
Dvorak DVAWR zhahk, duh
  VAWR zhahk, VAWR zhak
Dwight DWIGHT
dynamism DIGH nuh miz 'm
Dyophysite digh AHF uh sight
Dyothelete digh AHTH uh leet
Dyothelite digh AHTH uh
  light
dysentery DIS uhn *ter* i
dysmas DIS muhs
dysteleogy *dis* tel i AHL o ji,
  -uh ji, *dis* tee li-

Eadmer ED mur
Eanes EE uh neez
earthen UR thuhn
Easter EES tur
Ebal EE buhl
Ebed EE bed
Ebed-melech *ee* bed MEE lek,
  -MEL ek
Ebel AY buhl
Eben- EB uhn
Eben-bohan *eb* uhn BO han

Eben-ezel *eb* uhn EE zuhl
Eben-ezer eb uhn EE zur
Eben-zoheleth *eb* uhn ZO huh
  luhth
Eber EE bur
Eberhard AY bur hahrt
Ebert AY burt
Ebez EE bez
Ebiasaph i BIGH uh saf
Ebionism EE bi uhn iz 'm
Ebionite EE bi o night, -uh
  night
ebony EB uhn i
Ebron EE bruhn
Ebronah i BRO nuh
Ecanus i KAY nuhs
Ecbatana ek BAT uh nuh
ecce homo *ek* ay HO mo
ecclesia i KLEE zhi uh, -zi
  uh
Ecclesiastes i *klee* zi AS teez
ecclesiastical i *klee* zi AS ti
  kuhl, -k'l
Ecclesiasticus i *klee* zi AS ti
  kuhs
ecclesiology i *klee* zi AHL, o ji,
  -uh ji
Eck EK
Eckermann EK ur mahn
Eckhardt, Eckhart EK hahrt
eclectic ek LEK tik
eclecticism ek LEK ti siz 'm
ecphonesis ek fo NEE sis,
  -suhs
ecstasy EK stuh see
ecstatic ek STAT ik

KEY: bee, bit, bet, bay, bat, boot, butcher, bone, saw, ah, turn, uh huh, sigh,
cow, boy, thin, th in then, shoe, zh in azure, chop, sing, hw in when.

ectene   EK teen
ecthesis   EK thi sis
ecumenical   ek yoo MEN i kuhl
ecumenicity   *ek* yoo men IS i ti
Edar   EE dur
Eddias   i DIGH uhs
Eddinus   ED i nuhs, -uh nuhs
Eddy   ED i
Edelmann   ED 'l mahn
Eden   EE d'n
Eder   EE dur
Edes   EE duhz
Edessa   i DES uh
Edias   ed IGH uhs
edict   EE dikt
edification   *ed* i fi KAY shuhn,
   ed uh fuh-
Edmer   ED mur
Edmund   ED muhnd
Edna   ED nuh
Edom   EE duhm
Edomite   EE duhm ight
Edos   EE dahs
Edrei   ED ri igh
Eduth   EE duhth
Edward   ED wurd
Edwards   ED wurdz
Edwy   ED wi
efficacious   *ef* i KAY shuhs
effluvium   e FLOO vi uhm
efflux   ef LUHKS
Egbert   EG burt
Egede   AY guh duh
Egerton   EJ ur tuhn
Eginhard   AY gin hahrt
Eglah   EG luh

Eglaim   EG lay im
Eglath   EG lath
Eglath-shelishiyah   *eg* lath shel
   i SHIGH yuh
Eglon   EG lahn
ego   EE go, EG o
egoism   EE go iz 'm, EG o-
Egypt   EE jipt, -juhpt
Egyptian   ee JIP shuhn
Ehi   EE high
Ehud   EE huhd
Eichhorn   IGHK hawrn
eidetic   igh DET ik
Ein   IGHN, AY in
Einsiedeln   IGHN zee duhln
Eker   EE kur
Ekkehard   EK uh hahrt
Ekrebel   EK ri bel
Ekron   EK rahn
Ekronite   EK rahn ight
El   EL
Ela   EE luh
Eladah   EL uh duh
Elah   EE luh
Elam   EE luhm
Elamite   EE luhm ight
Elanite   EE luhn ight
élan vital   ay *lahn* vee TAL
Elasa, Elasah   EL uh suh
Elath   EE lath
Elberith   el BEE rith
El-beth-el   el BETH uhl
Elcia   EL shi uh
Eldaah   el DAY uh
Eldad   EL dad
elder   EL dur

Elead   EL i uhd, -ad
Eleadah   *el* i AY duh
Elealeh   *ee* li AY le, *el* i-
Eleasa, Eleasah   *el* i AY suh, i
   LEE uh suh
Eleatic   *el* i AT ik
Eleazar   *el* i AY zur
Eleazurus   *el* i ay ZYOO ruhs
elect   i LEKT
election   i LEK shuhn
electrum   i LEK truhm
elegie   EL i ji, -uh ji
El Elohe Israel   *el* i LO he IZ
   ruh el, *el* EL o-
El Elyon   *el*   i LIGH uhn
elenchus   i LENG kuhs
Eleph   EE lef
Elephantine   *el* uh fan TIGH
   ni, -TEE ni
Eleusinian   *el* yoo SIN i uhn
Eleusis   el YOO sis, -suhs
Eleutheropolis   *el yoo* thi
   RAHP o lis, -uh luhs
Eleutherus   i LYOO thur uhs
Elfric   EL frik
Elhanan   el HAY nan, -nuhn
Eli   EE ligh
Eli, Eli, lama sabachthani   AY
   li   AY li   LAH mah   sah *bahk*
   tah NEE, EE ligh-
Eliab   i LIGH uhb, -ab
Eliada, Eliadah   i LIGH uh duh
Eliadas   i LIGH uh duhs, -das
Eliadun   i LIGH uh duhn
Eliah   i LIGH uh
Eliahba   i LIGH uh buh

Eliakim   i LIGH uh kim
Eliali   i LIGH uh ligh
Eliam   i LIGH am, -uhm
Eliaonias   i *ligh* uh o NIGH
   uhs
Elias   i LIGH uhs
Eliasaph   i LIGH uh saf
Eliashib   i LIGH uh shib
Eliasib   i LIGH uh sib
Eliasibus   *ee* li AS i buhs
Eliasimus   *ee* li AS i muhs
Eliasis   i LIGH uh sis
Elias Levita   ee LIGH uhs   li
   VIGH tuh
Eliatha, Eliathah   i LIGH uh
   thuh
Elidad   i LIGH dad
Eliehoenai   i *ligh* uh HO i nigh
Eliel   EE li el, i LIGH uhl
Elienai   *el* i EE nigh, -nay igh
Eliezer   *el* i EE zur
Eligius   i LIJ i uhs
Elihaba   i LIGH huh buh
Elihoenai   *el* i ho EE nigh,
   -nay igh
Elihoreph   *el* i HO ref
Elihu   i LIGH hyoo, EL i hyoo
Elijah   i LIGH juh
Elika   i LIGH kuh, EL i kuh
Elim   EE lim
Elimelech   i LIM uh lek
Elioenai   i *ligh* o EE nigh, -nay
   igh
Elionas   *el* i O nuhs
Eliphal   i LIGH fal, EL i fal
Eliphalat   i LIF uh lat

KEY: b*ee*, b*i*t, b*e*t, b*ay*, b*a*t, b*oo*t, b*u*tcher, b*o*ne, s*aw*, *ah*, t*ur*n, *uh* h*uh*, s*igh*,
c*ow*, b*oy*, *th*in, *th* in *th*en, *sh*oe, *zh* in a*z*ure, *ch*op, si*ng*, *hw* in *wh*en.

Eliphalet   i LIF uh let
Eliphaz   EL i faz
Elipheleh   i LIF uh le
Eliphelehu   i LIF uh li *hyoo*
Eliphelet   i LIF uh let
Elisabeth   i LIZ uh beth, -buhth
Eliseus   *el* i SEE uhs
Elisha, Elishah   i LIGH shuh
Elishama, Elishamah   i LISH
   uh mah, -muh
Elishaphat   i LISH uh fat
Elisheba   i LISH i bah, -buh
Elishua   *el* i SHOO uh, i LISH
   oo uh
Elisimus   ee LIS i muhs
Eliu   i LIGH oo
Eliud   i LIGH uhd
Elizabeth   i LIZ uh beth,
   -buhth
Elizaphan   *el* i ZAY fuhn, i LIZ
   uh fan
Elizur   i LIGH zur
Elkanah   el KAY nuh
Elkesaite   el KEE say ight
Elkiah   el KIGH uh
Elkoshite   EL kahsh ight
Ellasar   el LAY sahr, el LAH
   sahr
Ellerian   e LER i uhn
Elliott   EL i uht
Ellora   i LO ruh, i LAWR uh
Elmadam   el MAY dam, -duhm
Elmo   EL mo
Elmodam   el MO dam
Elnaam   el NAY am
Elnathan   el NAY thuhn

Elohim   e LO him, el o HIM,
   EL o him
Eloi   ay LO igh, -i
Elon   EE lahn
Elon-beth-hanan   ee lahn beth
   HAY nan, -nuhn
Elonite   EE lahn ight
Eloth   EE lahth, -loth
Elpaal   el PAY al
Elpalet   el PAY let, EL puh let
El-paran   el PAY ruhn
Elpelet   EL pel uht
Elphinstone   EL fin *ston*,
   -stuhn
El Shaddai   el SHAD ay igh,
   -SHAD igh
Elteke, Eltekeh   EL ti kuh
Eltekon   EL ti kahn
Eltolad   el TO lad
Elul   i LOOL
Eluzai   i LYOO zay igh, -zigh
Elvira   el VIGH ruh
Ely   EE li
Elymaean   *el* i MEE uhn
Elymais   *el* i MAY is
Elymas   EL i mas
Elymean   *el* i MEE uhn
Elyon   i LIGH ahn
Elzabad   el ZAY bad, EL zuh
   bad
Elzaphan   el ZAY fuhn, EL zuh
   fan
Emadabun   i MAY duh buhn
Ematheis   *ee* muh THEE uhs,
   -is
embolism   EM bo liz 'm

KEY: b*ee*, b*i*t, b*e*t, b*ay*, b*a*t, b*oo*t, b*u*tcher, b*o*ne, s*aw*, *ah*, t*ur*n, *uh* h*uh*, s*igh*,
c*ow*, b*oy*, *th*in, *th* in *th*en, *sh*oe, *zh* in a*zu*re, *ch*op, si*ng*, *hw* in *wh*en.

Embury   EM bur i
Emek-Keziz   *ee* mek KEE ziz
emerod   EM ur ahd
Emerson   EM ur s'n
Emim   EE mim
eminence   EM uh nuhns
Emmanuel   e MAN yu el, i-
Emmaus   e MAY uhs, EM ay
  uhs
Emmer   EM ur
Emmeruth   EM ur uhth
Emmons   EM uhnz
Emmor   EM ur, -awr
Emory   EM uh ri
emotion   i MO shuhn
emotive   i MO tiv
empathic   em PATH ik
empathy   EM puh thi
Empedocles   em PED o kleez
emperor   EM pur ur
empirical   em PIR i kuhl
empiricism   em PIR uh siz 'm
Ems Congress   EMZ KAHNG
  gruhs
Emser   EM zur
emulation   em yu LAY shuhn
En-   EN, AYN
Enaim   i NAY im
Enam   EE nam, -nuhm
Enan   EE nan, -nuhn
Enasibus   i NAS i buhs, -uh
  buhs
encore   ahng KAWR, -KOR
Encratite   EN kruh tight
encyclical   en SIK li kuhl, en
  SIGH kli kuhl

Encyclopaedist, Encyclopedist
  en *sigh* klo PEE dist
Endor   EN dawr
Eneglaim   en EG lay im, *en* eg
  LAY im
Enemessar   *en* i MES ur
Eneneus, Enenius   i NEE ni us
energism   EN ur jiz 'm
energumen   *en* ur GYOO muhn
Enfantin   ahn fahn TAN
Engaddi   en GAD igh
En-gannim   en GAN im
En-gedi   en GEE digh, -di, en
  GED i
Engelbert   ENG 'l burt, ENG
  guhl burt
Engelhardt   ENG 'l hahrt,
  ENG guhl hahrt
Enhaddah   en HAD uh
Enhakkore   en HAK o ri
Enhazor   en HAY zawr
enhypostasia   en *high* po STAY
  shi uh, -si uh
Enmishpat   en MISH pat
Ennatan   EN uh tan
Ennodius   i NO di uhs
Enoch   EE nuhk
Enos   EE nahs, -nuhs
Enosh   EE nahsh
Enrimmon   en RIM uhn
Enrogel   en RO guhl
Enshemesh   en SHEE mesh
entablature   en TAB luh chur,
  -tyoor
Entappuah   en TAP yu uh, *en*
  ta PYOO uh

KEY: b*ee*, b*i*t, b*e*t, b*ay*, b*a*t, b*oo*t, b*u*tcher, b*o*ne, s*aw*, *ah*, t*ur*n, *uh* h*uh*, s*igh*,
c*ow*, b*oy*, *th*in, *th* in *th*en, *sh*oe, *zh* in a*z*ure, *ch*op, si*ng*, *hw* in *wh*en.

entelechy   en TEL i ki, -uh ki
enthymeme   EN thi meem
entrophy   EN tro pi
enuresis   *en* yu REE sis, -suhs
environment   en VIGH ruhn
muhnt
environmentalism   en *vigh*
ruhn MEN t'l iz 'm
epact   EE pakt
Epaenetus   i PEE ni tuhs, -nuh
tuhs
epagoge   *ep* uh GO ji
Epaphras   EP uh fras
Epaphroditus   i *paf* ro DIGH
tuhs
eparch   EP ahrk
eparchy   EP ahr ki
Epée   ay PAY
ephah   EE fuh
Ephai   EE figh, -fay igh
Epher   EE fur
Ephes-dammim   *ee* fes DAM
im
Ephesian   i FEE zhuhn, -zi
uhn
Ephesus   EF uh suhs
Ephlal   EF lal
Ephod   EE fahd, EF ahd
ephor   EF awr, -ur
ephphatha   EF uh thuh
Ephraem   EE fruh em
Ephraim   EE fray im, EE fri
uhm
Ephraimite   EE fray im ight,
EE fri uhm ight
Ephrain   EE fray in

Ephrata, Ephratah   EF ruh
tuh
Ephrath   EE frath
Ephrathah   EF ruh thuh, ef
RAH thuh
Ephrathite   EF ruh thight, EE
fruh-
Ephron   EE frahn, EF rahn
epicheirema   *ep* i kigh REE
muh
Epiclesis   *ep* i KLEE sis, -suhs
Epictetus   *ep* ik TEE tuhs
Epicurean   *ep* i kyu REE uhn
Epicurus   *ep* i KYOO ruhs
epigonation   *ep* i go NAY shi
uhn, -shuhn
epigraphy   i PIG ruh fi
epilepsy   EP i *lep* si
epileptic   *ep* i LEP tik
epimanikion   *ep* i muh NIK i
ahn
Epimenides   *ep* i MEN i deez
Epiphanes   *i* PIF uh neez
Epiphanius   ep i FAY ni uhs
Epiphany   i PIF uh ni
epiphenominalism   *ep* i fi
NOM uh n'l iz 'm, -NAHM
uh n'l iz 'm
Epiphi   EP i figh, -uh figh
episcopacy   ee PIS ko puh si
Episcopal   ee PIS ko puhl
Episcopalian   i *pis* ko PAY li
uhn, -PAYL yuhn
Episcopius   *ep* is KO pi uhs
epistemic   *ep* i STEEM ik,
-STEM ik

KEY: b*ee*, b*i*t, b*e*t, b*ay*, b*a*t, b*oo*t, b*u*tcher, b*o*ne, s*aw*, *ah*, t*ur*n, *uh* h*uh*, s*igh*,
c*ow*, b*oy*, *th*in, *th* in *th*en, *sh*oe, *zh* in a*zh*ure, *ch*op, si*ng*, *hw* in *wh*en.

epistemology   i *pis* tuh MAHL
o ji, -uh ji
epistle   ee PIS 'l
epistolarium   i *pis* to LAR i
uhm, -LER i uhm
episyllogism   *ep* i SIL o jiz 'm
epoch   EP uhk, EE pahk
equipollence   *ee* kwi PAHL
uhns
equiprobabilism   *ee* kwi
PRAHB uh buhl iz 'm, *ek* wi-
Er   UR
era   EE ruh, ER uh
Eran   EE ran
Eranite   EE ruhn ight
Erasmus   i RAZ muhs
Erastianism   i RAS chuhn iz 'm,
-ti uhn iz 'm
Erastus   i RAS tuhs
Erech   EE rek, ER ek
eremite   ER uh might
Erfurt   ER fuit, -fuuit
Eri   EE righ
Eri-Aku   er i a KOO, *ee* ri ay
KYOO
Erigena   i RIJ i nuh, uh nuh
eristic   er IS tik
Erite   ER ight
Ernesti   ur NES ti
Eros   ER ahs, IR ahs
erotic   i RAHT ik, e-
Erpenius   ur PEE ni uhs
err   UR
Erskine   UR skin, -skuhn
Esaias   i ZAY uhs, i ZIGH uhs
Esarhaddon   *ez* ur HAD 'n

Esau   EE saw
Esay   EE zay
eschatology   *es* kuh TAHL o ji,
-uh ji
eschatological   *es* kuh to LAHJ
i kuhl, *es* kat uh-
eschew   es CHOO
Esdraelon   *es* dray EE lahn, *ez*-
Esdras   EZ druhs
Esdris   EZ dris, -druhs, ES-
Esebon   ES i bahn
Esebrias   *es* i BRIGH uhs, i
SEE bri uhs
Esek   EE sek
Eserebias   es *er* i BIGH uhs
Eshan   EE shan, -shuhn
Eshbaal   ESH bay uhl
Eshban   ESH ban
Eshcol   ESH kahl, -kawl
Eshean   ESII i uhn, EE shi uhn
Eshek   EE shek
Eshkalonite   ESH kuh lahn ight
Eshtaol   ESH tay ahl
Eshtaulite   *esh* tuh YOO light
Eshtemoa   *esh* ti MO uh
Eshtemoh   ESH ti mo
Eshton   ESH tahn
Esli   ES ligh
Esne   ES nuh
Esora   i SO ruh, i SAWR uh
esoteric   *es* o TER ik
espressivo   *es* pres SEE vo
espy   es PIGH
Esril   ES ril, EZ ril
Esrom   ES rahm, EZ rahm
essence   ES uhns

Essene   ES een, es EEN
Esther   ES tur
esthesis   es THEE sis, -suhs
Etam   EE tam
eternal   i TUR nuhl, -n'l
eternity   i TUR nuh ti
Etham   EE tham
Ethan   EE thuhn
Ethanim   ETH uh nim
Ethanus   i THAY nuhs
Ethelbert   ETH uhl burt
Ethbaal   eth BAY uhl, ETH
  bay uhl
ether   EE thur
ethic   ETH ik
ethical   ETH i k'l
Ethiopia   *ee* thi O pi uh
Ethiopic   *ee* thi AHP ik, -OP
  ik
Eth-Kazin   eth KAY zin, -zuhn
Ethma   ETH muh
Ethnan   ETH nan
ethnarch   ETH nahrk
Ethni   ETH nigh
ethnic   ETH nik
ethnocentrism   *eth* no SEN
  triz 'm
ethnology   eth NAHL o ji, -uh
  ji
ethos   EE thahs
etiology   *ee* ti AHL o ji, -uh ji
étude   ay TOOD
Eubulus   yoo BYOO luhs
Eucharist   YOO kuh rist
euchologion   *yoo* ko LO ji ahn
Euclid   YOO klid

eudaemonism, eudemonism
  yoo DEE muhn iz 'm
Eudocia   yoo DO shuh, -shi uh
Eudoxius   yoo DAHK si uhs
Euergetes   yoo ER juh teez
eugenics   yoo JEN iks
Eugenius   yoo JEE ni uhs,
  -nyuhs
Eugippius, Eugyppius   yoo JIP
  i uhs
Euhemerism   yoo HEE mur iz
  'm, yoo HEM ur-
Euhemerus   yoo HEE mur uhs,
  yoo HEM ur uhs
Eulalia   yoo LAY li uh
Eulalius   yoo LAY li uhs
eulogia   yoo LO ji uh
Eumenes   YOO mi neez
Eunatan   yoo NAY tuhn
Eunice   YOO nis, -nuhs
Eunomian   yoo NO mi uhn
Eunomius   yoo NO mi uhs
eunuch   YOO nuhk
Euodia   yoo O di uh
Euodias   yoo O di uhs
Eupator   YOO puh tawr
Euphemia   yoo FEE mi uh
euphemism   YOO fi miz 'm,
  YOO fuh-
Euphrates   yoo FRAY teez
Eupolemus   yoo PAHL i muhs
Euraquilo   yu RAK wi lo
Euroclydon   yoo RAHK li dahn
Eusebian   yoo SEE bi uhn
Eusebius   yoo SEE bi uhs
Eustathian   yoo STAY thi uhn

KEY: b*ee*, b*i*t, b*e*t, b*ay*, b*a*t, b*oo*t, b*u*tcher, b*o*ne, s*aw*, *ah*, t*ur*n, *uh* h*uh*, s*igh*,
c*ow*, b*oy*, *th*in, *th* in *th*en, *sh*oe, *zh* in a*zh*ure, *ch*op, si*ng*, *hw* in *wh*en.

Eustathius yoo STAY thi uhs
Eutyches YOO ti keez, -tuh
  keez
Eutychianism yoo TIK i uhn iz
  'm
Eutychus YOO ti kuhs
Evagrius Ponticus i VAY gri
  uhs PAHN ti kuhs, i VAG
  ri-
Evagrius Scholasticus -sko LAS
  ti kuhs
evangel i VAN juhl
evangeliary *ee* van JEL i er i
evangelical *ee* van JEL i kuhl,
  ev uhn-
evangelism ee VAN juhl iz 'm
evangelist ee VAN juhl ist
evangelistarium ce *van* juhl is
  TAR i uhm, -TER i uhm
Eve EEV
evensong EE vuhn *sawng*
Evi EE vigh
evil EE v'l, -vil
Evilmerodach *ee* vil mi RO
  dak, -MER o dak
evolution *ev* o LYOO shuhn,
  -LOO shuhn
Ewald AY vahlt
ewe YOO
ewer YOO ur
Ewing YOO ing
exalt eg ZAWLT
exaltation *eg* zawl TAY shuhn
exarch ek SAHRK
ex cathedra eks kuh THEE
  druh, eks KATH i druh

excommunication *eks* kuh
  myoo ni KAY shuhn
execration *eks* i KRAY shuhn
exegesis *ek* suh JEE sis, -suhs
exegetical *ek* si JET i k'l
exemplarism eg ZEM plur iz 'm
exequator *ek* si KWAY tur
Exeter EKS uh tur
exhort eg ZAWRT
exhortation *eg* zawr TAY
  shuhn, *ek* sawr-
exile EK sighl, EG zighl
existentialism *eg* zis TEN
  shuhl iz 'm, *ek* sis-
exode EK sod
Exodus EK so duhs, -suh
  duhs
exomologcsis *ek* so *mahl* o JEE
  sis, -suhs
ex opere operato *eks* AIIP i
  ray *ahp* i RAY to
exorcise EK sawr sighz
exorcism EK sawr siz 'm
exoteric eks o TER ik
expiate EKS pi ayt
expiation *eks* pi AY shuhn
exposition *eks* po ZISH uhn
expository eks PAHZ i *to* ri,
  -*taw* ri
extol eks TAHL, -TOL,
  -TAWL
extravagantes eks *trav* uh GAN
  teez
extreme unction -UHNGK
  shuhn
extrinsic eks TRIN sik

KEY: b*ee*, bi*t*, be*t*, b*ay*, b*a*t, b*oo*t, b*u*tcher, b*o*ne, s*aw*, *ah*, t*ur*n, *uh* h*uh*, s*igh*,
c*ow*, b*oy*, *th*in, *th* in *th*en, *sh*oe, *zh* in a*z*ure, *ch*op, si*ng*, *hw* in *wh*en.

extroversion *eks* tro VUR shuhn, -zhuhn

extrovert *eks* tro VURT, EKS truh vurt

exult eg ZUHLT, ig-

exultation *eg* zuhl TAY shuhn, *ek* suhl-

exultet eg ZUHL tet

Ezar EE zur

Ezbai EZ bay igh, -bigh

Ezbon EZ bahn

Ezechias *ez* uh KIGH uhs, *ez* i-

Ezecias *ez* uh SIGH uhs, *ez* i-

Ezekias *ez* uh KIGH uhs, *ez* i-

Ezekiel i ZEEK yuhl, i ZEE ki uhl

Ezel EE zel

Ezem EE zem

Ezer EE zur

Ezerias *ez* i RIGH uhs

Ezias i ZIGH uhs

Ezion-geber *ee* zi ahn GEE bur

Eznite EZ night

Ezora i ZO ruh, i ZAWR uh

Ezra, Ezrah EZ ruh

Ezrahite EZ ruh hight

Ezri EZ righ

Ezril EZ ril

Faber FAH bur

Fabian FAY bi uhn

fable FAY b'l

Fabricius fa BRISH i uhs

façade fuh SAHD

Facciolati *fah* cho LAH ti

faïence fa YAHNS, figh AHNS

fain FAYN

Fairbairn FER bern

faith FAYTH

fakir fa KIR, FAY kur

Falasha fah LAH shuh

faldstool FAWLD stool

Falk FAWLK

fallacy FAL uh si

falsetto fawl SET o

familist FAM uh list, -luhst

famine FAM in, -uhn

famish FAM ish

fanatic fuh NAT ik

fanaticism fuh NAT uh siz 'm

fanon FAN uhn

Farel fah REL

Farrar FAR ur, fuh RAHR

farthing FAHR ~~th~~ing

fatalism FAY t'l iz 'm

Fatima fa TEE muh, fuh-, FAT i muh

Faucher fo SHAY

Fauchet fo SHAY

Faust FOWST

Faustus FOWS tuhs, FAWS tuhs

Fawkes FAWKS

Fayum figh YOOM

Fayumic figh YOOM ik

featly FEET li

Febronianism fi BRO ni uhn iz 'm

Fechner FEK nur

feign FAYN

Feith FIGHT

Felix   FEE liks
Fellenberg   FEL uhn *berk*
Fenelon   fan LAWN
fenestella   *fen* es TEL uh, *fen* is-, *fen* uhs-
feretory   FER i *to* ri, *-taw* ri, -tur i
Ferguson   FUR guh s'n
feria   FEE ri uh
Ferm   FERM
fermentarian   *fur* men TAR i uhn, -TER i uhn
fermentum   fur MEN tuhm
Ferrand   fuh RAWN
Ferrari   fuh RAH ri
Ferré   fuh RAY
Ferrar   FER ur
Ferrara   fuh RAH ruh
Ferrer   fuh RER
Fesch   FESH
Fessler   FES lur
festal   FES tuhl, -t'l
Festus   FES tuhs
fetish   FEE tish, FET ish
fetter   FET ur
feudal   FYOO d'l
Feuerbach   FOY ur bahk
Feuillant   fu yuh YAWN
fiacre   fi AH kur
fibula   FIB yoo luh
Fichte   FIK tuh, FISH tuh
Ficino   fi CHEE no
fideism   FIGH dee iz 'm
Fidejussor   *figh* di JUHS awr
fief   FEEF
filioque   *fil* i O kwi, *figh* li-

Fillan   FIL uhn
finial   FIN i uhl, FIGH ni uhl
finite   FIGH night
Finley   FIN li
firkin   FUR kin
firmament   FUR muh muhnt
Firmicus Maternus   FUR mi kuhs   may TUR nuhs
Firmilian   fur MIL i uhn
fistula   FIS choo luh, -tyoo luh
fitch   FICH
Flaccus   FLAK uhs
Flacian   FLAY shuhn
Flacius Illyricus   FLAY shi uhs i LIR i kuhs
flagellant   FLAJ uh luhnt, fluh JEL uhnt
flagellation   *flaj* uh LAY shuhn
flagon   FLAG uhn
flamen   FLAY muhn
Flavel   FLAV uhl, -'l
Flavian   FLAY vi uhn
Flavianus   *flay* vi AY nuhs
Fléchier   flay shi AY, flay SHAY
Fletcher   FLECH ur
Fleury   flur EE
Fliedner   FLEED nur
Florence   FLAHR uhns, FLAWR uhns
Florentine   FLAHR uhn teen, -tighn, -tin, FLAWR-
Florian   FLO ri uhn, FLAW-
florilegia   *flo* ri LEE ji uh, *flawr* i-
Florus   FLO ruhs, FLAW ruhs

KEY: b*ee*, b*i*t, b*e*t, b*ay*, b*a*t, b*oo*t, b*u*tcher, b*o*ne, s*aw*, *ah*, t*u*rn, *uh* h*uh*, s*igh*, c*ow*, b*oy*, *th*in, *th* in *th*en, *sh*oe, *zh* in a*zh*ure, *ch*op, si*ng*, *hw* in *wh*en.

flourish FLUR ish
Foliot FAHL i aht
font FAHNT
Fontevrault fawn ti VRO
forbear fawr BER
Forbes FAWRBZ
foreordain *for* awr DAYN,
  fawr-
foreordination *for* awr duh
  NAY shuhn, *fawr-*
formalism FAWR muhl iz 'm
Formosus fawr MO suhs
formulary FAWR myu *ler* i
fornication *fawr* nuh KAY
  shuhn
Forsyth fawr SIGHTH
Fortescue FAWR tes kyoo,
  -tuhs kyoo
Fortunatus *fawr* chu NAY
  tuhs, *fawr* tyu-
forum FO ruhm, FAWR uhm
Fosdick FAWZ dik, FAHZ dik
fosse FAHS
Fossor FAHS ur
Foucher foo SHAY
Fouquet foo KAY
Fourier foo RYAY
Fourmont foor MAWN, foor
  MON
Fox, Foxe FAHKS
fraction FRAK shuhn
Frances FRAN suhs
Francis FRAN suhs, -sis
Franciscan fran SIS kuhn
Francis Xavier -ZAY vi ur,
  -ZAV yur

Francke FRAHNGK,
  FRAHNG kuh
Frankfurt FRAHNGK foort,
  FRANGK furt
Frankfurter FRANGK fur tur
frankincense FRANGK in sens
Fraser FRAY zur
fraternity fruh TUR nuh ti
Fraticelli *frat* i SEL i, *frah* ti
  CHEL li
Frayssinous fray see NOO
Frederick FRED ur ik, FRED
  rik
Frelinghuysen FRAY ling *high*
  z'n
Frere FRIR, FREER
fresco FRES ko
Freud FROYD
Frey FRIGH
friar FRIGH ur
Frideswide FRIGH duh *swee*
  duh
Friedländer FREED len dur,
  -lan dur
Friedrich FREE drik
Friends FRENDZ
Fries FREES
Frith, Fryth FRITH
Fritzsche FRITSH, FRICH
Froben FRO buhn
Froissart FROY sahrt, frwah
  SAHR
Fromm FRAHM
frontal FRUHN tuhl, -t'l
Frossard fro SAHR
Froude FROOD

KEY: bee, bit, bet, bay, bat, boot, butcher, bone, saw, ah, turn, uh huh, sigh,
cow, boy, thin, th in then, shoe, zh in azure, chop, sing, hw in when.

frowardness   FRO wurd nes,
  -nis, -nuhs
Frumentius   froo MEN shuhs
Fulbert   ful BER
Fulda   FOOL dah, FUL duh
Fulke   FULK
Fuller   FUL ur
functionalism   FUHNGK
  shuhn 'l iz 'm
fundamentalism   *fuhn* duh
  MEN t'l iz 'm
funeral   FYOO nur uhl
Fyne   FIGHN

Gaal   GAY al, -uhl
Gaash   GAY ash
Gaba   GAY buh
Gabael   GAB ay el
Gabatha   GAB uh thuh
Gabbai   GAB ay igh, ga BAY
  igh
Gabbatha   GAB uh thuh
Gabbe   GAB i
Gabdes   GAB deez
Gabinius   ga BIN i uhs
Gabler   GAH blur
Gabrias   GAY bri uhs
Gabriel   GAY bri uhl
Gad   GAD
Gadara   GAD uh ruh
Gadarene   *gad* uh REEN,
  GAD uh reen
Gaddi   GAD igh
Gaddial   GAD i al
Gaddis   GAD is
Gadi   GAY digh

Gadite   GAD ight
Gadsden   GADZ duhn
Gage   GAYJ
Gaham   GAY ham
Gahar   GAY hahr
Gai   GA igh
Gaillard   gah YAHR
gainsay   GAYN say
Gairdner   GERD nur, GAHRD
  nur
Gaisford   GAYZ furd
Gaius   GAY uhs, GIGH uhs
Galaad   GAL ay ad
Galal   GAY lal
Galatia   guh LAY shuh
Galatians   gu LAY shuhnz
galbanum   GAL buh nuhm
Galeed   GAL i ed
Galen   GAY luhn
Galenist   GAY luhn ist, -uhst
Galerius   guh LEE ri uhs, guh
  LER i uhs
Galgala   GAL guh luh
Galilean   *gal* i LEE uhn
Galilee   GAL i lee
Galileo   *gal* i LEE o
gall   GAWL
Galla   GAL uh
Gallaudet   *gal* uh DET
Gallican   GAL i kuhn
Gallim   GAL im
Gallio   GAL i o
Galluppi   guh LOO pi
Gallus   GAL uhs
Gamad   GAY mad
Gamael   GAM ay uhl

KEY: b*ee*, b*i*t, b*e*t, b*ay*, b*a*t, b*oo*t, b*u*tcher, b*o*ne, s*aw*, *ah*, t*ur*n, *uh* h*uh*, s*igh*,
c*ow*, b*oy*, *th*in, *th* in *th*en, *sh*oe, *zh* in a*zh*ure, *ch*op, si*ng*, *hw* in *wh*en.

Gamala   GAM uh lah
Gamaliel   guh MAY il uhl, guh MAYL yuhl
Gamba   GAHM bah, GAM buh
Gammadim   GAM uh dim
Gamul   GAY muhl, GAM 'l
gamut   GAM uht
Gar   GAHR
Gareb   GAY reb
gargoyle   GAHR goyl
Garizim   GAR uh zim
Garmite   GAHR might
garner   GAHR nur
Garnier   *gahr* ni AY, GAHR ni ay
Garve   GAHR ve, -vuh
Gas   GAS
Gascoigne   GAS koyn
Gashmu   GASH myoo
Gasquet   gas KAY
Gassendi   ga SEN di
Gatam   GAY tam, -tuhm
Gath   GATH
Gath-hepher   *gath* HEE fur
Gath-rimmon   *gath* RIM uhn
Gauden   GAWD 'n
Gaul   GAWL
Gaulonitis   *gawl* on IGH tis, -tuhs
Gaussen   go SAHN, go SEN
Gautier   go TYAY
Gaza   GAY zuh
Gazara   guh ZAY ruh
Gazathite   GAY zuhth ight
gazelle   guh ZEL

Gazer   GAY zur
Gazera   guh ZEE ruh
Gazez   GAY zez
Gazite   GAY zight
Gazzam   GAZ am, -uhm
Geba   GEE buh, GAY buh
Gebal   GEE bal, -buhl
Gebalite   GEE buhl ight
Geber   GEE bur
Gebhard   GEP hahrt
Gebim   GEE bim
Geko   GEK o
Gedaliah   *ged* uh LIGH uh
Geddes   GED is, GED eez
Geddur   GED ur
Gedeon   GED i uhn
Geder   GEE dur
Gederah   gi DEE ruh
Gederathite   guh DIR uh thight, guh DEER-
Gederite   guh DIR ight, guh DEER ight
Gederoth   gi DEE rahth, -roth
Gederothaim   *ged* i ro THAY im, gi *dee* ro-
Gedor   GEE dawr
Ge-Harashim   *gee* ha RAY shim
Gehazi   gi HAY zigh
Gehenna   gi HEN uh, guh-
Geibel   GIGH buhl
Geiger   GIGH gur
Geiler von Kaisersberg   GIGH lur fahn KIGH zurs berg, -berk
Gelasian   ji LAY shuhn
Gelasius   ji LAY si uhs

KEY: b*ee*, b*i*t, b*e*t, b*ay*, b*a*t, b*oo*t, b*u*tcher, b*o*ne, s*aw*, *ah*, t*ur*n, *uh* h*uh*, s*igh*, c*ow*, b*oy*, *th*in, *th* in *th*en, *sh*oe, *zh* in a*zh*ure, *ch*op, si*ng*, *hw* in *wh*en.

Geliloth   gi LIGH lahth, -loth
Gellert   GEL urt
Gemalli   gi MAL igh
Gemara   gi MAH rah, gi MAW rah
Gemariah   *gem* uh RIGH uh
Gematria   gi MAY tri uh
Gemistus   ji MIS tuhs
Gemshorn   GEMZ *hawrn*
Genesis   JEN uh suhs, -i sis
Genesius   je NEE shi uhs
Geneva   ji NEE vuh, juh-
Genevieve   *jen* uh VEEV, JEN uh veev
Geniza, Genizah   ge NEE zah
Gennadius   je NAY di uhs
Gennaeus   ge NEE uhs
Gennesar   ge NEE sahr
Gennesaret   ge NES uh ret
Gennesareth   ge NES uh reth
Genneus   ge NEE uhs
Gentile   JEN tighl
Gentilly   zhahn tee YEE, JEN til i
Genubath   gi NYOO bath
genuflectente   *jen* yu flek TEN ti
genuflection, genuflexion   *jen* yu FLEK shuhn
Geoffrey   JEF ri
Geon   GEE ahn
Gera   GEE ruh
gerah   GEE ra, -ruh
Gérando   zhe rahn DO, je RAHN do
Gerar   GEE rahr

Gerard   juh RAHRD
Gerasa   GER uh suh
Gerasene   GER uh seen
Gerberon   zherb RAWN
Gerbert   GER burt
Gerdil   zher DEEL
Gergesene   *gur* guh SEEN, GUR guh seen
Gergesite   GUR guh sight
Gerhard, Gerhardt   GER hahrt
Gerizim   gi RIGH zim, GER i zim
Gerlach   GER lahk
Germain   zher MAN
Germanus   jur MAY nuhs
Geron   GEE ruhn
Gerrenian, Gerrhenian   ge REE ni uhn, guh-
Gershom   GUR shuhm
Gershomite   GUR shuhm ight
Gershon   GUR shahn
Gershonite   GUR shuhn ight
Gerson (Biblical)   GUR suhn, -sin
Gerson (Jean)   zher SAWN, -SON, jer
Gertrude   GUR trood
Geruth Chimham   GEE rooth KIM ham
Gervaise   zher VAYS
Gervase   jer VAYS
Gerzite   GUR zight
Gesem   GE sem, -suhm
Gesenius   guh SEE ni uhs
Geshan   GEE shan, -shuhn
Geshem   GEE shem, -shuhm

KEY: b*ee*, b*i*t, b*e*t, b*ay*, b*a*t, b*oo*t, b*u*tcher, b*o*ne, s*aw*, *ah*, t*ur*n, *uh* h*uh*, s*igh*, c*ow*, b*oy*, *th*in, ᵗℏ in *th*en, *sh*oe, *zh* in a*z*ure, *ch*op, si*ng*, *hw* in *wh*en.

Geshur   GEE shur
Geshuri   gi SHOO righ
Geshurite   GESH yu right, gi
  SHOO right
Gestalt   gi SHTAHLT, gi
  STAWLT
Gether   GEE thur
Gethsemane   geth SEM uh ni
Geuel   gi YOO uhl, -el,
  GYOO-
Geulinx   GYOO lingks
Gezer   GEE zur
Gezrite   GEZ right
Gförer   GFER ur
ghetto   GET o
Ghibelline   GIB uh lin, -leen,
  -lighn
ghost   GOST
Giah   GIGH uh
Gib   GIB
Gibbar   GIB ahr
Gibbethon   GIB i thahn, -uh
  thahn
Gibbon   GIB uhn
Gibea, Gibeah   GIB i uh
Gibeath   GIB i ath
Gibeathelohim   *gib* i ath EL o
  him
Gibeath-Ha-Araloth   GIB i
  uhth ha AR uh lahth, -loth
Gibeathite   GIB i uhth ight
Gibeon   GIB i uhn
Gibeonite   GIB i uhn ight
Giblite   GIB light
Gichtel   GIK tel
Giddalti   gi DAL tigh

Giddel   GID uhl, -'l
Gideon   GID i uhn
Gideoni   *gid* i O nigh
Gidom   GIGH dahm
gier-eagle   JIR *ee* g'l, JEER-
Gieseler   GEE zuh ler
Gifford   GIF urd
Gihon   GIGH hahn
Gil   HEEL
Gilalai   GIL uh ligh, gi LAY
  ligh
Gilboa   gil BO uh
Gildas   GIL duhs
Gilead   GIL i uhd
Gileadite   GIL i uhd ight
Giles   JIGHLZ
Gilgal   GIL gal
Gilgamesh   GIL guh mesh
Gilo   GIGH lo
Giloh   GIGH lo
Gilonite   GIGH lo night
Gilpin   GIL pin
Gimel   GIM uhl, -'l
Gimzo   GIM zo
gin   JIN
Ginath   GIGH nath
Ginnetho   GIN i tho
Ginnethoi   GIN i thoy
Ginnethon   GIN i thahn
Gioberti   jo BER ti
Giovanni Capistrano   jo VAH
  ni   kah pi STRAH no
Giraldus Cambrensis   ji RAL
  dus   kam BREN sis
Girgashite   GUR guh shight
Girzite   GUR zight

KEY: b*ee*, b*i*t, b*e*t, b*ay*, b*a*t, b*oo*t, b*u*tcher, b*o*ne, s*aw*, *ah*, t*ur*n, *uh* h*uh*, s*igh*,
c*ow*, b*oy*, *th*in, *th* in *th*en, *sh*oe, *zh* in a*z*ure, *ch*op, si*ng*, *hw* in *wh*en.

Gishpa GISH puh
Gispa GIS puh
Gittah-Hepher *git ah HEE fur*
Gittaim GIT ay im, gi TAY im
Gittite GIT ight
Gittith GIT ith
Gizonite GIGH zo night, gigh ZO night
Gizrite GIZ right
glacis GLAY sis, GLAS is, -uhs
Gladstone GLAD stuhn, -ston
Glagol GLAG uhl
Glagolitic glag o LIT ik
Glanvil, Glanvill GLAN vil
Glasite GLAS ight
Glastonbury GLAS tuhn *ber* i, -bur i
glebe GLEEB
glede GLEED
glissando gli SAHN do
glistering GLIS tur ing
Gloria in Excelsis GLO ri uh in ek SEL sis, GLAWR i uh-
Gloria Patri -PAH tri, -PAT ri
glossolalia *glahs* o LAY li uh, *glaws* uh-
Gloucester GLAHS tur
glyptic GLIP tik
gnash NASH
gnosiology *no* si AHL o ji, -uh ji, *no* zi-
gnosis NO sis, -suhs
Gnostic NAHS tik
gnosticism NAHS tuh siz 'm
goah GO a

goad GOD
Goath GO ath
Gob GAHB
God GAHD
godliness GAHD li nes, -nis, -nuhs
Godspeed GAHD *speed*
Godwin GAHD win
goel GO el
Goethe GAY ti, GUR tuh
Goettingen, Göttingen GURT ing uhn
Gog GAHG, GAWG
Goiim GOY im
Golan GO lan
Golgotha GAHL go thuh, -guh thuh
Goliath go LIGH uhth, guh-
Gomer GO mur
Gomorrah go MAHR uh, go MAWR uh, guh-
gonfalon CAHN ful lahn, -luhn
Gonzaga gon ZAH guh
Gonzalez gahn ZAH layz
gopher GO fur
gorget GAWR jet, -jit
Gorgias GAWR ji uhs
Gorkum GAWR kuhm
Görres GER es
Gorton GAWR t'n
Gortonian gawr TO ni uhn
Gortyna gawr TIGH nuh
Goshen GO shuhn
Gospel, gospel GAHS puhl
Gothic GAHTH ik

KEY: b*ee*, b*i*t, b*e*t, b*a*y, b*a*t, b*oo*t, b*u*tcher, b*o*ne, s*aw*, *ah*, t*ur*n, *uh* h*u*h, s*igh*, c*ow*, b*oy*, *th*in, *th* in *th*en, *sh*oe, *zh* in a*zu*re, *ch*op, si*ng*, *hw* in *wh*en.

Gotholias *gahth* o LIGH uhs, *gahth* uh-
Gothoniel go THO ni uhl, go THAHN i uhl, guh-
Gotthard GAHTH ahrd
Gottschalk GAHTS chawk
Gounod GOO no
gourd GORD, GAWRD
Gousset goo SAY
goyim GOY im
Gozan GO zan
Graal GRAYL
Graba GRAY buh
grace GRAYS
gradine gruh DEEN
gradual GRAD ju uhl
graffiti gra FEE ti
Grafton GRAF tuhn
Grail GRAYL
Grammont GRAM ahnt
Grammontine *gram* uhn TEEN
Grandier grahn DYAY
Grandmont GRAND mahnt
Grandmontine *grand* muhn TEEN
Granvelle grahn VEL
Gratian GRAY shi uhn, -shuhn
Gratry grah TREE
gravamen gruh VAY men, -muhn
greaves GREEVZ
Grecia GREE shi uh, -shuh
Grecian GREE shuhn
Grégoire gray GWAHR

Gregorian gre GO ri uhn, gre GAWR i uhn
Gregorovius *greg* o RO vi uhs
Gregory GREG o ri, -uh ri
gremial GREE mi uhl
Grieg GRIG, GREEG
Griesbach GREES bahk
Groce-Teste GROS test
Grocyn GRO sin
Gross GROS
Grosseteste, Grostest GROS test
Grotius GRO shi uhs
Grynaeus grigh NEE uhs
Guastalline gwahs TAHL in, -een
Gude GOO de, -duh
Gudgodah guhd GO duh
Guelph GWELF
Guibert de Nogent gi BER duh no ZHAWN
Guido GWEE do
Guignes gee NYAY
guile GIGHL
guilt GILT
Guise GEEZ, GWEEZ
Gundulf GUHN duhlf
Guni GYOO nigh
Gunite GYOO night
Gur GUR
Gur-Baal *gur* BAY uhl
Gustavus guhs TAY vuhs, guhs TAH vuhs
Gustavus Adolphus -a DAHL fuhs
Gutenberg GOO t'n burg

KEY: bee, bit, bet, bay, bat, boot, butcher, bone, saw, ah, turn, uh huh, sigh, cow, boy, thin, th in then, shoe, zh in azure, chop, sing, hw in when.

Guthlac GOOTH lahk
Gutzlaff GOOTS lahf
Guyon GIGH uhn, GEE uhn
gyrovague JIGH ro vayg

ha HAH
Haahashtari *hay* uh HASH tuh righ
Ha-Ammonai hay AM o nigh
Ha-Araloth hay AR uh lahth, -loth
Habaiah huh BAY yuh, huh BIGH yuh
Habakkuk HAB uh kuhk, huh BAK uhk
Habaziniah *hab* uh zi NIGH uh
Habbacuc HAB uh kuhk, huh BAK uhk
habergeon HAB ur juhn
Habiri HAH bi ree
Habiru HAH bi roo
Habor HAY bawr
Hacaliah *hak* uh LIGH uh
Hachiliah *hak* uh LIGH uh
Hachmoni HAK mo nigh, hak MO nigh
Hachmonite HAK mo night
Hadad HAY dad
Hadadezer *had* ad EE zur
Hadadrimmon *hay* dad RIM uhn
Hadar HAY dahr
Hadarezer *had* uh REE zur
Hadashah huh DASH uh
Hadassah huh DAS uh

Hadattah huh DAT uh
Hades HAY deez
Hadid HAY did
Hadlai HAD ligh, -lay igh
Hadoram huh DO ram
Hadrach HAY drak, HAD rak
Hadrian HAY dri uhn
Hagab HAY gab
Hagaba, Hagabah HAG uh buh
Hagar HAY gahr
Hagarene *hag* uh REEN, HAG uh reen
Hagarite HAG ahr ight, HAG uh right
Hagenau HAH guh now
Hagerite HAG uh right
Haggada, Haggadah huh CAH dah
Haggai HAG ay igh, HAG igh
Haggeri HAG uh righ, huh GEE righ
Haggi HAG igh
Haggiah huh GIGH uh
Haggite HAG ight
Haggith HAG ith
Hagia HAY gi uh
Hagiographa *hag* i AHG ruh fuh
Hagri HAG righ
Hagrite HAG right
Ha-Hiroth ha HIGH rahth, -roth
Hahn HAHN
Hai HAY igh, HIGH
Ha-Jehudijah *ha* ji hyu DIGH juh

KEY: bee, bit, bet, bay, bat, boot, butcher, bone, saw, ah, turn, uh huh, sigh, cow, boy, thin, th in then, shoe, zh in azure, chop, sing, hw in when.

Hakkatan HAK uh tan
Hakkoz HAK ahz
Hakupha huh KYOO fuh
Halah HAY luh
Halak HAY lak
Halakah, Halakha hah lah KAH
Haldane HAWL dayn
Hales HAYLZ
Halhul HAL huhl
Hali HAY ligh
Halicarnassus *hal* i kahr NAS uhs
Hallel ha LAYL, HAL el
hallelujah *hal* i LOO yuh, *hal* uh-
Halloesh huh LO esh, ha-
Hallohesh huh LO hesh, ha-
hallow HAL o
hallowed HAL od, -o uhd
Ham HAM
Haman HAY muhn
Hamann HAH mahn
Hamath HAY math
Hamathite HAY muhth ight
Hamath-Zobah HAY math ZO buh
Hammath HAM ath, -uhth
Hammeah ha MEE uh, HAM i uh
Hammedatha *ham* i DAY thuh
Hammelech HAM uh lek
Hammer-Purgstall HAHM ur POORG stahl
Hammiphkad ha MIF kad

Hammolecheth, Hammoleketh ha MAHL i keth, ha MO li keth
Hammon HAM uhn
Hammoth-Dor HAM uhth *dawr*
Hammuel HAM yu el
Hammurabi *ham* uh RAH bi
Hamonah huh MO nuh
Hamon-Gog HAY mahn *gahg*
Hamor HAY mawr
Hampden HAMP duhn
Hamran HAM ran
Hamuel HAM yu el, huh MYOO uhl
Hamul HAY muhl
Hamulite HAY muhl ight
Hamutal huh MYOO t'l
Hanameel HAN uh meel, huh NAM i el
Hanamel HAN uh mel
Hanan HAY nan
Hananeel huh NAN i el, HAN uh neel
Hananel HAN uh nel
Hanani huh NAY nigh
Hananiah *han* uh NIGH uh
Handel HAN d'l, HEN d'l
Hanes HAY neez
Haniel HAN i el
Hannah HAN uh
Hannathon HAN uh thahn
Hanniel HAN i el
Hanoch HAY nahk
Hanochite HAY nahk ight
Hanun HAY nuhn

KEY: b*ee*, b*i*t, b*e*t, b*a*y, b*a*t, b*oo*t, b*u*tcher, b*o*ne, s*aw*, *ah*, t*ur*n, *uh* h*uh*, s*igh*, c*ow*, b*oy*, *thi*n, *th* in *the*n, *sh*oe, *zh* in a*z*ure, *ch*op, si*ng*, *hw* in *wh*en.

Hapharaim   *haf* uh RAY im
Haphraim   haf RAY im, HAF
ray im
Haphtharah   *hahf* tah RAH
Happizzez   HAP i zez
Hara   HAY ruh, HAR uh
Haradah   huh RAY duh, HAR
uh dah
Haram   HAY ram, HAR
uhm
Haran   HAY ruhn, HER uhn
Hararite   HA ruh right
Harbaugh   HAHR baw
Harbona, Harbonah   hahr BO
nuh
Hardouin   ahr DWAN
Hareph   HAY ref, HER uhf
Hareth   HAY reth, HER uhth
Harhaiah   hahr HAY uh, hahr
HIGH uh
Harhas   HAHR has
Harhur   HAHR hur
Harim   HAY rim, HER im
Hariph   HAY rif, HER if
harlot   HAHR luht
harlotry   HAHR luht ri
Har-Magedon   *hahr* muh GED
'n
Harms   HAHRMZ
Harnack   HAHR nahk
Harnepher   HAHR nuh fur
Harod   HAY rod, HER uhd,
-rahd
Harodite   HAY rahd ight, HER
uhd-
Haroeh   huh RO e

Harorite   HAY ro right, HER
o-
Haroseth   huh RO seth, HER o
seth
Harosheth   huh RO sheth,
HER o sheth
harp   HAHRP
Harsha   HAHR shuh
Harsith   HAHR sith
hart   HAHRT
Harum   HAY ruhm, HER uhm
Harumaph   huh ROO maf,
-muhf
Haruphite   huh ROO fight
Haruz   HAY ruhz, HER uhz
Harvard   HAHR vurd
Hasadiah   *has* uh DIGH uh
Hasenuah   *has* i NYOO uh
Hashabiah   *hash* uh BIGH uh
Hashabna, Hashabnah   huh
SHAB nuh
Hashabneiah   *hash* uhb ni
IGH uh
Hashabniah   *hash* uhb NIGH
uh
Hashbadana   hash BAD uh nuh,
hash buh DAY nuh
Hashbaddana   hash BAD uh
nuh
Hashem   HAY shem
Hashmona   hash MO nuh
Hashub   HAY shuhb, HASH
uhb
Hashubah   huh SHOO buh
Hashum   HAY shuhm, HASH
uhm

KEY: b*ee*, b*i*t, b*e*t, b*ay*, b*a*t, b*oo*t, b*u*tcher, b*o*ne, *saw*, *ah*, t*ur*n, *uh* huh, *sigh*,
c*ow*, b*oy*, *th*in, *th* in *th*en, *sh*oe, *zh* in a*z*ure, *ch*op, si*ng*, *hw* in *wh*en.

Hashupha   huh SHOO fuh
Hasidaean, Hasidean   *has* i
DEE uhn, *has* uh-
Hasmonaean, Hasmonean   haz
mo NEE uhn
Hasrah   HAZ ruh, HAS ruh
Hasse   HAHS uh
Hassenaah   *has* i NAY uh, *has*
uh-
Hassenuah   *has* i NYOO uh,
has uh-
Hasshub   HASH uhb
Hassophereth   *has* o FEE reth,
-ruhth
Hasupha   huh SYOO fuh
Hatach   HAY tak
Hathach   HAY thak
Hathath   HAY thath
Hatipha   huh TIGH fuh
Hatita   huh TIGH tuh
Hatsi-Hammenuchoth   *hat* si
ham uhn YOO kahth,
-koth
Hattemist   HAT uhm ist
Hattil   HAT il, -uhl
Hatto   HAH to
Hattush   HAT uhsh
Hauran   HOW rahn, HAWR
ahn
Havilah   HAV i lah, -uh lah
Havoth-Jair   *hay* vahth JAY ir,
hay voth-
Havvah   HAV uh
Havvoth-Jair   *hav* ahth JAY ir
Haweis   HOYS
Haydn   HIGH d'n, HAY d'n

Hazael   HAZ ay el, HAY zay el,
huh ZAY el
Hazaiah   huh ZAY yuh, huh
ZIGH yuh
Hazar   HAY zahr
Hazar-Addar   *hay* zahr AD ahr
Hazar-Enan   *hay* zahr EE nuhn
Hazar-Gaddah   *hay* zahr GAD
uh
Hazar-Hatticon   *hay* zahr HAT
i kahn, -uh kahn
Hazar-Maveth   *hay* zahr MAY
veth, -vuhth
Hazar-Shual   *hay* zahr SHOO
uhl
Hazar-Susa, -Susah   *hay* zahr
SYOO suh, -SOO suh
Hazar-Susim   hay zahr SYOO
sim, -SOO sim
Hazazon-Tamar   *haz* uh zahn
TAY mur
Hazelelponi   *haz* uh lel PO
nigh
Hazer   HAY zur
Hazer-Hatticon   *hay* zur HAT i
kahn
Hazerim   huh ZEE rim
Hazeroth   huh ZEE rahth,
-roth
Hazezon-Tamar   *haz* i zahn
TAY mur
Haziel   HAY zi el
Hazo   HAY zo
Hazor   HAY zawr
Hazor-Hadattah   *hay* zawr huh
DAT uh

KEY: b*ee*, b*i*t, b*e*t, b*ay*, b*a*t, b*oo*t, b*u*tcher, b*o*ne, s*aw*, *ah*, t*ur*n, *uh* h*uh*, s*igh*,
c*ow*, b*oy*, *th*in, ᵺ in *th*en, *sh*oe, *zh* in a*z*ure, *ch*op, si*ng*, *hw* in *wh*en.

Hazzelelponi   *haz* uh lel PO
nigh
he (Hebrew letter)   HAY
heathen   HEE thuhn
heaven   HEV uhn, -'n
heave-offering   HEEV-
Heber   HEE bur
Heberite   HEE bur ight
Hebraic   hee BRAY ik
Hebrew   HEE broo
Hebrews   HEE brooz
Hebron   HEE bruhn
Hebronite   HEE bruhn ight
Heckewelder   HEK uh *vel* dur
hectare   HEK ter
Hegai   HEG ay igh, HEE gigh
hege   HEE gi
Hegel   HAY guhl
Hegemonides   *hej* i MAHN
uh deez, *hej* uh-
Hegesippus   *hej* i SIP uhs
Hegira   hi JIGH ruh, HEJ i ruh
Heidegger   HIGH *deg* ur
Heidelberg   HIGH d'l burg
Heinicke   HIGH ni kuh
Helah   HEE lah
Helam   HEE luhm
Helbah   HEL buh
Helbon   HEL bahn
Helchiah   hel KIGH uh
Helchias   hel KIGH uhs
Heldai   HEL day igh, -digh
Heleb   HEE leb
Heled   HEE led
Helek   HEE lek
Helekite   HEE luhk ight

Helem   HEE lem
Helena   HEL uh nuh
Heleph   HEE lef
Helez   HEE lez
Heli   HEE ligh
Helias   hi LIGH uhs
Heliodorus   *hee* li o DAWR
uhs
Heliopolis   *hee* li AHP o lis,
-uh luhs
Helkai   HEL kay igh, -kigh, hel
KAY igh
Helkath   HEL kath
Helkath-Hazzurim   *hel* kath
HAZ yu rim
Helkias   hel KIGH uhs
Hellenic   he LEN ik, he LEEN
ik
Hellenism   HEL uhn iz 'm,
HEL een-
Hellenistic   *hel* uh NIS tik
Helmont   HEL mahnt
Helon   HEE lahn
helve   HELV
Helvetic   hel VET ik
Helvetius   hel VEE shi uhs
Helvidius   hel VID i uhs
Hemam   HEE mam
Heman   HEE man, -muhn
Hemath   HEE math
Hemdan   HEM dan
Hen   HEN
Hena   HEE nuh
Henadad   HEN uh dad
Hengstenberg   HENG stuhn
berk, -burg

KEY: b*ee*, b*i*t, b*e*t, b*ay*, b*a*t, b*oo*t, b*u*tcher, b*o*ne, s*aw*, *ah*, t*ur*n, *uh* h*uh*, s*igh*,
c*ow*, b*oy*, *th*in, th in *then*, *sh*oe, *zh* in a*z*ure, *ch*op, si*ng*, *hw* in *wh*en.

Henke   HENG ki
henna   HEN uh
Hennepin   HEN i pin
Henoch   HEE nahk
Hepher   HEE fur
Hepherite   HEE fur ight
Hephzibah   HEF zi buh, -zuh
buh
Heracles, Herakles   HER uh
kleez
Heracleon   hi RAK li ahn
Heracleonite   hi RAK li uhn
ight
Heraclitus   *her* uh KLIGH
tuhs
Herbart   HER bahrt
Herbelot   *er* bi LO
Hercules   HUR kyu leez
Heres   HEE reez, -res
Heresh   HEE resh
heresiarch   hi REE si ahrk,
HER uh si ahrk
heresy   HER uh si
Hereth   HEE reth
heretic   HER uh tik
heretical   hi RET i kuhl, huh-
hermaphrodite   hur MAF ro
dight
Hermas   HUR muhs, -mas
hermeneutic   *hur* mi NYOO
tik, *hur* muh-, -NOO tik
Hermes   HUR meez
Hermes   (German theologian)
HER muhs
Hermian   HUR mi uhn
Hermogenes   hur MAHJ i neez

Hermogenian   *hur* mo JEE ni
uhn
Hermon   HUR muhn
Hermonite   HUR muhn ight
Herod   HER uhd
Herodian   hi RO di uhn, huh-,
he-
Herodias   hi RO di uhs, huh-,
he-
Herodium   hi RO di uhm, he-
Herrnhut   HERN *hoot*
Heruli   HER yu ligh
Hervey   HAHR vi, HUR vi
Hesed   HEE sed
Heshbon   HESH bahn
Heshmon   HESH mahn
Hess   HES
Hesse   HES
Hesychast   HES i kast
Hesychius   he SIK i uhs
heterodox   HET ur o dahks, -uh
dahks
Heth   HETH
Hethlon   HETH lahn
Hetzel   HET s'l
hewer   HYOO ur
Hewit, Hewitt   HYOO it, -uht
Hexateuch   HEK suh tyook,
-took
Heylin, Heylyn   HIGH lin
Hezeki   HEZ i kigh
Hezekiah   *hez* i KIGH uh
Hezion   HEE zi ahn
Hezir   HEE zur
Hezrai   HEZ ray igh, -righ
Hezro   HEZ ro

KEY: b*ee*, b*i*t, b*e*t, b*ay*, b*a*t, b*oo*t, b*u*tcher, b*o*ne, s*aw*, *ah*, t*ur*n, *uh* h*uh*, s*igh*,
c*ow*, b*oy*, *th*in, *th* in *then*, *sh*oe, *zh* in a*z*ure, *ch*op, si*ng*, *hw* in *wh*en.

Hezron   HEZ rahn
Hezronite   HEZ rahn ight,
-ruhn ight
Hiddai   HID ay igh, hi DAY
igh
Hiddekel   HID i kel
Hiel   HIGH el
Hierapolis   *high* ur AHP o lis,
-uh luhs
hierarchy   HIGH ur *ahr* ki
hieratic   *high* ur AT ik
hiereel   high ER i el
Hieremoth   high ER uh mahth,
-moth
Hicrielus   high *er* i EE luhs
Hiermas   high UR muhs
Hierocles   high ER o kleez
hieroglyphic   *high* ur o GLIF
ik, *high* ro-
Hieronymite   *high* ur AHN i
might, high RAHN-
Hieronymus   *high* ur AHN i
muhs, high RAHN-
Higgaion   hi GAY yahn,
-GIGH ahn
Hilarion   hi LER i ahn, -uhn
Hilarius   hi LER i uhs
Hilary   HIL uh ri
Hildebert   HIL duh burt
Hildebrand   HIL duh brand
Hilen   HIGH len
Hilkiah   hil KIGH uh
Hillel   HIL el
Hin   HIN
Hincmar   HINGK mahr
hind   HIGHND

Hinnom   HIN ahm
Hippo   HIP o
Hippolytus   hi PAHL i tuhs
Hirah   HIGH ruh
Hiram   HIGH ruhm
Hircanus   hur KAY nuhs
Histriomastix   *his* tri o MAS
tiks
Hittite   HIT ight
Hivite   HIGH vight
Hivvite   HIV ight
Hizki   HIZ kigh
Hizkiah   hiz KIGH uh
Hizkijah   hiz KIGH juh
Hoadley, Hoadly   HOD li
hoary   HOR i, HAWR i
Hoba   HO buh
Hobab   HO bab
Hobah   HO buh
Hobaiah   ho BAY yuh, ho
BIGH uh
Hobbes   HAHBZ
Hocking   HAHK ing
Hod   HAHD
Hodaiah   ho DAY yuh, ho
DIGH uh
Hodaviah   *ho* duh VIGH uh
Hodesh   HO desh
Hodevah   HO di vah, ho DEE
vuh
Hodiah   ho DIGH uh
Hodijah   ho DIGH juh
Hoffman   HAWF muhn, -mahn
Hoglah   HAHG luh
Hoham   HO ham
Hohenlohe   ho uhn LO i

KEY: b*ee*, b*i*t, b*e*t, b*ay*, b*a*t, b*oo*t, b*u*tcher, b*o*ne, s*aw*, *ah*, t*ur*n, *uh* h*uh*, s*igh*,
c*ow*, b*oy*, *th*in, **th** in *th*en, *sh*oe, *zh* in a*zh*ure, *ch*op, si*ng*, *hw* in *wh*en.

hoise   HOYZ
Holbach   awl BAK
holm-tree   HOM-
Holofernes   *hahl* o FUR neez,
   hahl uh-
Holon   HO lahn
holyday   HO li *day*
Homam   HO mam
homiletic   *hahm* i LET ik,
   hahm uh-
homilist   HAHM uh list
homily   HAHM uh li
Homoiousian   *ho* moy OO si
   uhn
homologoumena   *hahm* o lo
   GOO mi nuh, *hahm* uh-
Homoousian   *ho* mo OO si uhn
Honorius   ho NO ri uhs, ho
   NAWR i uhs
Hontheim   HONT highm
hoopoe   HOO poo
Hophni   HAHF nigh
Hophra   HAHF ruh
Hor   HAWR
Horam   HO ram
Horeb   HO reb, HAWR eb
Horebite   HO reb ight, HAWR
   eb ight
Horem   HO rem
Horesh   HO resh, HAWR esh
Hor-Haggidgad   *hawr* huh GID
   gad
Hori   HO righ
Horim   HO rim
Horite   HO right
Hormah   HAWR muh

Hormisdas   hawr MIS duhs
Horonaim   *hahr* o NAY im,
   hawr-
Horonite   HAWR o night,
   HAHR-
Horseleach   HAWRS *leech*
Hosah   HO suh
Hosai   HO say igh
hosanna   ho ZAN uh
Hosea   ho ZEE uh, ho ZAY uh
hosen   HO z'n
Hoshaiah   ho SHAY yuh, ho
   SHIGH uh
Hoshama   HAHSH uh muh
Hoshea   ho SHE uh
Hosius   HO see oos
hospice   HAHS pis
hospitaller   HAHS pit 'l ur
Hotham   HO tham
Hothan   HO than
Hothir   HO thur
Hottinger   HAHT ing ur
Hough   HAHK, HAWK
Hozai   HO zay igh
Hrabannus   rah BAH noos
Huber   HOO bur
Huc   OOK
Huesca   WAYS kuh
Hugo   HYOO go
Huguenot   HYOO guh naht
Hukkok   HUHK ahk
Hukok   HYOO kahk
Hul   HUHL
Huldah   HUHL duh
Hulse   HUHLS
humanism   HYOO muhn iz 'm

KEY: b*ee*, b*i*t, b*e*t, b*ay*, b*a*t, b*oo*t, b*u*tcher, b*o*ne, s*aw*, *ah*, t*ur*n, *uh* h*u*h, s*igh*,
c*ow*, b*oy*, *th*in, *th* in *th*en, *sh*oe, *zh* in a*z*ure, *ch*op, si*ng*, *hw* in *wh*en.

humanist HYOO muhn ist, -uhst
humble HUHM b'l, UHM b'l
Hume HYOOM
humility hyoo MIL uh ti
Humtah HUHM tuh
Hupfeld HOOP felt, -feld
Hupham HYOO fam, -fuhm
Huphamite HYOO fuhm ight
Huppah HUHP uh
Huppim HUHP im
Hur HUR
Hurai HYOO ray igh, -righ, hyu RAY igh
Huram HYOO ram, -ruhm
Huri HYOO righ
Hushah HYOO shuh
Hushai HYOO shigh, -shay igh
Husham HYOO sham, -shuhm
Hushathite HYOO shuhth ight
Hushim HYOO shim
Hushshathite HUHSH shath ight
Huss HUHS
Hussite HUHS ight
Hutten HOOT 'n
Huz HUHZ
Huzzab HUHZ ab, -uhb
hyacinth HIGH uh sinth
Hyades HIGH uh deez
Hydaspes high DAS peez
hyena high EE nuh
Hyksos HIK sos, -sahs
Hymenaeus, Hymeneus high muh NEE uhs

hymn HIM
hymnology him NAHL o ji, -uh ji
hyperdulia *high* pur dyu LIGH uh
hypocrisy hi PAHK ruh si
hypocrite HIP o krit, -uh krit
hypostasis high PAHS tuh sis, hi-
Hypsistarian hip sis TER i uhn
Hyrcanus hur KAY nuhs
hyssop HIS uhp
Hystaspes his TAS peez

Iacimus igh AS i muhs, -uh muhs
Iacubus igh AK yu buhs
Iadinus igh AD i nuhs, -uh nuhs
iambic igh AM bik
Iamblichus igh AM bli kuhs
Ibas IGH buhs
ibex IGH beks
Ibhar IB hahr
ibis IGH bis, -buhs
Iblcam IB li uhm
ibn-Baruch *ib* 'n BAY rook
ibn-Gabirol, ibn-Gebirol *ib* 'n guh BEE rawl
Ibneiah ib NEE yuh, ib ni IGH uh
Ibnijah ib NIGH juh
ibn-Thofail, ibn-Tofeil *ib* 'n TO fayl
ibn-Tumart *ib* 'n TOO mahrt
Ibri IB righ

KEY: b*ee*, b*i*t, b*e*t, b*a*y, b*a*t, b*oo*t, b*u*tcher, b*o*ne, s*aw*, *ah*, t*ur*n, *uh* huh, s*igh*, c*ow*, b*oy*, *th*in, *th* in *th*en, *sh*oe, *zh* in a*zh*ure, *ch*op, si*ng*, *hw* in *wh*en.

Ibsam   IB suhm
Ibzan   IB zan
Ichabod   IK uh bahd
Ichthus   IK thuhs
Ichthys   IK this
icon   IGH kahn
Iconium   igh KO ni uhm
iconoclast   igh KAHN o klast
iconostasis   *igh* ko NAHS tuh
   sis, -suhs
Ida   IGH duh
Idalah   ID uh luh, IGH duh
   luh, i DAY luh
Idbash   ID bash
Iddo   ID o
idealism   igh DEE uhl iz 'm
ideology   *id* i AHL o ji, -uh ju,
   igh di-
idiorrhythmic   *id* i o RITH
   mik, -RITH mik
idol   IGH duhl, -d'l
idolatry   igh DAHL uh tri
Iduel   ID yu el, -uhl
Idumaea   *id* yu MEE uh, *igh*
   dyu-
Idumaean   *id* yu MEE uhn
Ieddias   yed IGH uhs, *igh* uh
   DIGH uhs
Iezer   igh EE zur
Iezerite   igh EE zur ight
Igal   IGH gal
Igdaliah   *ig* duh LIGH uh
Igeal   IGH gi uhl, -ji uhl
Ignatian   ig NAY shuhn
Ignatius   ig NAY shi uhs,
   -shuhs

Ignorantine   *ig* no RAN tin,
   -teen, -tighn
Iim   IGH im
Ije Abarim   *igh* ji   AB uh rim
Ijon   IGH jahn
Ikhnaton   ik NAH tuhn, -t'n
Ikkesh   IK esh
Ikonobortsi   igh KAHN o
   bawrt si
Ilai   IGH lay igh, -ligh
Iliadun   i LIGH uh duhn, IL i
   ad uhn
illative   IL uh tiv, i LAY tiv
illicit   i LIS it, -uht
Illyricum   i LIR i kuhm
image   IM ij
imagery   IM ij ri
Imalcue   *igh* mal KYOO ee,
   igh muhl-
Imla, Imlah   IM luh, -lah
immaculate   i MAK yu lit, -luht
immanent   IM uh nuhnt
Immanuel   i MAN yu uhl, -el
Immer   IM ur
immersion   i MUR shuhn
immolation   *im* o LAY shuhn
immortality   im awr TAL uh ti
Imna   IM nuh
Imnah   IM nah, -nuh
Imnite   IM night
impanation   *im* puh NAY
   shuhn
impious   IM pi uhs
implead   im PLEED
impluvium   im PLOO vi uhm
impost   IM post

KEY: b*ee*, b*i*t, b*e*t, b*a*y, b*a*t, b*oo*t, b*u*tcher, b*o*ne, s*aw*, *ah*, t*ur*n, *uh* huh, s*igh*,
c*ow*, b*oy*, *th*in, t*h* in *th*en, *sh*oe, *zh* in a*z*ure, *ch*op, si*ng*, *hw* in *wh*en.

imprecation *im* pri KAY shuhn
impressionism im PRESH uhn
  iz 'm
imprimatur *im* pri MAY tur
imputation *im* pyu TAY shuhn
Imrah IM ruh
Imri IM righ
incantation *in* kan TAY shuhn
incardination in *kahr* duh NAY
  shuhn
incarnation *in* kahr NAY shuhn
incense IN sens
incest IN sest
In Coena Domini in SEE nuh
  DAHM i nigh, -uh nigh
incontinency in KAHN tuh
  nuhn si
incunabula *in* kyu NAB yu luh
indenture in DEN chur, -tyoor
indeterminism in di TUR min
  iz 'm, -muhn iz 'm
Index IN deks
indiction in DIK shuhn
indite in DIGHT
induction in DUHK shuhn
indulgence in DUHL juhns
indult in DUHLT
inerrancy in ER uhn si
infallibility in *fal* uh BIL uh
  ti
inferiority in *fir* i AWR uh ti
infidel IN fuh duhl
infidelity *in* fuh DEL uh ti,
  in figh-
in fieri in FIGH uh righ
infinite IN fuh nit, -nuht

infralapsarian *in* fruh lap SER
  i uhn
Inge ING
Ingelheim ING g'l highm
Ingham ING uhm
Inglis ING g'lz, -gluhs, -glis
inhibition *in* hi BISH uhn
iniquity i NIK wi ti
innate IN ayt, in AYT
innocent IN o suhnt, -uh s'nt
inordinate in AWR duh nit,
  -nuht
Inquisition *in* kwuh ZISH uhn
inscription in SKRIP shuhn
inspiration *in* spuh RAY shuhn
instinct IN stingkt
insufflation in suh FLAY shuhn
intercession *in* tur SESH uhn
interdict IN tur dikt
intermezzo *in* tur MED zo
internuncio *in* tur NUHN shi o
interpretation in *tur* pri TAY
  shuhn
interregnum *in* tur REG nuhm
interstice in TUR stis, -stuhs
intinction in TINGK shuhn
intonation *in* to NAY shuhn
intrinsic in TRIN sik
introit in TRO it, IN troyt
introversion *in* tro VUR shuhn,
  -zhuhn
introvert *in* tro VURT, IN tro
  vurt
intuition *in* tyu ISH uhn, *in* tu-
intuitive in TYOO uh tiv, in
  TOO-

KEY: b*ee*, b*i*t, b*e*t, b*ay*, b*a*t, b*oo*t, b*u*tcher, b*o*ne, s*aw*, *ah*, t*ur*n, *uh* h*uh*, s*igh*,
c*ow*, b*oy*, *th*in, *th* in *th*en, *sh*oe, *zh* in a*zh*ure, *ch*op, si*ng*, *hw* in *wh*en.

investiture   in VES ti tyoor, -chur
invitatory   in VIGH tuh *to* ri, *-taw* ri
invocation   *in* vo KAY shuhn
Iob   YOB
Iona   igh O nuh
Ionia   igh O ni uh
Ionic   igh AHN ik
iota   igh O tuh, YO tuh
Iphdeiah   if di IGH uh
Iphedeiah   *if* i DEE yuh, -DIGH uh
Iphtah   IF tuh
Iphtah-El   IF tuh *el*
Ir-Ha-Heres   *ir* huh HEE rez
Ir   IR, UR, EER
Ira   IGH ruh
Irad   IGH rad, -ruhd
Iram   IGH ram, -ruhm
Irenaeus   *igh* ri NEE uhs, *igh* ruh-
irenical   igh REN ik 'l
Iri   IGH righ
Irijah   igh RIGH juh
Ir-Nahash   ur NAY hash, ir-
Irpeel   UR pi el, -uhl, IR-
Ir-Shemesh   ur SHEE mesh, ir-
Iru   IGH roo
Isaac   IGH zik
Isaiah   igh ZAY uh, -ZIGH uh
Iscah   IS kuh
Iscariot   is KER i uht
Isdael   IS day el, -uhl
Ish   ISH
Ishbaal   ISH bay uhl

Ishbah   ISH buh
Ishbak   ISH bak
Ishbi-Benob   ish bigh BEE nahb
Ish-Bosheth   ish BO sheth, -BAHSH eth, ISH *bo* sheth
Ishhod   ISH hahd
Ishi   ISH igh, IGH shigh
Ishiah   igh SHIGH uh
Ishija   igh SHIGH juh
Ishma   ISH muh
Ishmael   ISH may el, -mi uhl
Ishmaelite   ISH may el ight, -meel ight
Ishmaiah   ish MAY yuh, -MIGH uh
Ishmeelite   ISH meel ight
Ishmerai   ISH mi righ
Ishod   IGH shahd, ISH ahd
Ishpah   ISH puh, -pah
Ishpan   ISH pan
Ish-Sechel   ISH si kel
Ish-Tob   ISH tahb
Ishuah   ISH yu uh
Ishuai, Ishui   ISH yu igh
Ishvah   ISH vuh
Ishvi   ISH vigh
Ishvite   ISH vight
Isidore   IZ i dor, -dawr, IZ uh-
Islam   IS luhm, IZ-, is LAHM
Ismachiah   *is* muh KIGH uh
Ismael   IS may el, -mi uhl
Ismaerus   *is* muh EE ruhs
Ismaiah   is MAY yuh, -MIGH uh
Ispah   IS puh

KEY: b*ee*, b*i*t, b*e*t, b*ay*, b*a*t, b*oo*t, b*u*tcher, b*o*ne, s*aw*, *ah*, t*ur*n, *uh* h*uh*, s*igh*, c*ow*, b*oy*, *th*in, *th* in *th*en, *sh*oe, *zh* in a*zh*ure, *ch*op, si*ng*, *hw* in *wh*en.

Israel   IZ ray el, -ri uhl, IS-
Israelite   IZ ri uhl ight, IS-
Issachar   IS uh kahr
Isshiah   is SHIGH uh
Isshijah   is SHIGH juh
Issy   ee SEE
Istalcurus   *is* tal KYOO ruhs, is
tuhl-
Isuah   IS yu uh, igh SYOO uh
Isui   IS yu igh, igh SYOO igh
Isvah   IS vuh, -vah
Itala   IT uh la
Ithai   ITH ay igh, ITH igh, igh
THAY igh
Ithamar   ITH uh mahr
Ithiel   ITH i el
Ithlah   ITH luh
Ithma, Ithmah   ITH mah
Ithnan   ITH nan
Ithra   ITH ruh
Ithran   ITH ran
Ithream   ITH ri am, -uhm
Ithrite   ITH right
Itinerarium   igh *tin* ur ER i
uhm
Ittah-Kazin   *it* uh KAY zin,
-zuhn
Ittai   IT ay igh, IT igh, i TAY
igh
Ituraea   *it* yu REE uh
Ivah   IGH vuh
Ives   IGHVZ
Ivo   IGH vo
Ivvah   IV uh
Iyar   EE yahr
Iye-Abarim   igh ee AB uh rim

Iyim   IGH yim
Iyyar   EE yahr, ee YAHR
Izehar   IZ i hahr, IGH zi hahr
Izeharite   IZ i hahr ight, IGH
zi-
Izhar   IZ hahr
Izharite   IZ hahr ight
Izliah   iz LIGH uh
Izrahia, Izrahiah   iz ruh HIGH
uh
Izrahite   IZ ruh hight
Izri   IZ righ
Izziah   iz IGH uh

Jaakan   JAY uh kan, -kuhn
Jaakobah   *jay* uh KO buh
Jaala, Jaalah   JAY uh luh, jay
AY luh
Jaalam   JAY uh lam, jay AY
luhm
Jaanai   JAY uh nigh
Jaar   JAY ur
Jaare-Oregim   *jay* uh ri AWR i
jim, -uh jim
Jaareshiah   *jay* uh ri SHIGH uh
Jaasai   JAY uh sigh
Jaasau   JAY uh saw
Jaasiel   jay AY si el, jay AS i el
Jaasu   JAY uh syoo
Jaazaniah   jay *az* uh NIGH uh
Jaazer   JAY uh zur
Jaaziah   *jay* uh ZIGH uh
Jaaziel   jay AY zi el
Jabal   JAY bal, -buhl
Jabbock   JAB ahk
Jabesh   JAY besh

KEY: b*ee*, b*i*t, b*e*t, b*ay*, b*a*t, b*oo*t, b*u*tcher, b*o*ne, s*aw*, *ah*, t*ur*n, *uh* h*uh*, s*igh*,
c*ow*, b*oy*, *th*in, *th* in *th*en, *sh*oe, *zh* in a*zh*ure, *ch*op, si*ng*, *hw* in *wh*en.

Jabesh-Gilead *jay* besh GIL i uhd
Jabez JAY bez, -biz, -buhz
Jabin JAY bin
Jablonski yah BLAWN ski, juh-
Jabneel JAB ni el, -neel
Jabneh JAB ne
Jacan, Jachan JAY kan
Jacimus JAY si muhs
Jachin JAY kin
Jachinite JAY kin ight
jacinth JAY sinth, JAS inth
jackal JAK awl, -'l
Jacob JAY kuhb, -kuhp
Jacobi yah KO bi, juh-
Jacobin JAK o bin
Jacobite JAK o bight
jactitation *jak* ti TAY shuhn
Jacubus juh KYOO buhs
Jada JAY duh
Jadau JAY daw, juh DAY yoo
Jaddai JAD igh, -ay igh
Jaddua ja DYOO uh, JAD yu uh
Jaddus JAD uhs
Jadon JAY duhn
Jael JAY uhl
Jagur JAY gur
Jah JAH, YAH
Jahalelel juh HAL i lel, -uh lel
Jahath JAY hath
Jahaveh YAH ha ve
Jahaz JAY haz
Jahaza, Jahazah juh HAY zuh

Jahaziah *jay* huh ZIGH uh
Jahaziel juh HAY zi el
Jahdai JAH day igh, -digh
Jahdiel JAH di el
Jahdo JAH do
Jahleel JAH li el
Jahleelite JAH li el ight, -uhl ight
Jahmai JAH may igh, -migh
Jahn YAHN
Jahva YAH vah, -vuh
Jahve, Jahveh YAH ve
Jahvism YAH viz 'm
Jahweh YAH we, -way
Jahwism YAH wiz 'm
Jahzah JAH zuh
Jahzeel JAH zi el
Jahzeelite JAH zi el ight, -'l ight
Jahzeiah jah ZEE yuh, JAH zi yuh
Jahzerah JAH zuh ruh
Jahziel JAH zi el
Jair JAY ur
Jairite JAY ur ight
Jairus JAY uh ruhs, jay IGH ruhs, JIGH ruhs
Jakan JAY kan, -kuhn
Jakeh JAY ke
Jakim JAY kim
Jalam JAY lam, -luhm
Jalon JAY lahn
Jambres JAM breez
Jambri JAM brigh
James JAYMZ
Jamieson JAY mi suhn, JAM i-

KEY: b*ee*, b*i*t, b*e*t, b*ay*, b*a*t, b*oo*t, b*u*tcher, b*o*ne, s*aw*, *ah*, t*ur*n, *uh* h*uh*, s*igh*, c*ow*, b*oy*, *th*in, *th* in *th*en, *sh*oe, *zh* in a*zh*ure, *ch*op, si*ng*, *hw* in *wh*en.

Jamin   JAY min
Jaminite   JAY min ight
Jamlech   JAM lek
Jamnia   JAM ni uh
Jamnite   JAM night
Janai   JAY nay igh, -nigh
Janim   JAY nim
Janizary   JAN i *zer* i
Janna   JAN uh
Jannai   JAN ay igh
Jannes   JAN eez
Janoah   juh NO uh
Janohah   juh NO huh
Jansen   JAN s'n
Jansenism   JAN suhn iz 'm,
   JAN s'n-
Januarius   *jan* yu ER i uhs
Janum   JAY nuhm
Japheth   JAY feth, -fuhth
Japhetite   JAY fet ight, -fit ight
Japhia   juh FIGH uh, JAF i uh
Japhlet   JAF let
Japhleti   JAF li tigh, jaf LEE
   tigh
Japhletite   JAF li tight, jaf LEE
   tight
Japho   JAY fo
Jarah   JAY ruh
Jareb   JAY reb, JAR eb, -uhb
Jared   JAY red
Jaresiah   *jar* uh SIGH uh
Jarha   JAHR huh
Jarib   JAY rib, JAR ib
Jarimoth   JAR i mahth
Jarmuth   JAHR muhth
Jaroah   juh RO uh

Jasael   JAY say el, JAS ay el
Jasaelus   *jas* uh EE luhs
Jashar   JAY shur, JASH ur
Jashen   JAY shuhn, JASH uhn
Jasher   JAY shur, JASH ur
Jashobeam   juh SHO bi am,
   -uhm
Jashub   JAY shuhb, JASH
   uhb
Jashubi-Lehem   juh *shoo* bigh
   LEE hem
Jashubite   JAY shuhb ight
Jasiel   JAY si el, JAS i el
Jason   JAY suhn, -s'n
jasper   JAS pur
Jaspers   YAHS purs
jaspis   JAS pis
Jasubus   juh SYOO buhs
Jatal   JAY tal, -tuhl
Jathan   JAY thuhn
Jathbath   JATH bath
Jathniel   JATH ni el
Jattir   JAT ur
Javan   JAY van
javelin   JAV lin, JAV uh lin
Jazar   JAY zur
Jazer   JAY zur
Jaziel   JAY zi el
Jaziz   JAY ziz
Jearim   JEE uh rim
Jeaterai   ji AT i righ, -uh righ
Jeatherai   ji ATH i righ, -uh righ
Jebb   JEB
Jeberechiah   ji *ber* i KIGH uh
Jebus   JEE buhs
Jebusi   JEB yu sigh

KEY: b*ee*, b*i*t, b*e*t, b*a*y, b*a*t, b*oo*t, b*u*tcher, b*o*ne, s*aw*, *ah*, t*ur*n, *uh* h*uh*, s*igh*,
c*ow*, b*oy*, *th*in, *th* in *th*en, *sh*oe, *zh* in a*zh*ure, *ch*op, si*ng*, *hw* in *wh*en.

Jebusite   JEB yu zight
Jecamiah   *jek* uh MIGH uh
Jechiliah   *jek* i LIGH uh, *jek* uh-
Jecholiah   *jek* o LIGH uh, *jek* uh-
Jechoniah   *jek* o NIGH uh, *jek* uh-
Jechonias   *jek* o NIGH uhs, *jek* uh-
Jecoliah   *jek* o LIGH uh, *jek* uh-
Jeconiah   *jek* o NIGH uh, *jek* uh-
Jeconias   *jek* o NIGH uhs, *jek* uh-
Jedaiah   ji DAY yuh, -DIGH uh
Jeddu   JED oo
Jedediah   *jed* i DIGH uh, *jed* uh-
Jedeus   ji DEE uhs
Jedeiah   ji DEE yuh
Jediael   ji DIGH ay el
Jedidah   ji DIGH duh
Jedidiah   *jed* i DIGH uh, *jed* uh-
Jediel   JEE di el
Jeduthun   ji DYOO thuhn
Jeeli   ji EE ligh
Jeelus   ji EE luhs
Jeezer   ji EE zur
Jeezerite   ji EE zur ight
Jegar-Saha-Dutha   *jee* gahr *say* huh DYOO thuh
Jehaleel   ji HAY li el
Jehaleleel   ji huh LEE li el

Jehalelel, Jehallelel   ji HAL i lel
Jehdeiah   juh DEE yuh, JAY di yuh
Jehezekel   ji HEZ i kel, -uh kel
Jehezkel   ji HEZ kel
Jehiah   ji HIGH uh
Jehiel   ji HIGH el, -uhl
Jehieli   ji HIGH uh ligh
Jehizkiah   *jee* hiz KIGH uh
Jehoadah   ji HO uh duh
Jehoaddah   ji HO uh duh
Jehoaddan   *jee* ho AD uhn
Jehoaddin   *jee* ho AD in, -uhn
Jehoash   ji HO ash
Jehohanan   *jee* ho HAY nan
Jehoiarib   ji HOY uh rib
Jehonadab   ji HAHN uh dab
Jehonathan   ji HAHN uh than, -thuhn
Jehoahaz   ji HO uh haz
Jehoiachin   ji HOY uh kin
Jehoiada   ji HOY uh duh
Jehoiakim   ji HOY uh kim
Jehoram   ji HO ram, -ruhm
Jehoshabeath   *jee* ho SHAB i ath, ji *hosh* uh BEE ath
Jehoshaphat   ji HAHSH uh fat
Jehosheba   ji HAHSH i buh, *jee* ho SHEE buh
Jehoshua, Jehoshuah   ji HAHSH yu uh
Jehovah   ji HO vuh
Jehovah-Cidkenu   -TSID ki nyoo, -tsid KEE nyoo
Jehovah-Jireh   -JIGH re

KEY: b*ee*, b*i*t, b*e*t, b*ay*, b*a*t, b*oo*t, b*u*tcher, b*o*ne, s*aw*, *ah*, t*ur*n, *uh* h*uh*, s*igh*, c*ow*, b*oy*, *th*in, *th* in *th*en, *sh*oe, *zh* in a*zu*re, *ch*op, si*ng*, *hw* in *wh*en.

Jehovah-Nissi -NIS igh
Jehovah-Shalom -SHAY lahm
Jehovah-Shammah -SHAM
  uh
Jehovah-Tsidkenu -TSID ki
  nyoo, -tsid KEE nyoo
Jehovist ji HO vist
Jehozabad ji HAHZ uh bad,
  jee ho ZAY bad
Jehozadak ji HAHZ uh dak, *jee*
  ho ZAY dak
Jehu JEE hyoo
Jehubbah ji HUHB uh
Jehucal ji HYOO kal, -kuhl
Jehud JEE huhd
Jehudi ji HYOO digh
Jehudijah *jee* hyu DIGH juh
Jehuel ji HYOO el
Jehush JEE huhsh
Jeiel ji IGH el
Jekabzeel ji KAB zi el, -zeel
Jekameam *jek* uh MEE am
Jekamiah *jek* uh MIGH uh
Jekuthiel ji KYOO thi el
Jelf JELF
Jemimah ji MIGH muh, juh-
Jemnaan JEM nay uhn
Jemuel ji MYOO el
Jenyns JEN inz
jeopardy JEP ur di
Jephthah JEF thuh
Jephthae JEF thee
Jephunne, Jephunneh ji
  FUHN e
Jerah JEE ruh
Jerahmeel ji RAY mi el

Jerahmeelite ji RAY mi uhl
  ight
Jerechu JER i kyoo
Jerechus JER i kuhs
Jered JEE red
Jeremai JER i migh, *jer* i MAY
  igh, *jer* uh-
Jeremiah *jer* i MIGH uh, *jer*
  uh-
Jeremias *jer* i MIGH uhs, *jer*
  uh-
Jeremiel *jer* i MIGH el, *jer*
  uh-
Jeremoth JER i mahth, -moth
Jeremy JER uh mi
Jeriah ji RIGH uh
Jeribai JER i bigh, *jer* i BAY
  igh, *jer* uh-
Jericho JER i ko, -uh ko
Jeriel JEE ri el, JER i el
Jerijah ji RIGH juh
Jerimoth JER i mahth, -moth
Jerioth JER i ahth, -oth
Jeroboam *jer* o BO uhm, *jer*
  uh-
Jeroham ji RO ham
Jerome ji ROM, juh-
Jerubaal, Jerubbaal *jer* uh BAY
  uhl
Jerubbesheth, Jerubesheth *jer*
  uh BEE sheth, ji RUHB bi
  sheth, -buh sheth
Jeruel ji ROO el, JER oo el
Jerusalem ji ROO suh lem,
  -luhm, juh-
Jerusha, Jerushah ji ROO shuh

KEY: bee, bit, bet, b*a*y, b*a*t, boot, butcher, bone, s*aw*, *ah*, t*ur*n, *uh* huh, s*igh*,
cow, boy, *th*in, **th** in *th*en, *sh*oe, *zh* in a*zh*ure, *ch*op, si*ng*, *hw* in *wh*en.

Jesaiah   ji SAY yuh
Jeshaiah   ji SHAY yuh,
   -SHIGH yuh
Jeshanah   JESH uh nuh, ji
   SHAY nuh
Jesharelah   jesh uh REE luh
Jeshebeab   ji SHEB i ab
Jesher   JEE shur
Jeshimon   ji SHIGH mahn,
   JESH i mahn
Jeshishai   ji SHISH ay igh,
   -SHISH igh
Jeshohaiah   *jesh* o HAY yuh,
   -HIGH uh
Jeshua, Jeshuah   JESH yu uh, ji
   SHOO uh
Jeshurin   JESH yu rin, ji
   SHOO rin
Jeshurun   JESH yu ruhn, ji
   SHOO ruhn
Jesiah   ji SIGH uh
Jesias   ji SIGH uhs
Jesimiel   ji SIM i el
Jesse   JES i
Jessue   JES yu i
Jessop   JES uhp
Jesu   JEE zoo, -soo, YAY zoo,
   -soo
Jesuat, Jesuate   JEZ yu uht
Jesui   JES yu igh
Jesuit   JEZ yu it, JEZH-
Jesuite   JES yu ight
Jesurun   JES yu ruhn, ji SYOO
   ruhn
Jesus   JEE zuhs
Jether   JEE ther

Jetheth   JEE theth
Jethlah   JETH luh
Jethro   JETH ro, JEE thro
Jetur   JEE tur
Jeush   JEE uhsh
Jeuz   JEE uhz
Jew   JOO
Jewess   JOO es, -is, -uhs
Jewett   JOO et, -it, -uht
Jewry   JOO ri
Jezaniah   *jez* uh NIGH uh
Jezebel   JEZ uh bel, -b'l
Jezelus   ji ZEE luhs, JEZ i luhs
Jezer   JEE zur
Jezerite   JEE zur ight
Jezia, Jeziah   JEZ yuh
Jeziel   JEE zi el, ji ZIGH el
Jezlia, Jezliah   *jez* LIGH uh
Jezoar   ji ZO ur
Jezrahiah   *jez* ruh HIGH uh
Jezreel   JEZ ri el, -reel
Jezreelite   JEZ ri uhl ight, -reel
   ight
Jezreelitess   JEZ ri uhl *ight* es,
   -is, JEZ reel-
Jezrielus   *jez* ri EE luhs
Jibsam   JIB sam
Jidlaph   JID laf
Jimna, Jimnah   JIM nuh
Jimnite   JIM night
Jiphtah   JIF tuh
Jiphthahel   JIF thuh el
Joab   JO ab
Joachaz   JO uh kaz
Joachim   JO uh kim
Joachimite   JO uh kim ight

KEY: bee, bit, bet, bay, bat, boot, butcher, bone, saw, ah, turn, uh huh, sigh,
cow, boy, thin, ᵺ in then, shoe, zh in azure, chop, sing, hw in when.

Joacim   JO uh sim
Joadanus   *jo* uh DAY nuhs
Joah   JO uh
Joahaz   JO uh haz, jo AY haz
Joakim   JO uh kim
Joan   JON, JO uhn, jo AN
Joanan   jo AY nan
Joanna   jo AN uh
Joannan   jo AN uhn
Joannes   jo AN eez, -es
Joarib   JO uh rib
Joasaph   JO uh saf
Joash   JO ash
Joatham   JO uh tham
Joazabdus   *jo* uh ZAB duhs
Job   JOB
Jobab   JO bab
Joceline   JAHS uh lin
Jochanan   jo KAY nuhn
Jochebed   JAHK uh bed
Jod, Jodh   YOD, YOTH,
    JAHD
Joda   JO duh
Joed   JO ed
Joel   JO el, -uhl
Joclah   jo EE luh
Joezer   jo EE zur
Jogbehah   JAHG bi hah
Jogli   JAHG ligh
Joha   JO huh
Johanan   jo HAY nuhn
Johannes   jo HAN eez, yo
    HAHN is, -uhs
Johannine   jo HAN in, -ighn
Johannite   jo HAN ight
John   JAHN

Joiada   JOY uh duh
Joiakim   JOY uh kim
Joiarib   JOY uh rib
Joinville   zhwan VEEL
Jokdeam   JAHK di am
Jokim   JO kim
Jokmeam   JAHK mi am
Jokneam   JAHK ni am
Jokshan   JAHK shan
Joktan   JAHK tan
Joktheel   JAHK thi el, -theel
Jona   JO na
Jonadab   JAHN uh dab, JON-
Jonah   JO nuh
Jonam   JO nam
Jonan   JO nan
Jonas   JO nuhs
Jonathan   JAHN uh thuhn
Jonathas   JAHN uh thuhs
Jonath Elem Rehokim   JO nath
    EE lem   ri HO kim
Joppa   JAHP uh
Jorah   JO ruh
Jorai   JO ray igh
Joram   JO ram, -ruhm
Jordan   JAWR d'n
Jordanes   jawr DAY neez
Jordanis   jawr DAY nis
Joribas   JAHR i bas, -buhs
Joribus   JAHR i buhs
Jorim   JO rim
Jorkeam   JAWR ki am
Jorkoam   JAWR ko am
Jornandez   jawr NAN deez
Josabad   JAHS uh bad
Josabdus   jo SAB duhs

KEY: bee, bit, bet, bay, bat, boot, butcher, bone, saw, ah, turn, uh huh, sigh,
cow, boy, thin, th in then, shoe, zh in azure, chop, sing, hw in when.

Josaphat   JAHS uh fat
Josaphias   *jahs* uh FIGH uhs
Joscelin   JAHS uh lin
Jose (Biblical)   JO si
Josech   JO sek
Josedec, Josedech, Josedek
   JAHS uh dek
Joseph   JO zef, -zif, -zuhf
Joseph Barsabas, Barsabbas
   -bahr SAB uhs
Josephinism   JO zuh fin iz 'm,
   -feen iz 'm
Josephus   jo SEE fuhs
Joses   JO seez, JO zez
Joshabad   JAHSH uh bad
Joshah   JO shuh
Joshaphat   JAHSH uh fat
Joshaviah   *jahsh* uh VIGH
   uh
Joshbekashah   *jahsh* bi KAY
   shuh
Josheb-Basshebeth   *jo* sheb ba
   SHEE beth
Joshibiah   *jahsh* i BIGH uh
Joshua   JAHSH yu uh
Josiah   jo SIGH uh
Josias   jo SIGH uhs
Josibiah   *jahs* i BIGH uh, *jahs*
   uh-
Josiphiah   *jahs* i FIGH uh, *jahs*
   uh-
Jost   YOST
jot   JAHT
Jotapata   jo TAP uh tuh
Jotbah   JAHT buh
Jotbath   JAHT bath

Jotbatha, Jotbathah   JAHT buh
   thuh
Jotham   JO tham, -thuhm
Joubert   zhoo BER
Jouffroy   zhoo FRWAH
Jovian   JO vi uhn
Joviannus   jo vi AY nuhs
Jovinian   jo VIN i uhn
Jowett   JOW et, -it, -uht
Joye   JOY
Jozabad   JAHZ uh bad
Jozabdus   jo ZAB duhs
Jozacar, Jozachar   JAHZ uh
   kahr, JO zuh-
Jozadak   JAHZ uh dak, JO zuh-
Jubal   JOO buhl
jube   JOO bi
jubilate (Psalm 100)   *joo* bi
   LAH ti, -LAY ti
jubilee   JOO bi li, -buh li
Jubilees   JOO buh leez
Jucal   JOO kal, -kuhl
Juda   JOO duh
Judaea   joo DEE uh
Judah   JOO duh
Judah Ha-Levi   -hah LEE vigh
Judah Ha-Nasi   -hah NAH si
Judaism   JOO day iz 'm, -di iz
   'm
Judas   JOO duhs
Judas Barsabbas   -bahr SAB uhs
Judas Iscariot   -is KER i uht
Judas Maccabaeus   *-mak* uh
   BEE uhs
Juddah   JUHD uh
Jude   JOOD

KEY: bee, bit, bet, bay, bat, boot, butcher, bone, saw, ah, turn, uh huh, sigh,
cow, boy, thin, th in then, shoe, zh in azure, chop, sing, hw in when.

Judea joo DEE uh
Judges JUHJ iz, -uhz
judgment JUHJ ment, -muhnt
Judica JOO di kuh
judicial ju DISH uhl
Judith JOO dith, -duhth
Judson JUHD s'n
Juel JOO el, -uhl
jugglery JUHG lur i
Julia JOOL yuh
Julian JOOL yuhn
Juliana joo li AN uh, -AH nuh
Julius JOOL yuhs
Julius Africanus -af ri KAY
  nuhs
jumper JUHMP ur
Jung YUNG
Junia JOO ni uh
Junias JOO ni uhs
juniper JOO ni pur, -nuh
  pur
Junius JOON yuhs
jurisdiction jur is DIK shuhn
Jushab-Hesed joo shab HEE
  sed
justification juhs tuh fi KAY
  shuhn
Justin JUHS tin, -tuhn
Justina juhs TIGH nuh
Justinian juhs TIN i uhn
Justinus juhs TIGH nuhs
justle JUHS 'l
Justus JUHS tuhs
Juttah JUHT uh
Juvenal JOO vi nuhl, -vuh n'l
Juxon JUHK s'n

Kaaba KAH buh, KAY uh buh
Kab KAB
kabbala KAB uh luh, kuh
  BAHL uh
Kabzeel KAB zi el, -zeel
Kades KAY deez, -des
Kadesh KAY desh
Kadesh-Barnea kay desh
  BAHR ni uh
Kadmiel KAD mi el
Kadmonite KAD muhn ight
Kagawa KAH gah wah, kah
  GAH wah, kah gah wah
Kain KAYN
Kaiserberg KIGH zurs berk
Kaiserswerth KIGH zurs vert
Kaiwan KAY i wahn, KIGH
  wahn
Kallai KAL ay igh, KAL igh
Kamon KAY mahn
Kana, Kanah KAY nuh
Kanesian kuh NEE si uhn
Kanisic ka NIGH sik, ka NIS
  ik
Kanon KAN uhn
Kant KAHNT, KANT
Kantianism KAN ti uhn iz 'm
Kaph KAHF, KAF
Kappa KAP uh
Karaite KAY ruh ight
Karea, Kareah kuh REE uh,
  KAY ri uh
Kariathiarius kay ri ath i AY
  ri uhs
Karka KAHR kuh
Karkaa KAHR kay uh

KEY: bee, bit, bet, bay, bat, boot, butcher, bone, saw, ah, turn, uh huh, sigh, cow, boy, thin, th in then, shoe, zh in azure, chop, sing, hw in when.

Karkor   KAHR kawr
Karlstadt   KAHRL stad
Karnaim   kahr NAY im
Karnak   KAHR nak, -nahk
Karo   KAH ro
Kartah   KAHR tuh
Kartan   KAHR tan
Kastor   KAS tur
Kathenotheism   kuh THEN
o *thee* iz 'm
Kattath   KAT ath, -uhth
Keble   KEE b'l
Kedar   KEE dur
Kedemah   KED i muh, -uh muh
Kedemoth   KED i mahth, -uh
mahth, -moth, ki DEE moth
Kedesh   KEE desh
Kedesh-Naphtali   *kee* desh NAF
tuh ligh
Kehelathah   *kee* hi LAY thuh,
ki HEL uh thuh
Keilah   ki IGH luh
Keim   KIGHM
Keith   KEETH
Keithian   KEETH yuhn
Kelaiah   ki LAY yuh, -LIGH uh
Kelita   KEL i tuh, ki LIGH
tuh
Kemp, Kempe   KEMP
Kempis   KEMP uhs, -is
Kemuel   KEM yu el, ki MYOO
el
Kenan   KEE nan, -nuhn
Kenath   KEE nath
Kenaz   KEE naz
Kenez   KEE nez

Kenezite   KEE nez ight
Kenite   KEE night, KEN ight
Kenizzite   KEN i zight
Kennedy   KEN i di, -uh di
Kennet   KEN et, -it, -uht
Kennicott   KEN i kaht
kenosis   ki NO sis, -suhs
kenotic   ki NAHT ik
kenotism   KEN o tiz 'm
Kenrick   KEN rik
Kentigern   KEN ti gurn
Kepler   KEP lur
Keras   KEE ras, -ruhs
kere   kuh REE
Keren-Happuch   *ker* uhn HAP
uhk, *kee* ruhn-
keri   kuh REE
Kerioth   KEE ri ahth, -oth
Kerioth-Hezron   *kee* ri ath HEZ
rahn
kernos   KUR nahs
Keros   KEE rahs
Kesil   KEE zil
Kesitah   KES i tah, ki SEE tuh
Kessler   KES lur
Kerr   KUR
kerygma   ki RIG muh, kuh-
keryktik   ki RIK tik
kerystic   ki RIS tik
Keswick   KEZ ik
Ketab   KEE tab
kethib, kethibh   kuh THEEV
Kethubim, Ketubim   ke thoo
VEEM
Keturah   kuh TYOO ruh
Kezia, Keziah   ki ZIGH uh

KEY: bee, bit, bet, bay, bat, boot, butcher, bone, saw, ah, turn, uh huh, sigh,
cow, boy, thin, th in then, shoe, zh in azure, chop, sing, hw in when.

Keziz   KEE ziz
Khabiru   HAHB i roo
Khan   KAHN, KAN
Khapiru   HAHP i roo
Khatti   KAT tee
Khorsabad   KOR suh bahd,
  kor sah BAHD
Khufu   KOO foo
Kibroth-Hattaavah   *kib* rahth
  ha TAY uh vuh, *kib* roth-
Kibzaim   kib ZAY im, KIB zay
  im
Kiddush   KID ush, ki DOOSH
Kidron   KID rahn, -ruhn,
  KIGH druhn
Kierkegaard   KIR ke gawr,
  KEER-
Kilan   KIGH lan
Kildare   kil DER, -DAYR
Kilham   KIL uhm
Kilhamite   KIL uhm ight
Kimah   KIGH muh
Kimchi   KIM ki
Kinah   KIGH nuh
kine   KIGHN
kinesis   ki NEE sis, suhs, kigh
Kingsley   KINGZ li
Kir   KUR, KIR
Kirama   ki RAY muh, KIR uh
  muh
Kirchentag   KEER kuhn tahg
Kir-Hareseth   *kur* HAR uh seth
Kir-Haresh   -HAY resh
Kir-Heres   -HEE res, -rez
Kiriath   KIR i ath
Kiriathaim   *kir* i uh THAY im

Kiriath-Arba   *kir* i ath AHR buh
Kiriath-Arim   -AY rim
Kiriath-Baal   -BAY uhl
Kiriath-Huzoth   -HYOO zahth,
  -zoth
Kiriathiarus   *kir* i *ath* i AY ri uhs
Kiriath-Jearim   *kir* i ath JEE uh
  rim
Kiriath-Sannah   -SAN uh
Kiriath-Sepher   -SEE fur
Kirioth   KIR i ahth, -oth
Kirjath   KUR jath, KIR-
Kirjathaim   *kir* juh THAY im,
  kur-
Kirjath-Arba   -AHR buh
Kirjath-Arim   -AY rim
Kirjath-Baal   -BAY uhl
Kirjath-Huzoth   -HYOO zahth,
  -zoth
Kirjath-Jearim   -JEE uh rim, ji
  AY rim
Kirjath Sannah   SAN uh
kirk   KURK, KIRK
Kiseus   kis EE uhs
Kish   KISH
Kishi   KISH igh
Kishion   KISH i ahn
Kishon   KIGH shahn, KISH
  ahn
Kislev   KIS lef
kite   KIGHT
Kithlish   KITH lish
Kitron   KIT rahn
Kittim   KIT im
Kitto   KIT o
Klausner   KLOWS nur

KEY: b*ee*, b*i*t, b*e*t, b*a*y, b*a*t, b*oo*t, b*u*tcher, b*o*ne, s*a*w, *ah*, t*ur*n, *uh* h*uh*, s*igh*,
c*ow*, b*oy*, *th*in, *th* in *th*en, *sh*oe, *zh* in a*zu*re, *ch*op, si*ng*, *hw* in *wh*en.

kleptomania   *klep* to MAY ni uh
Klopstock   KLAHP stahk
Klosterneuburg   *klos* tur NOY boorg
Knapp   KNAHP (German), NAP (Anglicized)
knead   NEED
Knipperdolling   NIP ur *dahl* ing, KNIP-
Knobel   KNO bel, -buhl
knop   NAHP
Knox   NAHKS
Knudsen, Knudson   NOOD s'n
Koa   KO uh
Kohath   KO hath
Kohathite   KO hath ight, -uhth ight
Koheleth   ko HEL eth, -uhth
koinonia   *koy* no NEE uh, koy NO ni uh
Kolaiah   ko LAY yuh, -LIGH uh
konae   KO nee
König   KUR nig
koph   KOF
kor   KOR, KAWR
Korah   KO ruh, KAWR uh
Korahite   KO ruh hight
Koran   ko RAHN, -RAN, KO ran
Korathite   KO rath ight
Kore   KO ri
Korhite   KAWR hight
Koz   KAHZ

Krafft, Kraft   KRAHFT, KRAFT
Kralitz   KRAH lits
Krasinski   krah SIN ski
krasis   KRAY sis
Krause   KROW ze, -zuh
Krauss   KROWS
Krudener   KROO duh nur
Krug   KROOG
Krummacher   KROO mah kur
krypsis   KRIP sis, -suhs
kryptic   KRIP tik
Kue   KYOO i
Ku Klux Klan   KYOO kluks *klan*, KOO-
Kulturkampf   kul TOOR *kahmpf*
Kushaiah   kyu SHAY yuh, -SHIGH uh
Kuyper   KOY pur
Kyrie eleison   KIR i ee e LAY uh sahn

Laadah   LAY uh duh
Laadan   LAY uh dan
Labadie   la ba DEE
Laban   LAY buhn
Labana   LAB uh nuh
labarum   LAB uh ruhm
Labat   la BA
labis   LAY bis
Laccunus   LAK yu nuhs
Lacedaemonian, Lacedemonian   *las* i di MO ni uhn
La Chaise   la SHEZ
Lachish   LAY kish

KEY: bee, bit, bet, bay, bat, boot, butcher, bone, saw, ah, turn, uh huh, sigh, cow, boy, thin, th in then, shoe, zh in azure, chop, sing, hw in when.

Lachmann   LAHK mahn
Lacordaire   la kawr DER
Lactantius Firmianus   lak TAN
shi uhs *fur* mi AY nuhs
lacticinia   *lak* ti SIN i uh
lacuna   luh KYOO nuh
Ladan   LAY dan, -duhn
ladanum   LAD uh nuhm
Ladislas, Ladislaus   LAD is lahs
Lael   LAY uhl
Laetare   li TAY ri
Lafaye   lah FAY
Lagarde   la GAHRD
Lagrange   la GRAHNZH
Lahad   LAY had
Lahai-Roi   luh HIGH roy,
-HAY roy
Lahmam   LAH mam
Lahmas   LAH mas
Lahmi   LAH mi
Laish   LAY ish
Laishah   lay IGH shuh, LAY
ish uh
laissez faire   les ay FER, *les* i-
laity   LAY i ti, -uh ti
Lakkum, Lakum   LAK uhm
lama   LAH muh
La Marck   la MAHRK
Lambert   LAM burt
Lambeth   LAM beth, -buhth
Lambruschini   *lahm* broos KEE
ni
Lamech   LAY mek
Lamed, Lamedh   LAH med,
-meth
Lamentabili   lah men TAH bi li

Lamennais   la mi NAY
Lamentations   *lam* en TAY
shuhnz
Lammas   LAM uhs
Lamothe   la MOT
lampadary   LAM puh *der* i,
-dur i
Lampe   LAHM pe, -puh
Lampsacus   LAMP suh kuhs
Lamy   la MEE
Lanfranc   LAN frangk
Lange   LANG uh, LANG
Langham   LANG uhm
Langres   LAHNGR'
Langton   LANG tuhn
Laodicea   lay *ahd* i SEE uh
Laodiceans   lay *ahd* i SEE uhnz
Lao-tse, Lao-tzu   LOW tzuh
Lapide   LAP i day
lapis   LAY pis, -puhs, LAP is,
-uhs
lapis lazuli   LAP is LAZ yu
ligh, -li
Laplace   la PLAS
Lapidoth, Lappidoth   LAP i
dahth, doth
Lapsi   LAP sigh
lapwing   LAP wing
larghetto   lahr GET o
largo   LAHR go
Laromiguière   *lah* ro mi GYER
Lasaea   luh SEE uh
Lasalle   luh SAL
Las Casas   lahs KAHS ahs
lasciviousness   la SIV i uhs nes,
-nis, -nuhs

KEY: b*ee*, b*i*t, b*e*t, b*ay*, b*a*t, b*oo*t, b*u*tcher, b*o*ne, s*aw*, *ah*, t*ur*n, *uh* h*uh*, s*igh*,
c*ow*, b*oy*, *th*in, *th* in *th*en, *sh*oe, *zh* in a*zh*ure, *ch*op, si*ng*, *hw* in *wh*en.

Lasea   luh SEE uh
Lasha   LAY shuh
Laski   LAHS ki
Lasharon, Lassharon   luh
 SHAY rahn, -ruhn, -SHER
 uhn
Lasthenes   LAS thi neez
latchet   LACH et, -it, -uht
Lateran   LAT ur uhn
Latimer   LAT uh mur
latitudinarian   *lat* uh *tyoo* duh
 NER i uhn, *lat* uh *too-*
Latourette   *lah* tuh RET, *lat* uh
 RET
La Trappe   lah TRAHP
Latria   luh TRIGH uh
Laubach   LOW bahk
laud   LAWD
Laudian   LAWD i uhn
Launay   lo NAY
Laura   LAW ruh
laureate   LAW ri at, -it, -uht
Laurentius Valla   law REN
 shuhs VAHL uh
Lausanne   lo ZAN
lavabo   luh VAY bo
Lavater   LAH vuh tur, lah VAH
 tur
laver   LAY vur
layman   LAY man, -muhn
Lazarist   LAZ uh rist
Lazarite   LAZ uh right
Lazarus   LAZ uh ruhs
Leacock   LEE kahk
Leah   LEE uh
Leander   li AN dur

Leannoth   li AN ahth, -oth
leasing   LEEZ ing
leaven   LEV uhn
Lebana, Lebanah   li BAY nuh
Lebanon   LEB uh nuhn
Lebaoth   li BAY ahth, -oth
Lebbaeus   luh BEE uhs
Lebonah   li BO nuh
Lebrija, Lebrixa   lay BREE
 huh
Lebrun   luh BRUN
Lecah   LEE kuh
Leclerc   le KLER
Lecompte du Nuoy   luh *kahmp*
 duh NOY, -NOO i
lectern   LEK turn
lectionary   LEK shuhn *er* i
lector   LEK tur, -tawr
lectorium   lek TO ri uhm,
 -TAWR i uhm
leek   LEEK
Lees, lees   LEEZ
legalist   LEE guhl ist
legando   li GAHN do
legate   LEG it, -uht
legato   li GAH to, lay-
Lehabim   li HAY bim
Lehem   li HEM
Lehi   LEE high
Leibnitz   LIGHP nits
Leigh   LEE
Leighton   LAY t'n
Leipsic, Leipzig   LIGHP sik
Leitomischl   LIGHT o mish 'l
Leland   LEE luhnd
Lemelekh   li MEL ek, -ik

Lemuel   LEM yu uhl
Lenfant   lahn FAHN
Lenin   LEN in, -uhn
Lenoir   le NWAHR
lentil   LEN t'l
Leo   LEE o
Leonardo da Vinci   li o
   NAHR do   duh   VIN chi,
   lay-
Leonine   LEE o nighn
Leontius   li AHN shi uhs,
   -shuhs
Lepanto   lay PAHN to
leper   LEP ur
leprosy   LEP ro si, -ruh si
Lérins   lay RAN
Leshem   LEE shem
Lessau   LES aw
Lessing   LES ing
Lethech   LEE thek
Lettus   LET uhs
Letushim   li TYOO shim
Leucippus   lyu SIP uhs, lu-
Leummim   li UHM im, -uhm
Leveller   LEV uhl ur
Levi   LEE vigh
Leviathan   li VIGH uh thuhn
Levirate   LEV uh rayt, LEE
   vuh rayt
Levis   LEE vis, -vuhs
Levite   LEE vight
Levitical   li VIT i k'l
Leviticus   li VIT i kuhs
Leydecker   LIGH dek ur,
   LIGH di kur
Leyden, Leiden   LIGH d'n

Libanius   li BAY ni uhs
Libanus   LIB uh nuhs
libation   ligh BAY shuhn
libel   LIGH buhl, -b'l
liberalism   LIB ur uhl iz 'm
Liberian   ligh BIR i uhn
Liberius   ligh BIR i uhs, ligh
   BEER-
libertine   LIB ur teen, -tin
Libnah   LIB nuh
Libni   LIB nigh
Libnite   LIB night
libretto   li BRET o
Libya   LIB i uh, -yuh
licentiate   ligh SEN shi uht,
   -ayt
licentious   ligh SEN shuhs
Lichfield   LICH feeld
Liddel   LID'L, li DEL
Liddon   LID 'n
Lidebir   LID i bur
Liebknecht   LEEP nekt
ligature   LIG uh chur, -tyoor
Lightfoot   LIGHT fut
lign-aloes   lighn AL oz
Liguori   li CWAW ri
Liguorian   li GWO ri uhn, li
   GWAW-
ligure   LIG yur
Likhi   LIK high
Lilienthal   LEE li uhn tahl
Lilith   LIL ith, -uhth, LIGH
   lith, -luhth
limbo   LIM bo
Limborch   LIM bawrk
Linacre   LIN uh kur

KEY: bee, bit, bet, bay, bat, boot, butcher, bone, saw, ah, turn, uh huh, sigh,
cow, boy, thin, th in then, shoe, zh in azure, chop, sing, hw in when.

Lindisfarne   lin dis FAHRN
Lindsay, Lindsey   LIN zi
lineage   LIN ij
Lingard   LING gahrd
lintel   LIN t'l
Linus   LIGH nus
Lippi   LIP i
Lipsius   LIP si uhs
Lisle   LIGHL
Lismore   liz MOR, -MAWR
Liszt   LIST
litany   LIT uh ni
liturgical   li TUR ji kuhl
liturgiology   li *tur* ji AHL o ji,
    -uh ji
liturgy   LIT ur ji
Liutprand   LEE ut prahnt
Llandaff   lan DAF
Llorente   yo RAYN tay, lyo-
Lo-Ammi   lo AM igh
Lobo   LO bo
Locke   LAHK
loculus   LAHK yu luhs
Lod   LOD
Loddeus   lahd EE uhs
Lo-Debar   *lo* DEE bahr, LO di
    bahr
logia   LAHG i uh, LO gi uh
logic   LAHJ ik
logistic   lo JIS tik
logos   LAHG ahs, LO gahs, LO
    gos
logothete   LAHG o theet
loins   LOYNZ
Lois   LO is, -uhs
Loisy   lwah ZEE

Lolhard, Lollard, Lollhard
    LAHL urd
Lombard   LAHM burd, -bahrd,
    LUHM-
Longinus   lahn JIGH nuhs
Longobardi   *lahng* go BAHR
    digh
lor   LOR, LAWR
Lord   LAWRD
Loreto   lo RAY to
loric   LAHR ik
Lorsch   LAHRSH, LAWRSH
Lo-Ruhamah   *lo* roo HAY muh,
    -HAH muh
Lot   LAHT
Lothasubus   *lahth* uh SYOO
    buhs
lotus   LO tuhs
Lotze   LAWT suh
Lourdes   LOORD
Lowth   LOWTH
Loyola   loy O luh
Lozon   LO zahn
Lubim   LYOO bim, LOO-
Lucan, Lukan   LYOO kuhn,
    LOO-
Lucaris, Lukaris   LYOO kuh ris,
    LOO-
Luccock   LUHK ahk
lucernarium   *lyoo* sur NAY ri
    uhm, *loo*-
Lucia   LYOO shuh, LOO-
Lucian   LYOO shuhn, LOO-
Lucianic   *loo* shi AN ik
Lucifer   LYOO si fur, LOO
    suh fur

KEY: b*ee*, b*i*t, b*e*t, b*a*y, b*a*t, b*oo*t, b*u*tcher, b*o*ne, s*aw*, *ah*, t*u*rn, *uh* h*uh*, s*igh*,
c*ow*, b*oy*, *th*in, *th* in *th*en, *sh*oe, *zh* in a*zh*ure, *ch*op, si*ng*, *hw* in *wh*en.

Lucina   lo SIGH nuh
Lucius   LYOO shi us, -shuhs, LOO-
lucre   LYOO kur, LOO-
Lud   LUHD
Ludim   LYOO dim, LOO-
Ludolf   LOO dahlf
Lugo   LOO go
Luhith   LYOO hith, LOO-
Luitprand   LOO it prahnt
Luke   LYOOK, LOOK
Lully   LUHL i
Lund   LUHND
Lupus   LYOO puhs, LOO-
lustration   luhs TRAY shuhn
lute   LYOOT, LOOT
Luther   LYOO thur, LOO-
Lutheran   LYOO thur uhn, LOO-
Luz   LUHZ
Lycaonia   lik ay O ni uh, ligh kay-
Lycia   LIS i uh, LISH uh
Lydda   LID uh
Lydia   LID i uh
Lyons   li AWN, -ON, LIGH uhnz
lyre   LIGHR
lyric   LIR ik
Lysanias   ligh SAY ni uhs
Lysias   LIS i uhs
Lysimachus   ligh SIM uh kuhs
Lystra   LIS truh

Maacah   MAY uh kuh
Maacath   MAY uh kath

Maacathite   may AK uh thight
Maachah   MAY uh kuh
Maachathi   may AK uh thigh
Maachathite   may AK uh thight
Maadai   *may* uh DAY igh, MAY uh digh
Maadiah   *may* uh DIGH uh
Maai   may AY igh, MAY igh
Maaleh-Acrabbim   MAY uh le a KRAB im, may AL e-
Maaleh-Adummim   -a DUHM im
Maani   MAY uh nigh
Maarath   MAY uh rath
Maareh-Geba   MAY uh re GEE buh, -GAY buh
Maasai   MAY uh sigh, may AS igh
Maaseas   *may* uh SEE uhs
Maaseiah   *may* uh SEE yuh, -SIGH uh
Maasiai   *may* uh SIGH igh
Maasias   *may* uh SIGH uhs
Maasmas   may AS muhs, MAY uhs muhs
Maath   MAY ath
Maaz   MAY az
Maaziah   *may* uh ZIGH uh
Mabdai   MAB day igh
Mabillon   mah bee YAWN, -YON
Mabnabedai   mab NAB i digh, -uh digh
macabre   muh KAH bur, -br'
Macalon   MAK uh lahn
Macarius   ma KAY ri uhs, muh-

KEY: b*ee*, b*i*t, b*e*t, b*a*y, b*a*t, b*oo*t, b*u*tcher, b*o*ne, s*aw*, *ah*, t*ur*n, *uh* h*uh*, s*igh*, c*ow*, b*oy*, *th*in, *th* in *th*en, *sh*oe, *zh* in a*zh*ure, *ch*op, si*ng*, *hw* in *wh*en.

Macauley   muh KAW li
Maccabaeus   *mak* uh BEE uhs
Maccabees   MAK uh beez
Macedo   mah SAY do
Macedonia   *mas* uh DO ni uh
Macedonius   *mas* uh DO ni uhs
Machaerus   ma KEE ruhs, muh-
Machbanai, Machbannai   MAK
   buh nigh
Machbena   mak BEE nuh
Machen   MAY chuhn
Machi   MAY kigh
Machiavelli   *mak* i uh VEL i
Machiavellian   *mak* i uh VEL i
   uhn, -yuhn
Machiavellism   *mak* i uh VEL
   iz 'm
Machir   MAY kir
Machirite   MAY kir ight, -kur
   ight
Machmas   MAK muhs
Machnadebai   mak NAD i bigh
Machpelah   mak PEE luh
Mackay, McKay   muh KIGH,
   muk KAY
Mackenzie   muh KEN zi
Mackey, Mackie   MAK i
Macintosh   MAK in tahsh,
   -tawsh
Mackonochie   muh KAHN o
   ki, -uh ki
MacLaren   muh KLAR uhn,
   -KLER uhn
Macleod   muh KLOWD, mak
   LOWD
Macon   mah KAWN, -KON

Maconah   may KO nuh
Macrina   ma KRIGH nuh,
   muh-
Macrobius   ma KRO bi uhs,
   muh-
macrocosm   MAK ro kahz 'm
Macron   MAY krahn, MAK
   rahn
Madai   MAD ay igh, MAY
   digh
Madiabun   muh DIGH uh
   buhn
Madiah   muh DIGH uh
Madian   muh DIGH uhn
Madmannah   mad MAN uh
Madmenah   mad MEE nuh
Madon   MAY dahn
Madonna   muh DAHN uh
Madras   muh DRAS
madrigal   MAD ri guhl
Maelus   may EE luhs
maestoso   *mah* es TO so, *migh-*
maestro   MIGHS tro
Maffei   mah FAY ee
Magadan   MAG uh dan, ma
   GAY duhn, muh-
Magbish   MAG bish
Magdala   MAG duh luh
Magdalen   MAG duh len, -lin,
   -luhn
Magdalen (college)   MAWD
   lin
Magdalena   mahg duh LAY
   nuh
Magdalene   MAG duh leen,
   mag duh LEE ni

KEY: b*ee*, b*i*t, b*e*t, b*ay*, b*a*t, b*oo*t, b*u*tcher, b*o*ne, s*aw*, *ah*, t*ur*n, *uh* h*uh*, s*igh*,
c*ow*, b*oy*, *th*in, **th** in *th*en, *sh*oe, *zh* in a*z*ure, *ch*op, si*ng*, *hw* in *wh*en.

Magdeburg MAHG duh boorg

Magdiel MAG di el

Maged MAY ged

Magi MAY jigh

magic MAJ ik

magnifical mag NIF i kuhl

Magnificat mag NIF i kat

Magnus MAHG noos, MAG nuhs

Magog MAY gahg

Magor-Missabib MAY gahr MIS uh bib

Magpiash MAG pi ash

Magus MAY guhs

Magyar MAG yahr

Mahalab muh HAY lab, MAY huh lab

Mahalah muh HAY luh, MAY huh lah

Mahalaleel muh HAY luh *lee* el, muh HAL uh leel

Mahalalel muh HAY luh lel

Mahalath MAY huh lath

Mahalcel muh HAY li el

Mahali MAY huh ligh

Mahanaim *may* huh NAY im

Mahanch-Dan MAY huh ne *dan*

Maharai muh HAR ay igh, muh HER-

Mahath MAY hath

Mahavite MAY huh vight

Mahazioth muh HAY zi ahth, -oth

Maher-Shalal-Hash-Baz *may* hur *shal* al HASH baz

Mahlah MAH luh

Mahli MAH ligh

Mahlite MAH light

Mahlon MAH lahn

Mahol MAY hahl

Mahseiah mah SEE yuh, -SIGH uh

Mai MAH ee, MIGH

Maianeas migh AN i uhs

Maiannas migh AN uhs

Maimbourg mam BOOR

Maimonides migh MAHN i deez, -uh deez

Maine de Biran *mayn* duh bi RAHN

Maintenon mant NAWN

Maistre, de duh MAYSTR'

Maitland MAYT luhnd

Major MAY jur

Majoristic *may* jur IS tik

majuscule muh JUHS kyool

Makaz MAY kaz

Makebate MAYK *bayt*

Maked MAY ked

Makheloth mak HEE lahth

Makkedah ma KEE duh

Maktesh MAK tesh

Malabar MAL uh bahr

Malachi MAL uh kigh

Malachy MAL uh ki

Malcam, Malcham MAL kam, -kuhm

Malchiah mal KIGH uh

Malchiel MAL ki el

KEY: bee, bit, bet, bay, bat, boot, butcher, bone, saw, ah, turn, uh huh, sigh, cow, boy, thin, th in then, shoe, zh in azure, chop, sing, hw in when.

Malchielite   MAL ki el ight,
-uhl ight
Malchijah   mal KIGH juh
Malchiram   mal KIGH ram,
-ruhm
Malchi-Shua   *mal* kigh SHOO
uh
Malchus   MAL kuhs
Malebranche   mahl BRAHNSH
malefactor   MAL i *fak* tur,
MAL uh-
Maleleel   muh LEE li el, MAL
i leel
malevolent   muh LEV o luhnt,
-uh luhnt
malice   MAL is, -uhs
mall   MAWL
Mallos   MAL ahs, -uhs
Mallothi   MAL o thigh
mallow   MAL o
Malluch   MAL uhk
Malluchi   MAL yu kigh
Mallus   MAL uhs
Malmesbury   MAHMZ ber i
Malobathron   *mal* o BATH
rahn
Maltanneus   *mal* ta NEE uhs,
mal tuh-
Maltese   MAWL teez, -tees,
MAHL-
Malthus   MAL thuhs
Malvern   MAWL vurn
Mamaias   muh MAY yas, -yuhs
Mamertine   MAM ur tighn
mammillarian   *mam* i LAY ri
uhn, *mam* uh LAR i uhn

Mammon   MAM uhn
Mamnitanaimus   *mam* nuh tuh
NAY muhs, -NIGH muhs
Mamnitanemus   *mam* nuh tuh
NEE muhs
Mamre   MAM ri
Mamuchus   ma MYOO kuhs,
muh-
Manaen   MAN uh en, -i en
Manahath   MAN uh hath
Manahathite   MAN uh hath
ight, muh NAY huh thight
Manahethite   muh NAY heth
ight, MAN uh heth ight
Manasseas   *man* uh SEE uhs
Manasseh   muh NAS uh
Manasses   muh NAS eez, -uhs
Manassite   muh NAS ight
manchet   MAN chet, -chit,
-chuht
Mandaean   man DEE uhn
Mandeville   MAN duh vil
mandra   MAN druh
mandrake   MAN drayk
mandyas   MAN di uhs
Maneh   MAN e
Manes   MAY neez
Manetho   MAN i tho, -uh tho
manger   MAYN jur
Mani   MAY nigh
Mani (Manichaeans)   MAH
nee
Manichaeism, Manicheism
man uh KEE iz 'm
Manichaeus   *man* i KEE uhs,
man uh-

KEY: bee, bit, bet, bay, bat, boot, butcher, bone, saw, ah, turn, uh huh, sigh,
cow, boy, thin, th in then, shoe, zh in azure, chop, sing, hw in when.

manifold MAN i fold, -uh fold
maniple MAN uh p'l
Manius MAY ni uhs
mankind *man* KIGHND
Manlius MAN li uhs
manna MAN uh
Manners-Sutton MAN urz SUHT 'n
Manoah muh NO uh
manse MANS
Mansel MAN sel, -suhl
Manson MAN suhn
Mant MANT
Mantegna mahn TAYN yuh
mantelet MAN t'l uht, MANT let, -lit, -luht
mantelleta *man* tuh LET uh
mantellone *man* ti LO nay
mantle MAN t'l
Manton MAN tuhn
manuductor *man* yu DUHK tur
manuscript MAN yu skript
Maoch MAY ahk
Maon MAY ahn
Maonite MAY ahn ight, may O night
Maphrian MAF ri uhn
Mara MAY ruh, MER uh
Marah MAY ruh, MER uh
Maralah MAR uh lah, muh RAY lah
Maranatha *mar* uh NATH uh
Marburg MAHR boorg
Marcan MAHR kuhn
marcando mahr KAHN do

Marcella mahr SEL uh
Marcellian mahr SEL i uhn
Marcellianus mahr *sel* i AY nuhs
Marcellinus *mah*r se LIGHN uhs, *mahr* suh-
Marcellus mahr SEL uhs
Marcheshvan mahr CHESH van
Marcian MAHR shi uhn, -shuhn
Marcion MAHR shuhn, -shi uhn
Marcionite MAHR shuhn ight
Marcosian mahr KO zhuhn
Marcus MAHR kuhs
Marcus Aurelius MAHR kuhs aw REE li uhs
Mardochaeus *mahr* do KEE uhs
Mardochai MAHR do kigh
Mardocheus *mahr* do KEE uhs
Mareal MAR i uhl
Maresha, Mareshah muh REE shuh
Margaret MAHR guh ret, -rit, -ruht
Marheineke mahr HIGH ni ke, -ki
Marheshvan mahr HESH van
Mari MAHR i
Maria mah REE uh, muh-
Mariana *mah* ree AH nah
Marianist MAR i uhn ist, MER-
Mariazell mah *ree* ah TSEL

Marimoth   MAR i mahth
Mariolatry   *mer* i AHL uh tri
Mariology   *mer* i AHL o ji, -uh
  ji
Marisa   MAR i suh, -uh suh
Marist   MER ist
Maritain   mar i TAN, -TAYN
Marius   MER i uhs
Mark   MAHRK
marl   MAHRL
Marmontel   mahr mawn TEL
Marot   mah RO
Marmoth   MAHR mahth,
  -moth
Maronite   MAR o night, MER-
Maroth   MAY rahth, -roth,
  MER ahth, -oth
Marprelate   MAHR *prel* it,
  -uht
marriage   MAR ij, MER-
Marrow   MAR o, MER-
Mars   MAHRZ
Marsden   MAHRZ duhn
Marsena   mahr SEE nuh,
  MAHR si nuh
Marsiglio   mahr SEEL yo
Martel   mahr TEL
Martensen   MAHR tuhn suhn
Martha   MAHR thuh
Mar Thoma   *mahr* TO muh
Martineau   MAHR ti no
Martini   mahr TEE nee
Martinist   MAHR tin ist, -t'n
  ist
Martinmas   MAHR tin muhs,
  -t'n muhs

Martyn   MAHR tin, -t'n
martyr   MAHR tur
martyrium   mahr TIR i uhm
martyrology   mahr tur AHL o ji,
  -uh ji
Marx   MAHRKS
Marxism   MAHRK siz 'm
Mary   MER i, MAY ri, MAR i
Masoloth   MAS uh lahth, -loth
Mascaron   mahs kah RAWN,
  -RON
Maschil   MAHS keel, -kil
Mash   MASH
Mashal   MAY shal
Masias   muh SIGH uhs
Masman   MAS muhn
Masora, Masorah   muh SO ruh,
  -SAWR uh
Masorete   MAS o reet
Masoreth, Massoreth   muh SO
  reth, -SAWR eth
Masoretic   *mas* o RET ik, *mas*
  uh-
Maspha   MAS fuh
Masrekah   MAS ri kuh
Massa, Massah   MAS uh
Massalian   ma SAY li uhn, muh-
Massebah   ma SEE bah, muh-
Massebath   ma SEE bath, muh-
Masseketh   MAS i keth
Massias   muh SIGH uhs
Massilian   muh SIL i uhn
Massillon   mah see YAWN,
  -YON
Massorete   MAS o reet
Massoretic   *mas* o RET ik

KEY: b*ee*, b*i*t, b*e*t, b*ay*, b*a*t, b*oo*t, b*u*tcher, b*o*ne, s*aw*, *ah*, t*ur*n, *uh* h*uh*, s*igh*,
c*ow*, b*oy*, *th*in, *th* in *th*en, *sh*oe, *zh* in a*zh*ure, *ch*op, si*ng*, *hw* in *wh*en.

Mastaba, Mastabah   MAS tuh
buh
mastic, mastick   MAS tik
mater dolorosa   MAY tur do lo
RO suh
materialism   muh TIR i uhl iz
'm
Maternus   may TUR nuhs
Mathanias   *math* uh NIGH uhs
Mathelas   ma THEE luhs, muh-
Mather   MATH ur
Mathilda   muh TIL duh
Mathurin   MATH yu rin
Mathurist   MATH yu rist
Mathusala   muh THYOO suh
luh
Matilda   muh TIL duh
Matin   MAT in
Matred   MAY tred
Matri   MAY trigh
matricula   muh TRIK yu luh
matrimony   MAT ri *mo* ni,
MAT ruh-
Matrite   MAY tright
matrix   MAY triks, MAT riks
Mattan   MAT uhn
Mattanah   MAT uh nuh
Mattaniah   *mat* uh NIGH uh
Mattatha   MAT uh thuh
Mattathah   MAT uh thuh
Mattathias   *mat* uh THIGH
uhs
Mattattah   MAT uh tuh
Mattenai   *mat* i NAY igh, MAT
i nigh
Matthan   MAT than

Matthanias   *mat* thuh NIGH
uhs
Matthat   MAT that
Matthelas   mat THEE luhs,
MAT thi luhs
Matthew   MATH yoo
Matthias   muh THIGH uhs
Mattin   MAT in
Mattinata   *mat* in AH tuh
Mattithiah   *mat* uh THIGH uh
mattock   MAT uhk
Maugham   MAWM
maul   MAWL
Maunday, Maundy   MAWN di
Maurice   MAW ris
Maurist   MAW rist
Mauritius   maw RISH i uhs
Maurus   MAW ruhs
Maury   mo REE
Mauzzim   MAWZ eem, -im,
MAWTS-
Maximilian   *mak* si MIL yuhn
Maximus   MAK si muhs
Mayence   mah YAHNS
Maynooth   may NOOTH
Mayr   MIGHR, MIGH ur
Mazarin   MAZ uh rin
Mazitias   *maz* i TIGH uhs,
maz uh-
Mazzaloth   MAZ uh lahth,
-loth
Mazzaroth   MAZ uh rahth,
-roth
Mazzebah   ma ZEE bah, -buh
McClintock   muh KLIN tahk,
-tik, -tuhk

KEY: b*ee*, b*i*t, b*e*t, b*a*y, b*a*t, b*oo*t, b*u*tcher, b*o*ne, s*aw*, *ah*, t*ur*n, *uh* h*uh*, s*igh*,
c*ow*, b*oy*, *th*in, **th** in *th*en, *sh*oe, *zh* in a*zh*ure, *ch*op, si*ng*, *hw* in *wh*en.

McCloskey   muh KLAHS ki
McIlvaine   *mak* il VAYN
McLeod   mak LOWD, muh
  KLOWD
Mead, Meade   MEED
Meah   MEE uh
Meani   mi AY nigh
Mearah   mi AY ruh
Mebunnai   mi BUHN igh, -ay
  igh
Mecca   MEK uh
Mecherah   mi KEE ruh
Mecherathite   mi KEE ruh
  thight
Mechitar   mek i TAHR
Mechitarist   MEK i *tahr* ist
Mechlin   MEK lin
Meconah   mi KO nuh
Medaba   MED uh buh
Medad   MEE dad
Medan   MEE dan
Mede   MEED
Medeba   MED i buh, -uh buh
Medhurst   MED hurst
Media   MEE di uh
Median   MEE di uhn
mediation   *mee* di AY shuhn
mediator   MEE di *ay* tur
Medici   MED i chee, MAY di-
mediety   mi DIGH uh ti
meditation   *med* uh TAY shuhn
Mediterranean   *med* uh tuh
  RAY ni uhn
Meeda   mi EE duh
Meedda   mi ED uh
megalithic   *meg* uh LITH ik

Megara   MEG uh ruh
Megarian   mi GER i uhn
Megaron   MEG uh rahn
Megiddo   mi GID o
Megiddon   mi GID ahn
Megillah   mi GIL uh
Megilloth   mi GIL oth
Mehetabeel   mi HET uh beel,
  muh-
Mehetabel   mi HET uh bel,
  muh-
Mehida   mi HIGH duh
Mehir   MEE hur
Meholah   mi HO luh
Meholathite   mi HO luh thight
Mehujael   mi HYOO jay el
Mehuman   mi HYOO man,
  -muhn
Mehunim   mi HYOO nim
Meier   MIGH ur
Meineke   MIGH ne ke, -ni ki
Meiners   MIGH nurs
Meisner, Meissner   MIGHS
  nur
Meister   MIGHS tur
Me-Jarkon   *mee* JAHR kahn
Mekhitar   mek i TAHR
Mekitarist   MEK i *tahr* ist
Mekonah   mi KO nuh
melancholia   *mel* uhn KO li uh
Melancthon   me LANGK
  thuhn, muh-
Melatiah   *mel* uh TIGH uh
Melchi   MEL kigh
Melchia, Melchiah   mel KIGH
  uh

KEY: bee, bit, bet, bay, bat, boot, butcher, bone, saw, ah, turn, uh huh, sigh,
cow, boy, thin, th in then, shoe, zh in azure, chop, sing, hw in when.

Melchias mel KIGH uhs
Melchiel MEL ki el
Melchiorite MEL ki awr ight,
 -kyawr ight
Melchisedec, Melchisedech
 mel KIZ uh dek
Melchishua *mel* ki SHOO uh
Melchite MEL kight
Melchizedek mel KIZ uh dek
Melea MEE li uh, MEL i uh
Melech MEE lek, MEL ek
Melekite MEL uh kight
Meletian mi LEE shi uhn,
 -shuhn
Meletius me LEE shi uhs,
 -shuhs
Melichu, Melicu MEL i kyoo
meliorism MEEL yo riz 'm
Melita MEL i tuh, -uh tuh
Melito MEL i to
Mellitus MEL i tuhs
melodia muh LO di uh
Melville MEL vil
Melzar MEL zahr
mem MEM
Memcroth MEM i rahth, roth
Memling MEM ling
Memmi MEM mi
Memmius MEM i uhs
memorial me MO ri uhl, muh
 MAWR i uhl
Memphis MEM fis, -fuhs
Memucan mi MYOO kan
Menahem MEN uh hem
Menaion mi NIGH ahn
Menan MEE nan

Mencke MENG ke, -ki, -kuh
Mendaen men DEE uhn
Mendelssohn MEN duhl son,
 -suhn
Mendez MEN dez, men DEZ
mendicant MEN di kant,
 -kuhnt
mene mene tekel upharsin
 MEE ni MEE ni TEK uhl
 yu FAHR sin, -suhn
Menelaus *men* i LAY uhs
Menes MEE neez
Menestheus mi NES thyoos,
 -thi uhs
Mengs MENGZ
Menhir MEN hir
meni ME nigh
Menippus me NIP uhs
Menna MEN uh
Menno MEN o
Mennonite MEN uhn ight
menologium *men* o LO ji uhm
mensa MEN suh
mensal MEN suhl, -s'l
mensa capitularis MEN suh
 kuh *pit* yu LAY ris, -kuh *pi* chu-
mensa episcopalis MEN suh
 ee *pis* ko PAY lis, -luhs
Menuhah men YOO hah
Menuhoth men YOO hahth,
 -hoth
Meonenim mi AHN i nim,
 -uh nim
Meonothai mi AHN o thigh,
 -uh thigh, mi O no, *mee* o
 NO-

KEY: bee, bit, bet, bay, bat, boot, butcher, bone, saw, ah, turn, uh huh, sigh,
cow, boy, thin, th in then, shoe, zh in azure, chop, sing, hw in when.

Mephaath   MEF ay ath, mi
FAY ath
Mephibosheth   me FIB o sheth,
muh-
Merab   MEE rab
Meraiah   mi RAY yuh, -RIGH
uh
Meraioth   mi RAY yahth,
-RIGH yoth
Meran   MEE ran
Merari   mi RAY righ
Merarite   mi RAY right
Merathaim   *mer* uh THAY im
Mercedarian   *mur* si DER i uhn
Mercier   mer SYAY
Mercurius   mur KYOO ri uhs
Mercury   MUR kyu ri
mercy   MUR si
Mered   MEE red
Meremoth   MER i mahth,
-moth
Meribah   MER i bah, muh
REE bah
Meribah-Kadesh   *mer* i bah
KAY desh
Meribath-Kadesh   *mer* i bath
KAY desh, *mer* uh-
Merib-Baal   *mer* ib BAY al,
-uhl
Meriboth-Kadesh   *mer* i bahth
KAY desh, *mer* uh-
Merino   me REE no, muh-
merit   MER it, -uht
Merle d'Aubigné   *merl* do
been YAY
Merlin   MUR lin

Merodach   mi RO dak, MER o
dak
Merodach-Baladan   -BAL uh
dan
Merom   MEE rahm
Meronathite, Meronothite   mi
RAHN uh thight
Meroz   MEE rahz
Merran   MER uhn
Mersenne   mer SEN
Meruth   MEE ruhth
Mesaloth   MES uh lahth, -loth
Mesech   MEE sek
Mesha   MEE shuh
Meshach   MEE shak
Meshech   MEE shek
Meshelemiah   mi *shel* uh
MIGH uh
Meshezabeel   mi SHEZ uh beel
Meshezabel   mi SHEZ uh bel
Meshillemith   mi SHIL uh
mith
Meshillemoth   mi SHIL uh
mahth, -moth
Meshobab   mi SHO bab
Meshullam   mi SHUHL uhm
Meshullemeth   mi SHUHL uh
meth
Mesmer   MES mur, MEZ mur
mesmerism   MES mur iz 'm,
MEZ-
Mesobaite   mi SO buh ight
Mesopotamia   *mes* o po TAY
mi uh, *mes* uh puh-
Mesrob   mes RAHB
Messiah   me SIGH uh, muh-

KEY: b*ee*, b*i*t, b*e*t, b*ay*, b*a*t, b*oo*t, b*u*tcher, b*o*ne, s*aw*, *ah*, t*ur*n, *uh* h*uh*, s*igh*,
c*ow*, b*oy*, *th*in, *th* in *th*en, *sh*oe, *zh* in a*zh*ure, *ch*op, si*ng*, *hw* in *wh*en.

Messianic   *mes* i AN ik
Messias   me SIGH uhs, muh-
metagnostic   *met* ag NAHS tik
metalogical   *met* uh LAHJ i k'l
metamorphosis   *met* uh
  MAWR fo sis, -fuh suhs,
  -mawr FO sis
metaphrast   MET uh frast
metaphysic   *met* uh FIZ ik
Metastasio   may tahs TAH zi o
mete   MEET
metempsychosis   me *temp* sigh
  KO sis, -suhs
Meterus   mi TEE ruhs
meteyard   MEET *yahrd*
Metheg-Ammah   *mee* theg AM
  uh, *meth* eg-
Metheghammah   *mee* theg
  HAM uh, *meth* eg-
Methoar   METH o ahr
methodism   METH uhd iz 'm
Methodist   METH uhd ist,
  uhst
Methodius   me THO di uhs
Methusael   mi THYOO say el
Methuselah   mi THYOO zuh
  luh, muh THOO-
Methushael   mi THYOO shay
  el
metropolitan   *met* ro PAHL uh
  tuhn
metropoliticum   *met* ro po LIT
  i kuhm
Mettray   met RAY
Metz   METS
Meunim   mi YOO nim

Meunite   mi YOO night
Meuzal   mi YOO zuhl
Meyer   MIGH ur
Me-Zahab   MEZ uh hab, mi
  ZAY hab
Mezarim   MEZ uh rim
Mezobaite   mi ZO bay ight
Mezzofanti   *med* zo FAHN ti
Miamin   MIGH uh min
Mibhar   MIB hahr
Mibsam   MIB sam
Mibzar   MIB zahr
Mica, Micah   MIGH kuh
Micaiah   migh KAY yuh,
  -KIGH uh
Micha   MIGH kuh
Michael   MIGH kay uhl, -k'l
Michael-Angelo   *migh* kuhl AN
  juh lo
Michaelis   *mee* chay AY lis
Michaelmas   MIGH k'l muhs
Michah   MIGH kuh
Michaiah   migh KAY yuh,
  -KIGH uh
Michal   MIGH kuhl
Micheas   migh KEE uhs
Michel   mi SHEL
Michelangelo   *migh* kuhl AN
  juh lo
Michelozzi   *mee* ke LAHT si
Michmas   MIK muhs
Michmash   MIK mash
Michmethah   MIK mi thuh
Michmethath   mik MEE thath
Michri   MIK righ
Michtam   MIK tam

KEY: bee, bit, bet, bay, bat, boot, butcher, bone, saw, ah, turn, uh huh, sigh,
cow, boy, thin, th in then, shoe, zh in azure, chop, sing, hw in when.

microcosm   MIGH kro kahz 'm
Middin   MID in
Midian   MID i uhn
Midianite   MID i uhn ight
Midianitish   MID i uhn *ight* ish
Midrash   MID rash
Migdal   MIG dal
Migdal-Eder   -EE dur
Migdal-El   -EL
Migdal-Gad   -GAD
Migdal-Sanna   -SAN uh
Migdol   MIG dahl, -dol
Migne   MEEN yuh
Migron   MIG rahn
Mijamin   MIJ uh min
Mikloth   MIK lahth, -loth
Mikneiah   mik NEE yuh,
   -NIGH uh
Milalai   *mil* uh LAY igh, MIL
   uh ligh
Milanese   *mil* uh NEEZ,
   -NEES
Milcah   MIL kuh
milch   MILCH
Milcom   MIL kahm, -kom
Mildred   MIL dred, -drid,
   -druhd
Miletus   migh LEE tuhs
Milic, Milicz   MEE lich
militant   MIL uh tuhnt
millenarian   *mil* uh NER i uhn
millennial   mi LEN i uhl
millennium   mi LEN i uhm
Millerite   MIL ur ight
millet   MIL et, -it, -uht
Millo   MIL o

Milman   MIL muhn
Milner   MIL nur
Milo   MIGH lo
Milon   MIGH lahn
Miltiades   mil TIGH uh deez
Milton   MIL tuhn
Milvian   MIL vi uhn
Mina   MIGH nuh
Minaean   mi NEE uhn
Minchah   min KAH
Miniamin   MIN yuh min, mi
   NIGH uh min
Minim   MIN im
Minish   MIN ish
minister   MIN is tur, -uhs tur
ministerial   *min* uhs TIR i uhl
ministerium   *min* uhs TIR i
   uhm, -TEE ri uhm
ministry   MIN is tri, -uhs tri
Minni   MIN igh
Minnith   MIN ith
Minorite   MIGH nur ight
Minster   MIN stur
Minucius   mi NYOO shi uhs,
   -shuhs
minuscule   mi NUHS kyool
minution   mi NYOO shuhn
Miphkad   MIF kad
miracle   MIR uh k'l, -i k'l
miraculous   mi RAK yu luhs,
   muh-
Miriam   MIR i uhm
Mirma, Mirmah   MUR muh
Misael   MIS ay el, MIGH say el
Misaias   mi SAY yuhs, -SIGH
   uhs

KEY: b*ee*, b*i*t, b*e*t, b*ay*, b*a*t, b*oo*t, b*u*tcher, b*o*ne, s*aw*, *ah*, t*ur*n, *uh* h*uh*, s*igh*,
c*ow*, b*oy*, *th*in, *th* in *th*en, *sh*oe, *zh* in a*zh*ure, *ch*op, si*ng*, *hw* in *wh*en.

misanthrope MIS uhn throp,
MIZ-

Miserere *miz* uh REE ri, -RAY
ri

misericord *miz* ur i KAWRD

Misgab MIS gab

Mishael MISH ay el, MIGH
shay el

Mishal MIGH shal

Misham MIGH sham

Misheal MISH i uhl, MIGH
shi uhl

Mishma MISH muh

Mishmannah mish MAN uh

Mishna, Mishnah MISH
nuh

Mishneh MISH ne

Mishor MIGH shawr

Mishraite MISH ray ight

misology mi SAHL o ji, -uh
ji

misoneism *mis* o NEE iz 'm,
migh so-

Mispar MIS pahr

Mispereth MIS pi reth, -puh
reth, mis PEE reth

Misrephoth-Maim *mis* ri fahth
MAY im

Missa MIS uh

Missabib MIS uh bib

Missa cantata MIS uh kan
TAY tuh, -TAH tuh

Missa capitularis -kuh *pit* yu
LAY ris, -kuh *pi* chu-

missal MIS uhl, -'l

Missa praesanctificatorum MIS

uh *pree* sangk *tif* i kuh TO
ruhm

Missa sicca -SIK uh

mission MISH uhn

missionary MISH uhn *er* i

Mitanni mi TAN i

mite MIGHT

miter MIGH tur

Mithcah MITH kah

Mithkah MITH kuh

Mithnite MITH night

Mithra MITH ruh, MIGH
thruh

Mithradates *mith* ruh DAY
teez

Mithraism MITH ray iz 'm,
MITH ruh-

Mithras MITH ras, -ruhs,
MIGH thras, -thruhs

Mithredath MITH ri dath

Mithridates *mith* ruh DAY
teez

mitre MICH tur

Mitylene mit uh LEE ni

Mizar MIGH zahr

Mizpah MIZ pah, puh

Mizpar MIZ pahr

Mizpeh MIZ pe

Mizraim MIZ ray im

Mizzah MIZ uh

Mnason NAY suhn, M'NAY-

Mneme NEE mi

mnemic NEE mik, NEM ik

mnemonic ni MAHN ik

Moab MO ab

Moabite MO ab ight, -uhb ight

Moabitess MO uhb ight es, -is, -uhs

Moadiah *mo* uh DIGH uh

Moberly MO bur li

Mochmur MAHK mur

Modad MO dad

modalism MO d'l iz 'm

modality mo DAL i ti, -uh ti

modernism MAHD urn iz 'm

Modin MO din

modulation *mahd* yu LAY shuhn, *mah* ju-

modus MO duhs

Moeth MO eth

Moffatt MAHF uht

Mogila mo GEE luh

Mogilas mo GEE luhs

Mohammed mo HAM uhd, mo HAHM uhd

Mohammedanism mo HAM uh duhn iz 'm, mo HAHM-

Mohl MOL

Möhler MOL ur, MUR lur

Mola MO luh

Moladah MAHL uh duh, mo LAY duh

Molay mo LAY

Molech MO lek

Moli MO ligh

Molid MO lid

Molina mo LEE nuh

Molinism MO lin iz 'm, MAHL in-

Molinos mo LEE nos

Moller MAHL ur, MOL ur

mollify MAHL i figh, -uh figh

Moloch MO lahk

molto MOL to

Molyneux MAHL i nuks

Momdis MAHM dis, -duhs

Mommsen MAHM zuhn

monachism MAHN uh kiz 'm

monad MO nad, MAHN ad

monadology *mahn* ad AHL o ji, -uh ji, *mo* nad-

monarchian mo NAHR ki uhn, mahn AHR-

monastery MAHN uhs *ter* i

monasticism mo NAS ti siz 'm, -tuh siz 'm

Moncada mon KAH dah

Moncrieff mahn KREEF

monergism MAHN ur jiz 'm

monism MO niz 'm, MAHN iz 'm

monition mo NISH uhn

monk MUHNGK

Monmouth MAHN muhth

Monod mo NO

monogamy mo NAHG uh mi, muh-

monolatry mo NAHL uh tri

monolith MAHN o lith, -uh lith

mono-personalism MAHN o PUR suhn 'l iz 'm

Monophysite mo NAHF i sight, -uh sight

monotheism MAHN o thee iz 'm

monotheistic *mahn* o thee IS tik

KEY: b*ee*, b*i*t, b*e*t, b*ay*, b*a*t, b*oo*t, b*u*tcher, b*o*ne, s*aw*, *ah*, t*ur*n, *uh* h*uh*, s*igh*, c*ow*, b*oy*, *th*in, *th* in *th*en, *sh*oe, *zh* in a*z*ure, *ch*op, si*ng*, *hw* in *wh*en.

Monothelet   mo NAHTH uh
  leet
Monotheletic   *mahn* o thee
  LET ik
Monothelitism   mo NAHTH
  uh li tiz 'm
Monseigneur   *mahn* say NYUR
Monsignor   mahn SEEN yawr,
  -yur
Monsignore   *mon* see NYO ray
Montagu, Montague   MAHN
  tuh gyoo
Montaigne   mahn TAYN
Montalembert   mawn tah lon
  BER
Montanism   MAHN tuhn iz 'm
Montanus   mahn TAY nuhs,
  MAHN tuh nuhs
Monte Casino, Cassino
  MAHN tay ka SEE no
Montefiore   *mahn* ti fi O ri,
  -AWR i
Montenegro   mon ti NAY gro
Montespan   mon tes PAHN
Montesquieu   mahn tes KYOO
Montfaucon   mawn fo KAWN
Montfort   MAHNT fort,
  mawn FOR
Montluc   mawn LUK
Montmorency   *mahnt* mo REN
  si
Montorsoli   mahn TAWR so li
Montserrat   mahnt si RAT
Mont St. Michel   mawn san mi
  SHEL
Moody   MOO di

Mooli   MO o ligh, -uh ligh
Moosias   *mo* o SIGH uhs
Moossias   mo AHS si uhs
Moph   MAHF
Mopsuestia   *mahp* soo ES ti uh
moral   MAH ruhl, MAW ruhl
morality   mo RAL i ti, -uh ti,
  mawr AL-
Morashtite   mo RASH tight
Moravian   mo RAY vi uhn,
  mawr AY-
Mordecai   MAWR di kigh,
  -kay igh
Moreh   MO re
Morendo   mo REN do
mores   MO reez, MAWR eez
Morcsheth   mo REE sheth
Moresheth-Gath   MO ri sheth
  gath, mo RESH eth *gath*
morganatic   mawr guh NAT ik
Morgenlied   MAWR guhn *leet*
Moriah   mo RICH uh, mawr
  IGH uh
Morisonianism   *mahr* uh SO ni
  uhn iz 'm, *mawr*-
Mormon   MAWR muhn
Morone   mo RO ne, -ni
Morosino   mo ro SEE no
mortal   MAWR tuhl, -t'l
mortality   mawr TAL i ti, -uh ti
mortify   MAWR ti figh
mortmain   MAWRT man
mortuary   MAWR tyu *er* i,
  MAWR chu-
mosaic   mo ZAY ik
Moser   MO zur

KEY: b**ee**, b**i**t, b**e**t, b**ay**, b**a**t, b**oo**t, b**u**tcher, b**o**ne, s**aw**, **ah**, t**ur**n, **uh** h**u**h, s**igh**,
c**ow**, b**oy**, **th**in, **th** in **th**en, **sh**oe, **zh** in a**z**ure, **ch**op, si**ng**, **hw** in **wh**en.

Mosera   mo SEE ruh
Moserah   MO si rah, -suh rah
Moseroth   mo SEE rahth, -roth,
   MO si-
Moses   MO ziz, -zis, -zuhz,
   -zuhs
Mosheim   MOS highm
Mosollam   mo SAHL uhm
Mosollamon   mo SAHL uh
   mahn
Mosollamus   mo SAHL uh
   muhs
mote   MOT
motet, motett   mo TET
motif   mo TEEF
motivation   mo ti VAY shuhn
motive   MO tiv
moto   MAW to, MO to
Mott   MAHT
mourn   MORN, MAWRN
Moya   MO yuh, MOY uh
Moza, Mozah   MO zuh
Mozarabian   moz uh RAY bi
   uhn
Mozarabic   moz AR uh bik,
   moz ER-
Mozart   MO zahrt, MOT sahrt
Mozzetta   mo ZET uh
Mucker   MUK ur
Muggletonian   muhg 'l TO ni
   uhn
Muhlenberg   MYOO luhn burg
Mulcaster   MUHL kas tur
mulct   MUHLKT
Muller   MUL ur, MUHL ur,
   MYOO lur

mullion   MUHL yuhn
mummer   MUHM ur
mummy   MUHM i
mumpsimus   MUHMP si
   muhs
Munden   MUN duhn
Munich   MYOO nik
muniment   MYOO ni muhnt
Munk   MUNGK
Munster   MUN stur
Munzer   MUNT zur
Muppim   MUHP im
Muratori   moo rah TO ri
Muratorian   myoo ru TO ri
   uhn, -TAWR i uhn
Murner   MOOR nur
murrain   MUR in
Musaeus   myoo SEE uhs
Mushi   MYOO shigh
Mushite   MYOO shight
Musselman, Mussulman
   MUHS uhl muhn, -'l muhn
Muth-Labben   muhth LAB en,
   -uhn
Mylitta   mi LIT uh
Myndus   MIN duhs
Myra   MIGH ruh
myrrh   MUR
myrtle   MUR t'l
Mysia   MISH i uh
mystagogue   MIS tuh gahg,
   -gawg
mystagogy   MIS tuh go ji
mystic   MIS tik
mysticism   MIS tuh siz 'm
myth   MITH

KEY: bee, bit, bet, bay, bat, boot, butcher, bone, saw, ah, turn, uh huh, sigh,
cow, boy, thin, th in then, shoe, zh in azure, chop, sing, hw in when.

mythology   mi THAHL o ji, -uh
ji

Naam   NAY am
Naamah   NAY uh muh
Naaman   NAY uh man, -muhn
Naamathite   NAY uh muh
thight
Naamite   NAY uh might, nay
AY might
Naarah   NAY uh ruh
Naarai   NAY uh righ
Naaran   NAY uh ran
Naarath   NAY uh rath
Naascnc   nay AS een
Naashon   nay ASH ahn, NAY
uhsh ahn
Naason   nay AS uhn
Naasson   nay AS ahn, -uhn
Naathus   NAY uh thuhs
Nabal   NAY bal
Nabarias   nab uh RIGH uhs
Nabataean, Nabatean   nab uh
TEE uhn
Nabathaean, Nabathean   nab
uh THEE uhn
Nabathitc   NAB uh thight
Nabla   NAB luh
Naboth   NAY bahth, -both
Nabuchodonosor   nab yu ko
DAHN o sawr
Nachtigall   NAHK ti gahl
Nachon   NAY kahn
Nachor   NAY kawr
Nacon   NAY kahn
Nadab   NAY dab

Nadabath   NAY duh bath
Nadabatha   nuh DAB uh thuh
Naggai   NAG igh, -ay igh
Nagge   NAG e
Nahalal   NAY huh lal
Nahaliel   nuh HAY li el, nuh
HAL i el
Nahallal   nuh HAL al
Nahalol   NAY huh lahl
Naham   NAY ham
Nahamani   nay huh MAY nigh
Naharai   NAY huh righ
Naharaim   nay huh RAY im
Nahari   NAY huh ri
Nahash   NAY hash
Nahath   NAY hath
Nahbi   NAH bigh
Nahor   NAY hawr
Nahshon   NAH shahn
Nahum   NAY huhm
Naidus   NAY uh duhs
Nain   NAY in, NAYN
Naioth   NAY ahth, -oth
Nanaea   na NEE uh
Nanea   nuh NEE uh
Nantes   NANTS, NAWNT
Naomi   na O mi, -migh
Naos   NAY ahs
Naphath   NAY fath
Naphath-Dor   NAY fath dawr
Naphish   NAY fish
Naphisi   NAF i sigh
Naphoth-Dor   NAY fahth
dawr
Naphtali   NAF tuh ligh
Naphthar   NAF thahr

KEY: bee, bit, bet, bay, bat, boot, butcher, bone, saw, ah, turn, uh huh, sigh,
cow, boy, thin, th in then, shoe, zh in azure, chop, sing, hw in when.

Naphtuhim   naf TYOO him,
NAF tyu him
Napier   NAY pi ur
Napoli di Romania   NAH po li
dee   ro mah NEE uh
Narbonne   nahr BAHN
Narcissus   nahr SIS uhs
nard   NAHRD
Nares   NERZ
Narses   NAHR seez
Narthex   NAHR theks
Nasbas   NAS bas, -buhs
nascent   NAY suhnt, NAS
uhnt
Nashon   NAY shahn
Nasi   NAH si
Nasith   NAY sith
Nasor   NAY sawr
Natalia   nuh TAY li uh, -TAYL
yuh
natalitia   *nay* tuh LISH uh
natatorium   nay tuh TO ri
uhm, -TAWR i uhm
Nathan   NAY thuhn
Nathanael   nuh THAN ay uhl,
-el
Nathanias   *nath* uh NIGH uhs
Nathan-Melech   NAY than
MEE lek
nativity   nuh TIV i ti, -uh ti
naturalism   NAT chu ruhl iz 'm
Naudé   no DAY
naught   NAWT
Naum   NAY uhm
Naumburg   NOWM boorg
Navarre   nuh VAHR

Navarrete, Navarette   nah vah
RAY tay
nave   NAYV
Nayler   NAY lur
Naylor   NAY lur, -lawr
Nazarene   *naz* uh REEN
Nazareth   NAZ uh reth, -ruhth,
NAZ ruhth
Nazirite   NAZ uh right
Neah   NEE uh
Neal, Neale   NEEL
Neander   ni AN dur
Neapolis   ni AP o lis, -uh luhs
Neariah   *nee* uh RIGH uh
Nebai   NEE bigh, ni BAY igh,
NEB ay igh
Nebaioth   ni BAY yahth, -yoth
Nebajoth   ni BAY jahth, -joth
Neballat   ni BAL uht
Nebat   NEE bat
Nebel   NEE bel
Nebo (Babylonian)   NAY bo
Nebo (Mount)   NEE bo
Nebuchadnezzar   *neb* yu kad
NEZ ur, *neb* uh-
Nebuchadrezzar   *neb* yu kad
REZ ur, *neb* uh-
Nebushasban   *neb* yu SHAS
ban
Nebushazban   *neb* yu SHAZ
ban
Nebuzaradan   *neb* yu zahr AY
dan, -AD uhn
necessitarian   ni *ses* uh TER i
uhn, nuh-
Necham   NEK uhm

KEY: b*ee*, b*i*t, b*e*t, b*ay*, b*a*t, b*oo*t, b*u*tcher, b*o*ne, s*aw*, *ah*, t*ur*n, *uh* h*uh*, s*igh*,
c*ow*, b*oy*, *th*in, *th* in *th*en, *sh*oe, *zh* in a*zh*ure, *ch*op, si*ng*, *hw* in *wh*en.

Necho, Nechoh   NEE ko
Necker   NEK ur
Neckham   NEK uhm
Neco   NEE ko
Necodan   ni KO dan
necrology   ne KRAHL o ji, -uh
ji
necromancy   NEK ro *man* si
Nedabiah   *ned* uh BIGH uh
Neemias   nee uh MIGH uhs
nessing   NEEZ ing
negation   ni GAY shuhn
Neginah   ne GEE nah
Neginoth   NEG i nahth,
-noth
Nehelem   ni HEL uhm
Nehelamite   ni HEL uh might,
nee huh LAY might
Nehemiah   *nee* huh MIGH uh,
nee uh-
Nehemias   *nee* huh MIGH uhs,
noo uh
Nehiloth   NEE hi lahth, -loth
Nehum   NEE huhm
Nehushta   ni HUHSH tuh
Nehushtan   ni HUHSH tan,
-tuhn
Neiel   ni IGH el
neigh   NAY, NEE
Neill   NEEL
Nekeb   NEE keb
Nekoda   ni KO duh
Nekodan   ni KO dan
Nemesis   NEM uh sis, -suhs
Nemesius   ni MEE si uhs,
-shuhs

Nemuel   NEM yu el, -uhl, ni
MYOO uhl
Nemuelite   NEM yu uhl ight
Nennius   NEN i uhs
neo-   NEE o
neology   ni AHL o ji, -uh ji
neonomian   *nee* o NO mi uhn
neophyte   NEE o fight
Neot   NEE aht, NEET
nephea   ni FEE uh
Nepheg   NEE feg
Nephesh   NEF esh
Nephi   NEE figh
Nephilim   NEF uh lim
Nephis   NEE fis
Nephisim   ni FIGH sim
Nephish   NEE fish
Nephishesim   ni FISH uh sim
Nephtali   NEF tuh ligh
Nephthai   NEF thigh, -thay igh
Nephthali   NEF thuh ligh
Nephthalim   NEF thuh lim
Nephthar   NEF thahr
Nephtoah   nef TO uh, NEF to
uh
Nephusim   ni FYOO sim
Nephushesim   ni FUHSH uh
sim
Nepos   NEE pahs
nepotism   NEP o tiz 'm
Ner   NUR
Nereus   NIR uhs, NEER uhs,
NEE ri uhs
Nergal   NER gahl
Nergal-Sharezer   NUR gahl
shuh REE zur

KEY: b*ee*, b*i*t, b*e*t, b*ay*, b*a*t, b*oo*t, b*u*tcher, b*o*ne, s*aw*, *ah*, t*ur*n, *uh* h*uh*, s*igh*,
c*ow*, b*oy*, *th*in, *th* in *th*en, *sh*oe, *zh* in a*zh*ure, *ch*op, si*ng*, *hw* in *wh*en.

Neri (Biblical)   NEE righ
Neri (Phillipe)   NAY ri
Neriah   ni RIGH uh
Nerias   ni RIGH uhs
Nero   NEE ro
Neronian   ni RO ni uhn
Nerva   nur vuh
Nestor   NES tur, -tawr
Nestorian   nes TO ri uhn, nes
   TAWR i uhn
Nestorius   nes TO ri uhs, nes
   TAWR i uhs
Netaim   NEE tay im, ni TAY
   im
Ne Temere   NEE TEM uh ri
Nethaneel   ni THAN i el, -uhl
Nethanel   ni THAN el, NETH
   uh nel
Nethaniah   neth uh NIGH uh
Nethinim   NETH uh nim
netophah   ni TO fuh
Netophas   ni TO fas
Netophathi   ni TAHF uh thigh
Netophathite   ni TAHF uh
   thight
Neuchatel, Neufchatel   ne shah
   TEL, nu-
Neukomm   NOY kahm
Neumann   NOY mahn
Neumark   NOY mahrk
neume   NYOOM
neurosis   nyu RO sis, -suhs,
   nuh-
neurotic   nyu RAHT ik, nuh-
Neuss   NOYS
Neustadt   NOY staht

Neuville   ne VEEL
Nevil, Neville   NEV il, -uhl
Newcomb, Newcombe, New-
   come   NYOO kuhm
Newell   NYOO uhl
Newton   NYOO t'n, NOO t'n
Neziah   ni ZIGH uh
Nezib   NEE zib
Nibhaz   NIB haz
Nibsham   NIB sham
Nibshan   NIB shan
Nicaea   nigh SEE uh
Nicaean   nigh SEE uhn
Nicander   ni KAHN dur, nigh
   KAN dur
Nicanor   nigh KAY nawr
Niccola Pisano   NEE ko lah pi
   ZAH no
Nicene   nigh SEEN, NIGH
   seen
Nicephorus   ni SEF o ruhs
Nicetas Acominatus   nigh SEE
   tuhs uh kahm i NAY tuhs
niche   NICH
Nicholas   NIK o luhs, -uh luhs
Nicholite   NIK o light, -uh
   light
Nicodemite   nik o DEEM ight
Nicodemus   nik o DEE muhs,
   nik uh-
Nicolai   NIK o ligh
Nicolaitan   nik o LAY uh tan,
   -tuhn
Nicolas   NIK o luhs, -'l uhs
Nicolaus   nik o LAY uhs
Nicole   ni KOL

KEY: bee, bit, bet, bay, bat, boot, butcher, bone, saw, ah, turn, uh huh, sigh,
cow, boy, thin, th in then, shoe, zh in azure, chop, sing, hw in when.

Nicopolis   ni KAHP o lis, -uh luhs
Nid, Nidd   NID
Niebuhr   NEE boor, -bur
Niemeyer   NEE migh ur
Niemöller   NEE mul ur, -muhl ur
Nietzsche   NEET chi
Niger   NIGH jur
nigh   NIGH
nihil   NIGH hil, NEE-
nihilianism   nigh HIL yuhn iz 'm
nihilism   NIGH uh liz 'm, NIGH hi-, NEE
Nikon   NEE kahn
Nile   NIGHL
Nilus   NIGH luhs
nimbus   NIM buhs
Nimes   NEEM
Nimrah   NIM ruh
Nimrim   NIM rim
Nimrod   NIM rahd
Nimshi   NIM shigh
Nineveh   NIN uh vuh
Ninevite   NIN uh vight
Ninian, Nynian   NIN i uhn
Nino   NEEN yo
Niobite   NIGH o bight
Niphis   NIGH fis
Nipter   NIP tur
Nirvana   nur VAH nuh, -VAN uh
Nisan   NIGH san
Nisibis   NIS uh bis
Nismes   NEEM

Nisroch   NIS rahk, NIZ-
Nithard   nee TAHR
nitre   NIGH tur
Nitrian   NIT ri uhn
Nitzsch   NITSH, NICH
Niza   NEET suh
No   NO
Noachian   no AY ki uhn
Noadiah   *no* uh DIGH uh
Noah   NO uh
Noailles   no IGH
No-Amon   *no* AY mahn
Nob   NAHB
Nobah   NO buh
Nobai   NO bigh, NAHB ay igh
nocturn, nocturne   NAHK turn
Nod   NAHD
Nodab   NO dab
Noe (Biblical)   NO ee
Noé (Marc)   no AY
Noeba   NO i buh
Noel   no EL
noesis   no EE sis, -suhs
noetic   no ET ik
Noetus   no EE tuhs
Nogah   NO guh
Nohah   NO hah, -huh
noisome   NOY suhm
nomianism   NO mi uhn iz 'm
nominalism   NAHM uh n'l iz 'm
nomocanon   no MAHK uh nahn
non   NAHN

KEY: b*ee*, b*i*t, b*e*t, b*a*y, b*a*t, b*oo*t, b*u*tcher, b*o*ne, s*aw*, *ah*, t*ur*n, *uh* h*u*h, s*igh*, c*ow*, b*oy*, *th*in, *th* in *th*en, *sh*oe, *zh* in a*z*ure, *ch*op, si*ng*, *hw* in *wh*en.

nonconformist *nahn* kuhn FAWRM ist
nonjurant nahn JUR uhnt
nonjuror nahn JUR ur
noology no AHL o ji, -uh ji
Nooma NO uh muh
Noph NAHF
Nophah NO fuh
Norbert NAWR bert, -burt
Nördlingen NURD ling uhn
Norwich NAWR ij, -ich
Nostradamus *nos* truh DAY muhs, -DAH muhs
notaricon, notarikon no TAR i kahn
notitia no TISH uh, -i uh
Notker NOT kur
Notre Dame NO truh DAHM, NO tur DAYM
Nott NAHT
nought NAWT
noumena NOO mi nuh
noumenon NOO mi nahn
nous NOOS
Novalis no VAH lis, -luhs
Novatian no VAY shi uhn, -shuhn
novena no VEE nuh
novice NAHV is, -uhs
noviciate, novitiate no VISH uht, -i uht
Noyon nwah YAWN, -YON
Nubia NYOO bi uh, NOO-
nullity NUHL uh ti
Numbers NUHM burz

Numenius nyu MEE ni uhs, nu-
numinous NYOO mi nuhs, NOO muh nuhs
numismatics *nyoo* miz MAT iks, *nyoo* mis-
Nun NUHN
nun (Hebrew letter) NOON
Nunc Dimittis NUHNGK di MIT is, -uhs
nuncio NUHN shi o
Nunez NOON yayz, -yez
nunnery NUHN ur i
nuptial NUHP shuhl
Nuremberg NYOO ruhm burg, NUR uhm-
Nygren NIGH gruhn, NEE-
nympha NIM fuh
nymphaeum nim FEE uhm
Nymphas NIM fuhs
Nymphoeum nim FEE uhm

Oabdius o AB di uhs
Oakeley OK li
Oakes OKS
Oates OTS
oath OTH
Obadiah *o* buh DIGH uh
Obal O buhl
obbligato *ahb* li GAH to, *ahb* luh-
Obdia ahb DIGH uh
Obed O bed
Obed-Edom o bed EE duhm
obedientiary o *bee* di EN shi *er* i

obeisance   o BAY suhns, -s'ns,
  o BEE-
obelisk   AHB uh lisk
Oberammergau   o bur AHM
  ur gow
Oberhausen   O bur *how* zuhn,
  -suhn
Oberlin (College)   O bur lin,
  -luhn
Oberlin (Jean)   o ber LAN
Obeth   O beth
Obil   O bil
obituary   o BIT chu *er* i
objective   ahb JEK tiv
oblata   ahb LAY tuh
oblate   AHB layt, ahb LAYT
oblation   ahb LAY shuhn
oblationarium   ahb *lay* shuhn
  ER i uhm
Oboth   O bahth, -both
obscurantist   ahb SKYOO rant
  ist
obsequium   ahb SEE kwi uhm
Observantine   ahb ZUR vuhn
  teen, -tin
Observantist   ahb ZUR vuhn
  tist
obversion   ahb VUR shuhn,
  -zhuhn
Ocampo   o KAHM po
Occam   AHK uhm
Occamism   AHK uhm iz 'm
occasionalism   o KAY zhuhn
  'l iz 'm
occult   o KUHLT, AHK uhlt
occurrent   o KUR ent, -uhnt

Ochiel   o KIGH el, -uhl
Ochielus   *o* kigh EE luhs
Ochino   o KEE no
Ochran   AHK ran
ochre   O kur
Ocidelus   ahs i DEE luhs, ahk-
Ocina   o SIGH nuh, AHS i
  nuh, AHK-
Ockham   AHK uhm
Ockhamism   AHK uhm iz 'm
Ockley   AHK li
Ocran   AHK ran, -ruhn
octateuch   AHK tuh tyook,
  -took
octavarium   ahk tuh VAR i
  uhm
octave   AHK tayv, -tiv
Octavian   ahk TAY vi uhn
Octavius   ahk TAY vi uhs
octet, octette   ahk TET
Octoechos   *ahk* to EE kahs
Odal   O duhl, -d'l
ode   OD
Oded   O ded
Odo   O do
Odollam   o DAHL uhm
Odomera   *ahd* o MEE ruh
Odonarkes   *ahd* o NAHR keez,
  ahd uh-
odylism   AHD uhl iz 'm
oeconomus   i KAHN o muhs,
  -uh muhs
oecumenical   ek yoo MEN i
  kuhl
oenomancy   EE no *man* si
oenomania   *ee* no MAY ni uh

KEY: b*ee*, b*i*t, b*e*t, b*a*y, b*a*t, b*oo*t, b*u*tcher, b*o*ne, s*aw*, *ah*, t*ur*n, *uh* h*uh*, s*igh*,
c*ow*, b*oy*, *th*in, *th* in *th*en, *sh*oe, *zh* in a*z*ure, *ch*op, si*ng*, *hw* in *wh*en.

Oesterley   ES tur li
Oetinger   ET ing ur
Offa   AHF uh, AWF uh
Offenbach   AHF uhn bahk
offertory   AHF ur *to* ri, AWF-,
   -*tawr* i
Og   AHG
Oggione   ahd JO ne
Ohad   O had
Ohel   O hel
Oholah   o HO luh
Oholiab   o HO li ab
Oholibah   o HAHL uh buh
Oholibamah   o *hahl* i BAY
   muh
ointment   OYNT ment, -muhnt
Oken   O ken, -kuhn
Olaf   O lahf, -luhf
Olamus   AHL uh muhs
Olearius   o li AY ri uhs
Oleaster   o li AS tur
Olevianus   o *lee* vi AY nuhs
Olga   AHL guh
Olier   o LYAY
Olin   O lin, -luhn
Oliva   o LEE vah
Oliver   AHL i vur, -uh vur
Olives   AHL ivz
Olivet   AHL i vet, -vuht
Olivetan   *ahl* i VEE tuhn, AHL
   i *vet* uhn
Olivier   o li VYAY
Olshausen   OLS how zuhn
Olympas   o LIM puhs
Olympiodorus   o *lim* pi o DO
   ruhs, -DAWR uhs

Olympius   o LIM pi uhs
Omaerus   *ahm* uh EE ruhs
Oman   O muhn
Omar (Biblical)   O mur
omega   o MEE guh, o MEG uh
omen   O men, -muhn
Omer   O mur
Omish   AHM ish
omnipotence   ahm NIP o tuhns,
   -uh tuhns
omnipresence   *ahm* ni PREZ
   ens, -uhns
omniscience   ahm NISH ens,
   -uhns
omophorion   o mo FO ri ahn,
   -FAWR i ahn
Omri   AHM righ
On   AHN, AWN
Onam   O nam
Onan   O nan
Oneida   o NIGH duh
Onesimus   o NES i muhs, -uh
   muhs
Onesiphorus   ahn i SIF o ruhs,
   -uh ruhs
Oniares   o NIGH uh reez, o ni
   AY reez
Onias   o NIGH uhs
Ono   O no
onolatry   o NAHL o tri, -uh tri
ontological   *ahn* to LAHJ i kuhl
ontologism   ahn TAHL o jiz
   'm, -uh jiz 'm
ontology   ahn TAHL o ji, -uh
   ji
onus   O nuhs

KEY: bee, bit, bet, bay, bat, boot, butcher, bone, saw, ah, turn, uh huh, sigh,
cow, boy, thin, th in then, shoe, zh in azure, chop, sing, hw in when.

onycha   AHN i kuh
onychomancy   *ahn* i ko MAN
   si, AHN i ko *man* si
onyx   AHN iks, O niks
ooscopy   o AHS ko pi
Oost   OST
Ophel   O fel, -fuhl
ophiomancy   AHF i o *man* si,
   O fi-
Ophir   O fur
Ophite   AHF ight, O fight
Ophni   AHF nigh
Ophrah   AHF ruh
opobalsamum   *ahp* o BAL suh
   muhm
optimism   AHP tuh miz 'm
opus   O puhs
oracle   AHR uh k'l, AWR-
orale   o RAY li
Orange   AHR uhnj, AWR-
Orangeman   AHR inj man,
   AWR-, -uhnj man
orant   O rant, -ruhnt
orarion   o RAY ri ahn
orarium   o RER i uhm
oration   o RAY shuhn, awr AY
   shuhn
orator   AHR uh tur, AWR-
Oratorian   *ahr* uh TO ri uhn,
   awr-, -TAWR i uhn
oratorio   *ahr* uh TO ri o, awr-,
   -TAWR i o
oratory   AHR uh *to* ri, AWR-,
   -*tawr* i
Orcagna   awr KAHN yah
ordain   awr DAYN

ordeal   awr DEEL, AWR deel,
   awr DEE uhl
Ordericus Vitalis   awr di RIGH
   kuhs   vi TAY lis, -luhs
Ordinal   AWR di n'l, -duh n'l
ordinance   AWR duh nuhns
ordinary   AWR di *ner* i, AWR
   d'n *er* i
ordination   *awr* duh NAY
   shuhn
Ordines Romani   AWR di neez
   ro MAY nigh
Ordo Romanus   AWR do ro
   MAY nuhs
Oreb   O reb
Oren   O ren
organ   AWR guhn
organicism   awr GAN uh siz
   'm
organism   AWR guhn iz 'm
organismic   *awr* guhn IZ mik
organon   AWR guh nahn
orgy   AWR ji
oriel   O ri el, -uhl
oriflamme   AWR i flam
Origen   AHR i jen, AWR , uh
   juhn
Origenian   *ahr* uh JEE ni uhn,
   awr-
Origenist   AHR uh jen ist,
   AWR-
Orion   o RIGH uhn
Orléans   awr lay ON, AWR li
   uhnz
Ormazd   AWR mazd
Orme   AWRM

KEY: b*ee*, b*i*t, b*e*t, b*ay*, b*a*t, b*oo*t, b*u*tcher, b*o*ne, s*aw*, *ah*, t*ur*n, *uh* h*uh*, s*igh*,
c*ow*, b*oy*, *th*in, *th* in *th*en, *sh*oe, *zh* in a*z*ure, *ch*op, si*ng*, *hw* in *wh*en.

Ornan AWR nan
Orosius o RO si uhs
Orpah AWR pah
Orpheus AWR fi uhs, AWR fyoos
Orphic AWR fik
Orthodox AWR tho dahks, AWR thuh-
orthography awr THAHG ruh fi
Orthosias *awr* tho SIGH uhs
orthron AWR thrahn
Orthros AWR thrahs
Orzechowski awr ze KAHV ski, -KOW ski
Orzichorius awr zi KO ri uhs, -KAWR i uhs
Osaias o ZAY yuhs, o SAY-
osculatorium *ahs* kyu luh TO ri uhm, -TAWR i uhm
Osea o ZEE uh, o SEE-
Oseas O ZEE uhs, o SEE-
Osee O zee, -see
Oshea o SHEE uh
Osiander o zi AHN dur
Osiris o SIGH ris
Osnapper ahs NAP ur
Osorio o SO ri o, o ZO-
ospray, osprey AHS pri
Ossat ahs SAH
ossifrage AHS uh frij
ossuarium *ahs* yu ER i uhm
ossuary AHS yu *er* i, AHSH yu-
ostensory ahs TEN so ri
Osterwald ahs tur VAHLD

ostiary AHS ti *er* i
ostraca AHS truh kuh
Oswald AHZ wahld
Otfried AHT freed
Othman awth MAHN
Othni AHTH nigh
Othniel ATH ni el
Otho O tho, AHT o
Othonias *ahth* o NIGH uhs
Ötinger ET ing ur
Otterbein AHT ur bighn
Otto AHT o
Ouseley OOZ li
Outram OO truhm, OW truhm
ovation o VAY shuhn
Overbeck O vur bek
Owen O uhn
Owtram OO truhm, OW truhm
Oxenstiern AHKS uhn stirn
Oxford AHKS furd
ox-goad AHKS *god*
Oxnam AHKS nuhm
Oxyrhynchus *ahk* si RING kuhs
Ozanam o zuh NAWM
Ozem o zem
Ozias o ZIGH uhs
Oziel O zi el
Ozni AHZ nigh
Oznite AHZ night
Ozora o ZO ruh

Paarai PAY uh righ
Pacatiana puh *kay* shi AY nuh

KEY: b*ee*, b*i*t, b*e*t, b*ay*, b*a*t, b*oo*t, b*u*tcher, b*o*ne, s*aw*, *ah*, t*ur*n, *uh* h*uh*, s*igh*, c*ow*, b*oy*, *th*in, ᵺ in *th*en, *sh*oe, *zh* in a*zh*ure, *ch*op, si*ng*, *hw* in *wh*en.

Pacca   PAHK kah
Pacheco   pah CHAY ko
Pachomius   pa KO mi uhs
Pachon   PAY kahn
pacifism   PAS uh fiz 'm
Padan   PAY dan
Paddan   PAY dan, PAD uhn
Paddan-Aram   PAY duhn AY ram, -ER uhm
Paderborn   PAH dur born, -bawrn
Padon   PAY dahn
padre   PAH dri, -dray
paedobaptism   *pee* do BAP tiz 'm
paedogogy   PED uh *go* ji, *-gahj* i
Paez   PAH ays
pagan   PAY guhn
Pagani   pah GAH ni
Paget   PAJ et, -it, -uht
Pagiel   PAY gi el, -ji el
Pahath-Moab   PAY hath MO ab
Pai   PAY igh
pain benit   PAN   bay NEE
Pajon   pah ZHAWN, -ZHON
palaeography   *pay* li AHG ruh fi
Palaestra, Palastra   puh LES truh
Palafox   pah lah FOH
Palal   PAY lal
Palamas   PAL uh muhs
palanquin   *pal* un KEEN
Palatine   PAL uh tighn, -tin
Paleario   pah lay AH ri o

paleography   *pay* li AHG ruh fi
Palermo   puh LUR mo, puh LER-
Palestina   *pal* uhs TIGH nuh
Palestine   PAL uhs *tighn*
Palestrina   *pah* les TREE nuh, *pal* uhs-
Paley   PAY li
Palgrave   PAL grayv
palimpsest   PAL imp sest
palingenesis   *pal* in JEN uh sis, -suhs
Palissy   pah li SEE
pall   PAWL
Palladio   pah LAH di o
Palladius   pa LAY di uhs
Pallavicino   *pah* lah vee CHEE no
pallium   PAL i uhm
Pallu   PAL yoo
Palluite   PAL yu ight
Palma   PAHL mah
palmer-worm   PAHM ur *wurm*
Palmyra   pal MIGH ruh
palsy   PAWL zi
Palti   PAL tigh
Paltiel   PAL ti el
Paltite   PAL tight
Pamphylia   pam FIL i uh
Panaetius   pa NEE shi uhs
Panagia   puh NAY gi uh
Pancras   PAN kruhs
Pancratius   pan KRAY shi uhs
pandect   PAN dekt
pane   PAYN
panegyric   *pan* uh JIR ik

KEY: b*ee*, b*i*t, b*e*t, b*ay*, b*a*t, b*oo*t, b*u*tcher, b*o*ne, s*aw*, *ah*, t*ur*n, *uh* h*uh*, s*igh*, c*ow*, b*oy*, *th*in, *th* in *th*en, *sh*oe, *zh* in a*zh*ure, *ch*op, si*ng*, *hw* in *wh*en.

panegyricon　*pan* uh JIR i kahn
panentheism　pan EN thi iz 'm
Panini　PAH ni ni
panlogism　PAN lo jiz 'm
pannag　PAN ag
Pannini　PAH ni ni
panoply　PAN o pli
panpneumatism　pan NYOO
　muh tiz 'm
panpsychism　pan SIGH kiz 'm
pantheism　PAN thi iz 'm
pantheistic　*pan* thi IS tik
pantheon　PAN thi ahn, pan
　THEE ahn
Panthéon　(Church in Paris)
　pawn tay AWN
pap　PAP
papacy　PAY puh si
papal　PAY puhl, -p'l
Paphos　PAY fahs
Papias　PAY pi uhs
Papin　PAY pin
Papini　pa PEE ni
Papist　PAY pist, -puhst
Pappenheim　PAHP uhn highm
Pappus　PAP uhs
papyrology　*pap* i RAHL o ji,
　pap uh RAHL uh ji
papyrus　puh PIGH ruhs
parabaptism　*par* uh BAP tiz
　'm, *per-*
parabolanus　*par* uh bo LAY
　nuhs
Paracelsus　*par* uh SEL suhs,
　per-
paraclete　PAR uh kleet, PER-

paradigm　PAR uh dim, -dighm,
　PER-
paradise　PAR uh dighs, -dighz,
　PER-
paradox　PAR uh dahks, PER-
Parah　PAY ruh, PAR uh
Paralipomenon　*par* uh li
　PAHM uh nahn, -nuhn
paralogism　puh RAL o jiz 'm,
　-uh jiz 'm
paramour　PAR uh moor, PER-
Paran　PAY ran, -ruhn
parapet　PAR uh pet, PER-
parapsychology　*par* uh sigh
　KAHL o ji, *per-*, -uh ji
parasceve　PAR uh seev, *par* uh
　SEE vi
parashah　PAR uh shah
parashioth　*par* uh SHEE oth
paratorium　*par* uh TO ri uhm,
　per-, -TAWR i uhm
Parbar　PAHR bahr
parchment　PAHRCH ment,
　-muhnt
parclose　PAHR *kloz, -klos*
Pardo　PAHR do
pardon　PAHR d'n
parish　PAR ish, PER-
parishioner　puh RISH uhn ur
parity　PAR i ti, PER-, -uh ti
Parmashta　pahr MASH tuh
Parmenas　PAHR mi nas
Parmenides　pahr MEN uh
　deez
Parmigiano　pahr mi JAH no
Parnach　PAHR nak

KEY: b*ee*, b*i*t, b*e*t, b*a*y, b*a*t, b*oo*t, b*u*tcher, b*o*ne, s*aw*, *ah*, t*ur*n, *uh* h*uh*, s*igh*,
c*ow*, b*oy*, *th*in, *th* in *th*en, *sh*oe, *zh* in a*zh*ure, *ch*op, si*ng*, *hw* in *wh*en.

parnas pahr NAHS, PAHR
nahs
Parnassus pahr NAHS uhs,
-NAS uhs
Parny pahr NEE
parochial puh RO ki uhl
Parosh PAY rahsh, PAR ahsh
Parousia puh ROO zhi uh,
-zhuh
Parsee PAHR si, pahr SEE
Parshandatha pahr shan DAY
thuh, pahr SHAN duh thuh
parsimony PAHR si mo ni,
PAHR suh-
parsin PAHR sin, -suhn
parson PAHR s'n
parsonage PAHR s'n ij
Parthenay pahrt NAY
Parthenius pahr THEE ni uhs
Parthenon PAHR thuh nahn
Parthian PAHR thi uhn
particularist pur TIK yu lur ist,
-ust
Paruah puh ROO uh
Parvaim pahr VAY im
parvis PAHR vis
Pasach PAY sak
Pascal PAS kuhl
Pasch PASK
paschal PAS kuhl
Pas-Dammim pas DAM im
Paseah puh SEE uh, PAS i uh
Pashhur, Pashur PASH ur
Passau PAS ow
Passion PASH uhn
passional PASH uhn 'l

passionato *pah* syo NAH to
Passionist PASH uhn ist
Passover PAS o vur
pastophorium *pas* to FO ri
uhm, -FAWR i uhm
pastor PAS tur
pastoral PAS tur uhl
pastorale *pas* to RAL, -RAH
lay
pastorate PAS tur it, -uht
Pastoureaux *pahs* too RO
Patara PAT uh ruh
Patarene, Patarine PAT uh
reen, -rin
paten PAT uhn
Pater Noster PAY tur NAHS
tur, PAT ur-
Patheus puh THEE uhs
Pathros PATH rahs
Pathrusim path ROO sim
Patmore PAT mor, -mawr
Patmos PAT muhs
patriarch PAY tri ahrk
patrician put TRISH uhn
Patrick PAT rik
patrimony PAT ri mo ni
Patripassian *pay* tri PAS i uhn,
pat ri-
patristic puh TRIS tik
Patrobas PAT ro buhs
Patroclus puh TRO kluhs, puh
TRAHK-, PAT ro-
patrology puh TRAHL o ji,
-uh ji
patronage PAY truhn ij, PAT
ruhn-

KEY: bee, bit, bet, bay, bat, boot, butcher, bone, saw, ah, turn, uh huh, sigh,
cow, boy, thin, th in then, shoe, zh in azure, chop, sing, hw in when.

Pau   PAY oo
Paul   PAWL
Pauli   POW li
Paulianist   PAWL i uhn ist,
  -uhst
Paulician   paw LISH uhn
Pauline   PAWL ighn, -een
Paulinus   paw LIGH nuhs
Paulist   PAWL ist
Paulus   PAWL uhs
pauperism   PAW pur iz 'm
Pavia   pah VEE uh
pax   PAKS, PAHKS
pax vobiscum   PAHKS vo BIS
  kuhm, PAKS-
Pazzi   PAHT see
pe   PAY
Peabody   PEE bah di, -buh di
pease   PEEZ
Peckham   PEK uhm
pectoral   PEK tur uhl
pedagogy   PED uh go ji, *-gahj*
  i
Pedahel   PED uh hel, pi DAH
  el
Pedahzur   pi DAH zur
Pedaiah   pi DAY yuh, pi DIGH
  uh
pedary   PED uh ri
Pedias   PED i uhs, pi DIGH
  uhs
pedobaptism   *pee* do BAP tiz 'm
Pekah   PEE kah
Pekahiah   *pek* uh HIGH uh, pi
  KAH yuh
Pekod   PEE kahd

Pelagia   pi LAY ji uh, puh-
Pelagianism   pi LAY ji uhn iz
  'm, puh-
Pelagius   pi LAY ji uhs, puh-
Pelaiah   pi LAY yuh, pi LIGH-
  uh
Pelaliah   *pel* uh LIGH uh
Pelatiah   *pel* uh TIGH uh
Peleg   PEE leg
Pelet   PEE let
Peleth   PEE leth
Pelethite   PEL uh thight, PEE
  leth ight
Pelias   pi LIGH uhs
pelican   PEL i kuhn
Pelishtim   PEL ish tim, puh
  LISH tim
Pella   PEL uh
Pelonite   PEL o night, PEE lo-,
  pi LO-
Pelusium   pi LYOO shi uhm,
  puh LOO si uhm
penal   PEE nuhl, -n'l
penance   PEN uhns
pendentive   pen DEN tiv
Peniel   pi NIGH uhl, PEN i el,
  -uhl
Peninnah   pi NIN uh
penitence   PEN i tuhns
penitentes   *pen* uh TEN teez
penitential   *pen* uh TEN shuhl
Penna   PEN ah, -uh
Penry   PEN ri
pentacle   PEN tuh k'l
Pentateuch   PEN tuh tyook,
  -took

Pentecost   PEN ti kahst, -kawst
pentecostal   *pen* ti KAHS t'l,
   -KAWS t'l
pentecostarion   pen ti kahs
   TAY ri ahn, -TER i ahn
Penuel   pi NYOO el
penury   PEN yu ri
Peor   PEE awr
Pepin   PEP in, -uhn
Pepusch   PAY poosh
Peraea   puh REE uh
Perazim   PER uh zim, pi RAY
   zim
percept   PUR sept
perclose   PUR *kloz, -klos*
perdendo   per DEN do
perdition   pur DISH uhn
Peregrinus   *per* i GRIGII nuhs
Pereira   pe RAY rah
peres   pi RAYS
Peresh   PEE resh
Perez (Biblical)   PEE rez
Pérez   PAY rays, per EZ
Perezite   PEE rez ight
Perez-Uzza, Perez-Uzzah   *pee*
   rez UIIZ uh
Perga   PUR guh
Pergamos   PUR guh mahs
Pergamum   PUR guh muhm
Pergolese   *per* go LAY say
peribolos   pi RIB o lahs, -uh
   lahs
pericopae, pericope   puh RIK o
   pi, -uh pi
Perida   pi RIGH duh, puh-
Perier   pay RYAY

peripatetic   *per* i puh TET ik,
   per uh-
peristyle   PER i stighl
Perizzite   PER i zight, puh RIZ
   ight
Perpetua   pur PET chu uh
Perpignan   per peen YAHN
Perron   pay RAWN, -RON
per saltum   pur   SAL tuhm
perseity   pur SEE uh ti
Persepolis   pur SEP o lis, -uh
   luhs
Perseus   PUR si uhs
Persia   PUR zhuh
Persian   PUR zhuhn, -shuhn
Persis   PUR sis
personalism   PUR suhn 'l iz 'm
personality   *pur* suhn AL i ti,
   -uh ti
Perth   PURTH
Perthes   PER tes
Peruda   pi ROO duh, puh-
Perugino   pay roo JEE no
Peruzzi   pay ROOT si
perverse   pur VURS
Pesaro   PAY sah ro
Peshito   pe SHEE to
Peshitta   pe SHEE tah
pessimism   PES uh miz 'm
Pestalozzi   *pes* tuh LAHT si
pestilence   PES ti luhns, -tuh
   luhns
pestle   PES 'l, -t'l
Peter   PEE tur
Pethahiah   *peth* uh HIGH uh
Pethor   PEE thawr

KEY: b*ee*, b*i*t, b*e*t, b*ay*, b*a*t, b*oo*t, b*u*tcher, b*o*ne, s*aw*, *ah*, t*ur*n, *uh* h*uh*, s*igh*,
c*ow*, b*oy*, *th*in, *th* in *th*en, *sh*oe, *zh* in a*zh*ure, *ch*op, si*ng*, *hw* in *wh*en.

Pethuel   pi THYOO el, -uhl
petition   pi TISH uhn, puh-
Petra   PEE truh
Petrarch   PEE trahrk
Petrie   PEE tri
Petrine   PEE trighn, -trin
Petrobrusian   *pet* ro BROO
zhuhn
petrography   pi TRAHG ruh fi
Petro-Johannite   *pee* tro jo
HAN ight
Petronius   pe TRO ni uhs
Peullethai   pi UHL uh thigh
Peulthai   pi UHL thigh
pew   PYOO
Pfaff   PFAHF, FAF
Pfeiffer   FIGHF ur
Phaath Moab   FAY ath   MO
ab
Phacareth   FAK uh reth
Phaedo   FEE do
Phaedrus   FEE druhs
phaenomenon   fuh NAHM uh
nahn, -nuhn
Phaisur   FAY sur, fay IGH sur
Phaldaius   fal DAY yuhs
Phaldeus   fal DEE uhs
Phaleas   fa LEE uhs, fuh-
Phalec   FAY lek
Phaleg   FAY leg
Phalias   fuh LIGH uhs
phallic   FAL ik
phallicism   FAL uh siz 'm
Phallu   FAL oo
phallus   FAL uhs
Phalti   FAL tigh

Phaltiel   FAL ti el
Phanar   FAN ur
Phantasiast   fan TAY zi ast
Phanuel   fuh NYOO uhl, FAN
yu el
Pharacim   FAR uh sim, FER-
Pharakim   FAR uh kim, FER-
Pharaoh   FER o, FAY ro
Pharaoh Hophra   -HAHF ruh
Pharaoh-Necoh   -NEK o, -NEE
ko
Pharathon   FAR uh thahn,
FER-
Pharathoni   *far* uh THO nigh,
fer-
Phares, Pharez   FAY reez
Pharida   fuh RIGH duh
Pharira   fuh RIGH ruh
Pharisaic   *far* uh SAY ik, *fer-*
Pharisee   FAR uh see, FER-
Pharosh   FAY rahsh
Pharpar   FAHR pahr
Pharzite   FAHR zight
Phasaelis   fuh SEE lis, -luhs
Phaseah   fuh SEE uh
Phaselis   fuh SEE lis, -luhs
Phasiron   FAS uh rahn
Phassaron   FAS uh rahn
Phassurus   fa SYOO ruhs, FAS
yu ruhs
Phebe   FEE bi
Phelonion   fi LO ni ahn, fuh-
Phenice   fi NIGH si
Phenicia   fuh NISH uh
phenomenalism   fuh NAHM
uh n'l iz 'm

phenomenology fuh *nahm* uh NAHL o ji, -uh ji

phenomenon fuh NAHM uh nahn, -nuhn

Pheresite FER uh sight

Pherezite FER uh zight

phiale FIGH uh li

Phi-Beseth FIGH bi seth, FIB uh seth

Phichol, Phicol FIGH kahl

Philadelphia *fil* uh DEL fi uh

Philalethe *fil* uh LEE thi

philanthropy fi LAN thuo pi, fuh LAN thruh pi

Philarches fi LAHR keez, fuh-

philaster fi LAS tur

Philemon fi LEE muhn, fuh-

Philetus fi LEE tuhs, fuh-

Philip FIL ip, -uhp

Philippi fi LIP igh, fuh-, FIL uh pigh

Philippians fi LIP i uhnz, fuh-

Philippist FIL uh pist

Philistia fi LIS ti uh, fuh-

Philistim fi LIS tim, fuh-

Philistine fi LIS tin, fuh-, FIL uhs *teen*, -tin

philocalian *fil* o KAL i uhn, *fil* uh-

Philo Judaeus FIGH lo ju DEE uhs

philologus fi LAHL o guhs, fuh LAHL uh guhs

philology fi LAHL o ji, fuh LAHL uh ji

Philometor *fil* o MEE tur

Philopatris fi LAHP uh tris, fuh-

philosophist fi LAHS o fist, fuh LAHS uh fist

philosophy fi LAHS o fi, fuh LAHS uh fi

Philostorgius *fil* o STAWR ji uhs, *fil* uh-

Philostratus fi LAHS truh tuhs

Philoxenian *fil* ahks EE ni uhn

Philoxenus fi LAHK si nuhs

philter, philtre FIL tur

Phinees FIN i es

Phinehas FIN i uhs

Phinoe FIN o i

Phlegon FLEE gahn, FLEG ahn, -uhn

Phoebe FEE bi

Phoenice fi NIGH si

Phoenicia fuh NISH uh

phoenix FEE niks

Phoros FO rahs

Photinian fo TIN i uhn

Photius FO shi uhs

phrenology fri NAHL o ji, -uh ji

Phrurai FROO righ, -ray igh

Phrygia FRIJ i uh

Phurah FYOO ruh

Phurim FYOO rim

Phut FUHT

Phuvah FYOO vuh

Phygelus fi JEL uhs

phylactery fi LAK tur i, fuh-

phylarch FIGH lahrk

Phylarches fi LAHR keez

pianissimo   *pee* uh NIS i mo,
  -uh mo
Piarist   PIGH uh rist
piazza   pi AHT sah
Piazzi   pi AHT si
Pi-Beseth   *pigh* BEE seth,
  -BES uhth
pica   PIGH kuh
Picard (sect)   PIK urd
Picard   pi KAHR, -KAHRD
Piccolomini   *pik* o LAHM uh
  ni
Pichler   PIK lur
Pico   PEE ko
Picot   pi KO
Pieta   pyay TAH
pietism   PIGH uh tiz 'm
pietistic   *pigh* uh TIS tik
piety   PIGH uh ti
Pi-Hahiroth   *pigh* huh HIGH
  rahth, -roth
pilaster   pi LAS tur, pigh-
Pilate   PIGH luht
Pildash   PIL dash
Pileha   PIL i hah, PIGH li hah
pilgrimage   PIL gruh mij
Pilha   PIL hah
pillar   PIL ur
Piltai   PIL tigh, pil TAY igh
Pim   PIM
pinion   PIN yuhn
Pinon   PIGH nahn
Pinturicchio   *peen* tu REEK i o
Piombo   pi AHM bo
Pira   PIGH ruh
Piram   PIGH ram

Pirathon   PIR uh thahn
Pirathonite   PIR uh thahn ight
Pirke Aboth, Pirqe Aboth   pir
  KAY   ah VOTH
Pisa   PEE zuh, -suh
Pisano   pi ZAH no
Piscina   pi SIGH nuh, pi SEE-
Pisgah   PIZ guh
Pishon   PIGH shahn
Pisidia   pi SID i uh, puh-
Pison   PIGH sahn
Pispa, Pispah   PIS pah, -puh
Pistoia, Pistoja   pis TO yuh
pistology   pis TAHL o ji, -uh ji
Pithom   PIGH thahm
Pithon   PIGH thahn
Pius   PIGH uhs
pizzicato   *pit* si KAH to
placebo   pluh SEE bo
Placentia   pla SEN shi uh, pluh-
placet   PLAY set, -sit, -suht
placido   plah CHEE do, -SEE
  do
plaister   PLAS tur
plait   PLAYT, PLAT
Planck   PLAHNGK
planeta   pla NEE tuh, pluh-
Plantin   PLAN tin, PLAHN tin
Plato   PLAY to
Platonic   pluh TAHN ik, play-
Platonism   PLAY t'n iz 'm
plead   PLEED
Pleiades   PLEE uh deez,
  PLIGH-
plenary   PLEE nuh ri, PLEN
  uh-

KEY: b*ee*, b*i*t, b*e*t, b*a*y, b*a*t, b*oo*t, b*u*tcher, b*o*ne, s*aw*, *ah*, t*ur*n, *uh* h*uh*, s*igh*,
c*ow*, b*oy*, *th*in, **th** in *th*en, *sh*oe, *zh* in a*zh*ure, *ch*op, si*ng*, *hw* in *wh*en.

pleroma   pli RO muh
Plessis-Mornay   ple SEE   mawr
　NAY
Pliny   PLIN i
Plotinus   plo TIGH nuhs
plumb   PLUHM
plummet   PLUHM it, -uht
pluralism   PLUR uhl iz 'm,
　PLOO ruhl-
plurality   plu RAL uh ti
Plutarch   PLOO tahrk
pluvial   PLOO vi uhl
pneuma   NYOO muh
pneumatology   *nyoo* muh
　TAHL o ji, -uh ji
Pneumatomachian   *nyoo* muh
　to MAY ki uhn
Pochereth   PAHK uh reth, PO
　kuh-, po KEE-
Pocherethhazzebaim   *po* kuh
　reth *haz* uh BAY im, *pahk* uh-,
　po *kee-*
Pocock, Pococke   PO kahk
pocular y   PAHK yu *ler* i
Poggio   PAHD jo
Poisson   pwah SAWN,
　-SON
Poissy   pwah SEE
Poitiers   pwah TYAY
polemic   po LEM ik
Polignac   po leen YAHK
Politian   po LISH uhn
polity   PAHL uh ti
Poliziano   po *leet* si AH no
Pollio   PAHL i o
Pollok   PAHL ahk, -uhk

pollution   po LOO shuhn, po
　LYOO-
Pollux   PAHL uhks
Polotsk, Polotzk   PO lahtsk
polyandry   PAHL i *an* dri, *pahl*
　i AN dri
Polycarp   PAHL i kahrp
Polycrates   po LIK ruh teez,
　puh-
polygamy   po LIG uh mi, puh-
polyglot   PAHL i glaht
polystaurion   *pahl* i STAW ri
　ahn
polytheism   PAHL uh thee iz
　'm
pome   POM
pomegranate   PAHM gran it,
　-uht, PUHM-
Pomeroy   PAHM uh roy,
　PUHM-, PAHM roy
Pomfret   PAHM fruht
pommel   PUHM uhl
Pompey   PAHM pi
Ponce   PON say
pontiff   PAHN tif
pontifical   pahn TIF i kuhl
pontificate   pahn TIF i kuht
Pontius   PAHN shuhs, -ti uhs
Pontus   PAHN tuhs
pope   POP
popery   POP ur i
popish   POP ish
Poratha   po RAY thuh, PAHR
　uh thuh, PAWR-
Porcius   PAWR shi uhs, -si uhs
porphyrian   pawr FIR i uhn

KEY: b*ee*, b*i*t, b*e*t, b*ay*, b*a*t, b*oo*t, b*u*tcher, b*o*ne, s*aw*, *ah*, t*u*rn, *uh* h*u*h, s*igh*,
c*ow*, b*oy*, *th*in, *th* in *th*en, *sh*oe, *zh* in a*zh*ure, *ch*op, si*ng*, *hw* in *wh*en.

porphyry   PAWR fuh ri, -fir i
Porta, della   *del* uh   POR tuh-,
   PAWR-
portando   pawr TAHN do
portatile   POR tuh til, -tighl,
   PAWR-
portative   POR tuh tiv, PAWR-
portico   POR ti ko, PAWR-
portionist   POR shuhn ist,
   PAWR-
Port-Royal   port ROY uhl,
   pawrt-
poser   POZ ur
Posidonius   *pahs* i DO ni uhs,
   pahs uh-
positivism   PAHZ uh tiv iz 'm
post hoc ergo propter hoc
   POST   HAKH   UR go
   PRAHP tur   HAHK
postil   PAHS til, -tuhl
postlude   POST lood, -lyood
postulant   PAHS tyu luhnt,
   -chu luhnt
postulate   PAHS tyu layt, -chu
   layt
potentate   PO tuhn tayt
Pothier   po TYAY
Potiphar   PAHT uh fur
Potiphera   po TIF ur uh
potsherd   PAHT *shurd*
pottage   PAHT ij
potter   PAHT ur
Prado   PRAH do
praemunire   *pree* myu NIGH
   ri
praepositus   pri PAHZ uh tuhs

Praetorian   pri TO ri uhn, pri
   TAWR i-
praetorium   pri TO ri uhm, pri
   TAWR i-
pragmatic   prag MAT ik
pragmatism   PRAG muh tiz 'm
praise   PRAYZ
prate   PRAYT
Praxean   PRAK si uhn
prayer   PRER
preach   PREECH
preadamic   *pree* uh DAM ik
Preadamite   pri AD uhm ight
prebend   PREB uhnd
prebendary   PREB uhn *der* i
precentor   pri SENT ur
precept   PREE sept
preceptory   pri SEP to ri, -tuh
   ri
preces   PREE seez
precisian   pri SIZH uhn
preciso   pray CHEE so
preconization   *pree* ko nuh ZAY
   shuhn, *pree* ko nigh-
predella   pri DEL uh
predestination   pri *des* ti NAY
   shuhn, pri *des* tuh-
predestine   pri DES tin, -tuhn
preeminence   pri EM uh nuhns
preexistence   *pree* eg ZIST uhns
preface   PREF is, -uhs
prejudice   PREJ u dis, -uh duhs
prelacy   PREL uh si
prelate   PREL it, -uht
prelude   PREL yood, -ood,
   PREE lyood, -lood,

KEY: b*ee*, b*i*t, b*e*t, b*ay*, b*a*t, b*oo*t, b*u*tcher, b*o*ne, s*aw*, *ah*, t*ur*n, *uh* h*uh*, s*igh*,
c*ow*, b*oy*, *th*in, *th* in *th*en, *sh*oe, *zh* in a*zh*ure, *ch*op, si*ng*, *hw* in *wh*en.

Premonstratensian   pri *mahn* struh TEN shuhn
Presburg   PRES boorg, -burg
presbyter   PREZ buh tur, PRES-
Presbyterian   *prez* buh TIR i uhn, *pres-*
presbyterium   *prez* buh TIR i uhm, *pres-*
presbytery   PREZ buh *ter* i, PRES-, -tur i
prescience   PREE shi uhns, PRESH i-
pressfat   PRES *fat*
presto   PRES to
prevenient   pri VEEN yuhnt
prevost   pri VO
pricket   PRIK ct, -it, -uht
Prideaux   PRID o
prie-dieu   *pree* DYOO
priest   PREEST
primacy   PRIGH muh si
prima facie   PRIGH muh FAY shi
primate   PRIGH mit, -mayt
primeval   prigh MEE vuhl
primogeniture   *prigh* mo JEN uh tyoor, -chur
Primus   PRIGH muhs
principality   *prin* suh PAL uh ti
prior   PRIGH ur
prioress   PRIGH ur es, -is, -uhs
priory   PRIGH o ri, -uh ri
Prisca   PRIS kuh
Priscilla   pri SIL uh
Priscillianist   pri SIL yuhn ist

privily   PRIV uh li
privy   PRIV i
probabilionist   *prahb* uh BIL yuhn ist
probabiliorist   *prahb* uh BIL yur ist
probabilism   PRAHB uh b'l iz 'm
Probus   PRO buhs
Prochorus   PRAHK o ruhs, -uh ruhs
proconsul   pro KAHN suhl
proctor   PRAHK tur
procurator   PRAHK yu *ray* tur
profane   pro FAYN
profess   pro FES
profession   pro FESH uhn
profligate   PRAHF luh gayt
prognosticate   prahg NAHS tuh kayt
prokeimenon   pro KIGH mi nahn
prolegomena   *pro* li GAHM uh nuh
prolocutor   pro LAHK yu tur
prologue   PRO lahg, -lawg
promulgate   pro MUHL gayt, PRAHM uhl gayt
pronaos   pro NAY ahs
pronto (music)   PRON to
propagate   PRAHP uh gayt
prophecy   PRAHF uh si
prophesy   PRAHF uh sigh
prophet   PRAHF it, -uht
prophetess   PRAHF uht es, -is
prophetic   pro FET ik

KEY: *b*ee, b*i*t, b*e*t, b*a*y, b*a*t, b*oo*t, b*u*tcher, b*o*ne, s*aw*, *ah*, t*ur*n, *uh* h*uh*, s*igh*, c*ow*, b*oy*, *th*in, *th* in *th*en, *sh*oe, *zh* in a*zh*ure, *ch*op, si*ng*, *hw* in *wh*en.

propitiation pro *pish* i AY shuhn
propitiatory pro PISH i uh *to* ri, *-tawr* i
prosar PRO zur
proselyte PRAHS uh light
proseucha pro SYOO kuh
proseuche pro SYOO ki
prostitute PRAHS tuh tyoot, -toot
prostitution *prahs* tuh TYOO shuhn, -TOO shuhn
prostrate PRAHS trayt
Protagoras pro TAG uh ruhs
Protestant PRAHT is tuhnt, -uhs tuhnt
protevangelium *pro* ti van JEL i uhm
prothesis PRAHTH i sis
prothonotary pro THAHN o *ter* i, pro tho NO-
proto- PRO to
protocol PRO tuh kahl
proto-Hattic PRO to HAT ik
protopapas *pro* to PAP uhs, -PAY puhs
protopresbyter pro to PREZ buh tur, -PRES buh tur
provender PRAHV uhn dur
Proverbs PRAHV urbz
Providence PRAHV uh duhns
provisor pro VIGH zur
provost PRAHV uhst, PRO vo, -vost
prozymite PRAHZ uh might
Prudentius proo DEN shi uhs

Prynne PRIN
psalmister SAHM is tur
psalmody SAHM uh di, SAL muh-
Psalms SAHMZ
psalter SAWL tur
psaltery SAWL tur i
Psaltiel SAWL ti el
Psellus SEL uhs
pseudepigrapha *syoo* duh PIG ruh fuh, *soo-*
pseudo- SYOO do, SOO do
pseudodoxy SYOO do *dahk* si, SOO-
pseudolatry syu DAHL uh tri, su-
pseudology syu DAHL o ji, su-, -uh ji
pseudomancy SYOO do *man* si, SOO-
psilanthropist sigh LAN thro pist
psyche SIGH ki
psychiatry sigh KIGH uh tri
psychical SIGH ki kuhl
psychoanalysis *sigh* ko uh NAL uh sis
psychology sigh KAHL o ji, -uh ji
psychomancy SIGH ki *man* si
psychometry sigh KAHM uh tri
psychopannychism *sigh* ko PAN i kiz 'm
psychosis sigh KO sis, -suhs

KEY: b*ee*, b*i*t, b*e*t, b*ay*, b*a*t, b*oo*t, b*u*tcher, b*o*ne, s*aw*, *ah*, t*ur*n, *uh* h*uh*, s*igh*, c*ow*, b*oy*, *th*in, *th* in *th*en, *sh*oe, *zh* in a*z*ure, *ch*op, si*ng*, *hw* in *wh*en.

psychosomatic *sigh* ko so MAT
ik

psychotherapy *sigh* ko THER
uh pi

Ptolemaeus tahl uh MEE
uhs

Ptolemaic *tahl* uh MAY ik

Ptolemais *tahl* uh MAY is,
-uhs

Ptolemee, Ptolemy, Ptolomee
TAHL uh mi

Pua, Puah PYOO uh

publican PUHB li kuhn

Publius PUHB li uhs

Pucelle poo SEL

Pudens PYOO denz

Pufendorf POO fuhn dorf,
-dawrf

Puget poo ZHAY

Pugin PYOO jin, -juhn

Puhite PYOO hight

Pul PUHL, PUL

Pulcheria pul KEE ri uh

pulpit PUL pit, -puht

Punite PYOO night

Punjabi puhn JAH bi

Punon PYOO nahn

Punti PUHN *tee*

Pur PUR

Purah PYOO ruh

Purchas PUR chuhs

purgation pur GAY shuhn

purgatory PUR guh *to* ri, -*tawr*
i

purge PURJ

purify PYOO ri figh, PYU-

purificator PYOO ruh fuh *kay*
tur, PYU-

Purim PYOO rim, POO rim

Puritan PYOO ri tuhn, PYU-

purloin pur LOYN

purslain, purslane PURS layn

purtenance PUR tuh nuhns

Pusey PYOO zi, -si

Puseyism PYOO zee iz 'm

Pushtu PUHSH too

Puteoli pyu TEE o ligh, -uh
ligh

Puthite PYOO thight

Putiel PYOO ti el

Puvah PYOO vuh

Pygarg PIGH gahrg

pyre PIGHR

Pyrrho PIR o

Pyrrhonism PIR o niz 'm

Pyrrhus PIR uhs

Pythagoras pi THAG uh ruhs,
puh-

python PIGH thahn

pyx PIKS

Qaraite KAY ruh ight

Qoph KOF

Qorban KAWR ban, -buhn

Quadragesima *kwahd* ruh JES
uh muh

quadratum kwahd RAY tuhm

quadratus kwahd RAY tuhs

quadrilateral *kwahd* ruh LAT
ur uhl

Quadrio KWAHD ri o

quadrisacramentarian *kwahd*

KEY: bee, bit, bet, bay, bat, boot, butcher, bone, saw, ah, turn, uh huh, sigh,
cow, boy, thin, th in then, shoe, zh in azure, chop, sing, hw in when.

ruh *sak* ruh men TAR i uhn,
-TER i uhn
quadrivium   kwahd RIV i uhm
quaestio   KWES chi o,
KWEES-
Quaker   KWAYK ur
Quandt   KWAHNT, KAHNT
quantum   KWAHN tuhm
quare impedit   KWAY ri   IM
pi duht
Quarles   KWAWRLZ,
KWAHRLZ
quarternion   kwawr TUR ni
ahn, -uhn
Quartodeciman   *kwawr* to DES
uh muhn
Quartus   KWAWR tuhs
quasi-   KWAY sigh, KWAH si
Quasimodo   *kwah* si MO do
Quatember   kwah TEM bur
Quaternion   kwah TUR ni uhn,
kwuh-
Quatremere   kaht ruh MER
Quedlinburg   KVED luhn
boorg
Quesnel   kay NEL, kee-
questman   KWEST muhn
Quevedo y Villegas   kay VAY
do ee   vil YAY gahs
quicunque vult   qui KUHNG
kwi   *vuhlt*
quiddity, quidity   KWID uh ti
quietism   KWIGH uht iz 'm
quinisext   KWIN i sekst
quinisextine   *kwin* i SEX tin,
-teen

Quinquagesima   *kwin* kwuh
JES uh muh
quinquarticular   *kwin* kwahr
TIK yu lur
Quinquatria   kwin KWAHT ri
uh
quinquennalia   *kwin* kwuh
NAY li uh
quintessence   kwin TES uhns
quintillanian   *kwin* til AY ni
uhn
Quintillian   kwin TIL i uhn
Quintus Memmius   KWIN
tuhs   MEM i uhs
quire   KWIGHR
Quirenius, Quirinius   kwi RIN
i uhs, kwuh-
quirk   KWURK
quiver   KWIV ur
Qumran   kum RAHN, KUM
rahn
quoin   KOYN, KWOYN
quotidian   kwo TID i uhn
quo vadis   *kwo* VAH dis, -VAY
dis

Raama, Raamah   RAY uh muh
Raamiah   *ray* uh MIGH uh
Raamses   ray AM seez
Rab   RAHB
Rabanus   rah BAH noos
Rabat   RAB uht
Rabbah   RAB uh
Rabbath   RAB bath, -uhth
rabbi   RAB igh
rabbinic   ra BIN ik, ruh-

KEY: bee, bit, bet, bay, bat, boot, butcher, bone, saw, ah, turn, uh huh, sigh,
cow, boy, thin, th in then, shoe, zh in azure, chop, sing, hw in when.

rabbinism RAB uhn iz 'm
Rabbith RAB ith
Rabboni ra BO nigh, ruh BO ni
Rab-Mag RAB mag
Rabsaces RAB suh seez, rab SAY seez
Rab-Saris RAB suh ris
Rabshakeh RAB shuh ke, rab SHAY ke
raca ruh KAH, RAY kuh
Racal RAY kal, -kuhl
Raccovian ruh KO vi uhn
Racha RAY kuh
Rachab RAY kab
Rachal RAY kuhl
Rachel RAY chuhl
Racine rah SEEN
Racovian ruh KO vi uhn
Radbertus rad BURT uhs
Raddai RAD ay igh, ruh DAY igh
Raffles RAF l'z
Ragau RAY gaw
Rages RAY jeez
Raguel ruh GYOO el
Rahab RAY hab
Raham RAY ham
Rahel RAY hel
Raikes RAYKS
raiment RAY muhnt
Raimondi righ MAHN di
Rakem RAY kem
Rakkath RAK ath, -uhth
Rakkon RAK ahn
Ram RAM

Rama, Ramah RAY muh
Ramath RAY math
Ramathaim ray muh THAY im
Ramathaim-Zophim -ZO fim
Ramathem RAM uh them
Ramathite RAY muh thight
Ramath-Lehi ray math LEE high
Ramath-Mizpeh ray math MIZ pe
Ramath-Negeb ray math NEE geb
Rameses RAM uh seez
Ramiah ruh MIGH uh
Ramist RAY mist
Ramoth RAY mahth, -moth
Rahmoth-Gilead -GIL i uhd
Ramus RAY muhs
Rancé rahn SAY
Ranke RAHN kuh, RAHNGK
ranter RANT ur
Rapha RAY fuh
Raphael RAF ay el, -uhl, RAY fay-
Raphah RAY fuh
Raphaim RAF ay im, ruh FAY im
Raphon RAY fahn
Raphu RAY fyu
Rappist RAP ist
rapport ra POR, -PAWR
Raratongan, Rarotongan rah ruh TON guhn, -TAHN guhn
Rashi RASH i, RAH shi
Raskolnik ras KAWL nyik
Rasses RAS eez

KEY: bee, bit, bet, bay, bat, boot, butcher, bone, saw, ah, turn, uh huh, sigh, cow, boy, thin, th in then, shoe, zh in azure, chop, sing, hw in when.

Ras Shamra rahs SHAHM
ruh
Rathumus ruh THYOO muhs
rationale (Ecclesiastical) *rash*
uhn AY li
rationalism RASH uhn 'l iz 'm
Ratisbon RAT is bahn
Rau ROW
Rauch ROWK
Raumer ROW mur
Rauschenbusch ROWSH uhn
bush, ROWS-
raven, ravin RAV in, -uhn
Ravenna ruh VEN uh
Ravenscroft RAY vuhnz krahft
Razis RAY zis
Reaia, Reaiah ri AY yuh, -IGH
uh
realism REE uhl iz 'm
Reba, Rebah REE buh
Rebecca ri BEK uh, ruh-
Rebekah ri BEK uh, ruh-
rebuke ri BYOOK
Recah REE kuh
recension ri SEN shuhn
Rechab REE kab
Rechabite REK uh bight
Rechah REE kuh
Recollet REK o let, -uh luht
recompense REK uhm pens
reconcile REK uhn sighl
reconciliation *rek* uhn *sil* i AY
shuhn
rectitude REK tuh tyood, -tood
rector REK tur
rectory REK to ri, -tuh ri

recursion ri KUR shuhn
recusant REK yu zuhnt
Redeemer ri DEEM ur
redemption ri DEMP shuhn
Redemptorist ri DEMP tur ist
redound ri DOWND
reductio ad absurdum ri
DUHK shi o ad ab SUR
duhm
Reelaiah *ree* el AY yuh, -IGH
uh
Reelias ri EL i uhs
Reesaias *ree* uh SAY yuhs,
-SIGH uhs
refectory ri FEK to ri, -tuh ri
referent REF ur uhnt
Reformation *ref* ur MAY
shuhn
refrigerium *ref* ruh JEE ri
uhm, -JIR i uhm
refute ri FYOOT
regale (Ecclesiastical), ri GAY
li
regalia ri GAYL yuh, ri GAY
li yuh
Regem REE gem
Regem-Melech *ree* gem MEE
lek, -MEL ek
regeneration ri *jen* ur AY
shuhn, *ree* jen-
Regensburg RAY gens boorg
regium donum REE ji uhm
DO nuhm
regnum REG nuhm
regression ri GRESH uhn
Rehabiah *ree* huh BIGH uh

Rehob   REE hahb
Rehoboam   *ree* huh BO uhm,
  ree uh-
Rehoboth   ri HO bahth, -both
Rehoboth-Ir   ri HO bahth UR,
  -IR
Rehum   REE huhm
Rei   REE igh
Reichardt   RIGH kahrt
Reichenau   RIGH kuh now
reign   RAYN
Reimarus   righ MAHR uhs
Reims   REEMZ
reincarnation   *ree* in kahr NAY
  shuhn
Rekem   REE kem
relativism   REL uh tiv iz 'm
relic   REL ik
religion   ri LIJ uhn
relicary   REL i *ker* i
reliquary   REL i *kwer* i
Rellyan   REL i uhn
Rellyanite   REL i uhn ight
Remaliah   *rem* uh LIGH uh
Rembrandt   REM brant
Remeth   REE meth, REM
  uhth
Remigius   ri MIJ i uhs, ruh-
Reminiscere   *rem* uh NIS uh
  ri
Remmon   REM ahn, -uhn
Remmon-Methoar   *rem* uhn
  METH o ahr, -mi THO ahr
remnant   REM nuhnt
Remoboth   REM o bahth,
  -both

remonstrant   ri MAHN struhnt,
  ruh-
Remphan   REM fan
Renaissance   *ren* uh ZAHNS,
  -SAHNS, REN uh *zahns*, ri
  NES uhns
Renan   ri NAN
renunciant   ri NUHN shi uhnt
reparation   *rep* uh RAY shuhn
repentance   ri PEN tuhns
Rephael   REE fay el, REF ay el
Rephah   REE fuh
Rephaiah   ri FAY yuh, -FICH
  uh
Rephaim   REF ay im, ri FAY
  im
Rephan   REE fan
Rephidim   REF uh dim
reposoir   ri po ZWAHR
repression   ri PRESH uhn
reprobate   REP ro bayt
requiem   REK wi uhm, REE
  kwi-
requite   ri KWIGHT
reredos   RIR dahs, REER-
rereward   RIR wurd
Resaias   ri SAY yuhs, -SIGH
  uhs
rescissory   ri SIS uh ri, ri SIZ-
rescript   REE skript
Resen   REE sen
Resh   RESH
Resheph   REE shef
Resolutioner   *rez* o LYOO
  shuhn ur, *rez* uh LOO-
respite   RES pit, -puht

KEY: b*ee*, b*i*t, b*e*t, b*a*y, b*a*t, b*oo*t, b*u*tcher, b*o*ne, s*aw*, *ah*, t*ur*n, *uh* h*uh*, s*igh*,
c*ow*, b*oy*, *th*in, *th* in *th*en, *sh*oe, *zh* in a*zh*ure, *ch*op, si*ng*, *hw* in *wh*en.

responsary, responsory   ri
   SPAHN suh ri
restitution   *res* tuh TYOO
   shuhn, -TOO shuhn
restorationist   *res* tuh RAY
   shuhn ist
resurrection   *rez* ur REK shuhn
retable   ri TAY b'l
retribution   *ret* ruh BYOO
   shuhn
Retz   RAYS, RETS
Reu   REE oo, ROO
Reuben   ROO ben, -bin, -buhn
Reubenite   ROO buhn ight
Reuchlin   ROYK lin, -luhn
Reuel   ROO el
Reumah   ROO muh
revel   REV uhl, -'l
Revelation   *rev* uh LAY shuhn
reverence   REV ur uhns
Rezon   REE zahn, -zuhn
Rhabanus   rah BAH noos
Rhegium   REE ji uhm
Rheims   REEMZ
Rhemish   REE mish
Rhesa   REE suh
rhetorian   re TO ri uhn,
   -TAWR i uhn
rhetoric   RET ur ik
rho   RO
Rhoda   RO duh
Rhodes   RODZ
Rhodocus   RAHD uh kuhs
Ribai   RIGH bigh, -bay igh, ri
   BAY igh
ribband   RIB uhnd, -uhn

Ribera   ri BAY ruh
Riblah   RIB luh
Ricci   REET chi
Richelieu   REESH loo
Richter   RIK tur
rie   RIGH
Rienzo   ri EN zo
righteous   RIGH chuhs
rigorist   RIG ur ist
Rimini   REE mi ni
Rimmon   RIM ahn, -uhn
Rimmonah   ri MO nuh
Rimmon-Methoar   *rim* uhn
   MEE tho ahr, -mi THO ahr
Rimmono   ri MO no
Rimmon-Parez   *rim* uhn   PAY
   reez, -PER ez
Rimmon-Perez   *rim* uhn   PEE
   rez, -PER ez
Rinnah   RIN uh
Riphath   RIGH fath
Ripon   RIP ahn
Rissah   RIS uh
rite   RIGHT
Rithmah   RITH muh
Ritschl   RICH 'l
ritual   RIT chu uhl
Rizia   RIZ i uh
Rizpah   RIZ pah
Roboam   ro BO uhm
Rocelin, Rocellin   rahs el AN
Roch   ROK
Rochet   RAHCH et, -it, -uht
rococo   ro KO ko, *ro* ko KO
Rodanim   RAHD uh nim
Rödiger   RED ig ur

KEY: b*ee*, b*i*t, b*e*t, b*ay*, b*a*t, b*oo*t, b*u*tcher, b*o*ne, s*aw*, *ah*, t*ur*n, *uh* h*uh*, s*igh*,
c*ow*, b*oy*, *th*in, *th* in *then*, *sh*oe, *zh* in a*z*ure, *ch*op, si*ng*, *hw* in *wh*en.

roe RO
roebuck RO *buhk*
rogation ro GAY shuhn
Rogelim RO guh lim, ro GEE lim
Rohgah RO guh
Roimus RO uh muhs
Rolle ROL
Rollin ro LAN
Romaic ro MAY ik
Romaine ro MAYN, -MAN
Romamti-Ezer ro *mam* tuh EE zur, -tigh EE zur
Romanesque *ro* muhn ESK
Romanic ro MAN ik
Romanism RO muhn iz 'm
Romano ro MAH no
Romans RO muhnz
romanticism ro MAN tuh siz 'm
Romanus ro MAY nuhs
Ronsdorfer RAHNZ dawrf ur
rood ROOD
Roos ROS
Roquette ro KET
Rosa RO sah, -zah
Rosales ro SAHL ays
Rosalie ROZ uh li
rosary RO zuh ri
Roscelin, Roscellin rahs el AN
Roscellinus *rahs* uh LIGH nuhs
Rosellini *ro* scl LEE ni
Rosenmuller RO zuhn *mul* ur, -*muhl* ur
Rosenthal RO zuhn tahl, -thahl

Rosetta ro ZET uh
rosette ro ZET
Rosh RAHSH, ROSH
Rosh Chodesh *rosh* KO desh
Rosh Hashanah *rosh* hah SHAH nah
Rosh Hashonoh *rosh* hah SHAW naw
Rosh Hodesh *rosh* KO desh
Rosicrucian *ro* zuh KROO shuhn
Rosminian rahz MIN i uhn
Rosmini-Serbati rahs MEE ni ser BAH ti
Rossi RAHS si
Rossignol rah SEEN yol, rah seen YOL
Roswitha ROS vee tah
rote ROT
Roth ROT, RAHTH
Rougemont roozh MAWN, -MON
Rousseau roo SO
Roussel roo SEL
rowan RO uhn
Rowe RO
Rowley RO li, ROW-
Royce ROYS
rubato roo BAH to
rubric ROO brik
rude ROOD
rudenture ru DEN chur
Rudolph ROO dahlf
rue ROO
Rufus ROO fuhs

KEY: b*ee*, b*i*t, b*e*t, b*a*y, b*a*t, b*oo*t, b*u*tcher, b*o*ne, s*aw*, *ah*, t*ur*n, *uh* huh, s*igh*, c*ow*, b*oy*, *th*in, *th* in *th*en, *sh*oe, *zh* in a*zh*ure, *ch*op, si*ng*, *hw* in *wh*en.

Ruhamah   ru HAY muh, -HAH
  muh
Rumah   ROO muh
rump   RUHMP
runagate   RUHN uh gayt
runnel   RUHN uhl, -'l
Rupert   ROO purt
ruridecanal   rur uh DEK uh
  nuhl, -n'l, -di KAY nuhl, -n'l
Russian   RUHSH uhn
Russo-   RUHS o
Ruth   ROOTH
Ruthenian   ru THEE ni uhn
Rutherglen   RUH~~TH~~ ur glen,
  RUHG luhn
Rycaut   ri KO
Ryswick   RIZ wik

Sa   SAH
Saadia Gaon   sah AHD yah
  gah ON
Sabachthani   sah *bahk* tah NEE
Sabaco   SAB uh ko
Sabaean   suh BEE uhn
Sabakon   SAB uh kahn
Sabanneus   *sab* uh NEE uhs
Sabannus   sa BAN uhs, suh-
Sabaoth   SAB ay ahth, -oth
Sabat   SAY bat
Sabateas, Sabateus   *sab* uh TEE
  uhs
Sabathus   SAB uh thuhs
Sabatier, Sabbatier   sah bah
  TYAY, sah *bah* ti AY
Sabatus   SAB uh tuhs
Sabban   SAB uhn

Sabbatarian   *sab* uh TER i uhn
Sabbatai Zevi, Sabbathai Zebi
  sah bah TIGH zi VEE
Sabbateus   *sab* uh TEE uhs
Sabbath   SAB uhth
Sabbathaist   *sab* uh THAY ist
Sabbatheus   *sab* uh THEE uhs
Sabbatian   sa BAY shuhn
sabbatical   suh BAT i kuhl, -k'l
Sabbatine   SAB uh tin, -teen
Sabbeus   sa BEE uhs
Sabean   sa BEE uhn
Sabeca   suh BEK uh
Sabellian   suh BEL i uhn
Sabellius   suh BEL i uhs
Sabi   SAY bigh
Sabian   SAY bi uhn
Sabias   sa BIGH uhs, suh-
Sabie   SAY bi ee
Sabina   suh BIGH nuh, suh
  BEE nuh
Sabotier   sa bo TYAY
Sabta, Sabtah   SAB tuh
Sabteca, Sabtecha, Sabtechah
  SAB ti kuh
Sacar   SAY kahr
sacerdos   SAS ur dahs
sacerdotal   *sas* ur DO tuhl, -t'l
Sachar   SAY kahr
Sacheverell   suh SHEV ur el
Sachia   sa KIGH uh, suh-
sackbut   SAK buht
sackcloth   SAK *klawth*, -*klahth*
sacrament   SAK ruh muhnt
sacramental   *sak* ruh MEN
  tuhl, -t'l

Sacramentarian *sak* ruh men
TER i uhn
sacramentary *sak* ruh MEN
tuh ri
sacrarium suh KRER i uhm
sacred SAY kred, -krid, -kruhd
sacrifice SAK ruh fighs, -ri fighs
sacrificial *sak* ruh FISH uhl
sacrilege SAK ruh lij, -lej
sacrilegious *sak* ruh LEE juhs,
-LIJ uhs
sacring bell SAY kring BEL
sacrist SAY krist
sacristan SAK ris tan
sacristy SAK ris ti
Sacy, de duh sah SEE
Sadamias *sad* uh MIGH uhs
Sadas SAY das
Saddeus sa DEE uhs
Sadduc SAD uk
Sadducee SAD ju see
Sadduk SAD uhk
Sadoc SAY dahk
saffron SAF ruhn
Saggitarius *saj* uh TAY ri uhs,
-TER i uhs
saint SAYNT
Saint Alban saynt AWL buhn
Saint Asaph saynt AZ uhf
Saint Denis san di NEE
Sainte-Chapelle *sant* shah PEL
Saint Germain des Prés san
zher *man* day PRAY
Saint Omer san to MER
Saint-Simon san si MON,
saynt SIGH muhn

saith SETH
Sakkuth SAK uhth
Sala, Salah SAY luh
Saladin SAL uh din
Salamiel suh LAY mi el
Salamis SAL uh mis, -muhs
Salasadai *sal* uh SAD ay igh
Salathiel suh LAY thi el
Salcah, Salchah SAL kuh
Salecah SAL i kuh
Salem SAY luhm
Salemas· SAL uh mas, sa LEE
muhs, suh-
Salesian suh LEE shuhn
salicet SAL i set
salicional suh LISH uhn uhl
Salim SAY lim
Salimoth SAL i mahth, -moth
Salisbury SAWLZ bur i
Sallai SAL ay igh, SAL igh
Sallu SAL yoo
Sallumus sal YOO muhs, suh
LOO muhs
Salma, Salmah SAL muh
Salmai SAL migh, -may igh
Salmanasar *sal* muh NAY sur
Salmasius sal MAY shi uhs
Salmon SAL mahn
Salmon (George) SAH muhn
Salmone sal MO ni
Saloas SAL o uhs
Salom SAY lahm
Salome suh LO mi
Salomon SAL o mahn, -uh
mahn
saltando sahl TAHN do

KEY: b*ee*, b*i*t, b*e*t, b*ay*, b*a*t, b*oo*t, b*u*tcher, b*o*ne, s*aw*, *ah*, t*ur*n, *uh* h*uh*, s*igh*,
c*ow*, b*oy*, *th*in, *th* in *th*en, *sh*oe, *zh* in a*z*ure, *ch*op, si*ng*, *hw* in *wh*en.

salt-wort   SAWLT *wurt*
Salu   SAY lyoo, -loo
Salum   SAY luhm
salutation   *sal* yu TAY shuhn
salvation   sal VAY shuhn
Salvianus   *sal* vi AY nuhs
Salviati   *sahl* vi AH ti
Salzburger   SAWLTS burg ur
Samael   SAM ay el, -i el
Samaias   suh MAY yuhs
Samaria   suh MAR i uh, suh
  MER-
Samaritan   suh MAR uh tuhn,
  suh MER-
Samatus   SAM uh tuhs
Sambation   *sam* buh TYON
Samech, Samekh   SAH mek
Sameius   suh MEE yuhs
Samellius   suh MEL i uhs
Sameus   sa MEE uhs, suh-
Samgar-Nebo   *sam* gahr NEE
  bo
Sami   SAY migh
Samis   SAY mis
Samlah   SAM luh
Sammus   SAM uhs
Samogitian   *sam* o JISH uhn
Samos   SAY mahs
Samosatenian   *sam* o suh TEE
  ni uhn
Samothrace   SAM o *thrays*
Sampsaean   samp SEE uhn,
  sam-
Sampsames   SAMP suh meez
Samson   SAMP s'n, SAM-
Samuel   SAM yu uhl

Sanaas   SAN ay uhs
Sanabassar   *san* uh BAS ur
Sanabassarus   *san* uh BAS uh
  ruhs
Sanasib   SAN uh sib
Sanballat   san BAL uht
San Benito   *san*   buh NEE
  to
sancte-bell   SANGK ti *bel*
sanctification   *sangk* tuh fi KAY
  shuhn
sanction   SANGK shuhn
Sanctology   sangk TAHL o ji,
  -uh ji
sanctuary   SANGK chu *er* i,
  -ur i
Sanctus   SANGK tuhs
sandal   SAN duhl, -d'l
Sandeman   SAN duh muhn
Sandemanian   *san* duh MAY ni
  uhn
Sandoval   sahn do VAHL
Sandys   SAN dis, SANDZ
Sanhedrim   SAN hi drim, -uh
  drim
Sanhedrin   SAN hi drin, -uh
  drin
Sankey   SANG ki
Sansannah   san SAN uh
Sanscrit   SAN skrit
santa croce   SAHN tah   KRO
  che
Santali   sahn TAH li
Santa Maria Maggiore   SAHN
  tah   mah REE ah   mahd JO
  re

KEY: b*ee*, b*i*t, b*e*t, b*a*y, b*a*t, b*oo*t, b*u*tcher, b*o*ne, s*aw*, *ah*, t*ur*n, *uh* h*uh*, s*igh*,
c*ow*, b*oy*, *th*in, t͟h in t͟hen, *sh*oe, *zh* in a*zh*ure, *ch*op, si*ng*, *hw* in *wh*en.

Santa Sophia   *sahn* tah   so FEE
   ah
Santayana   *san* tuh YAH nuh
Santos   SAHN tos
Saph   SAF
Saphat   SAY fat
Saphatias   *saf* uh TIGH uhs
Sapheth   SAY feth
Saphir   SAY fur
Saphuthi   SAF yu thigh, sa
   FYOO thi
Sapphira   suh FIGH ruh
Sara   SER uh, SAY ruh
Sarabaite   *sar* uh BAY ight,
   ser-
Sarabias   *sar* uh BIGH uhs,
   ser-
Saracen   SAR uh suhn, SER-
Sarah   SER uh, SAY ruh
Sarai   SAY righ, SER ay igh
Saraias   suh RAY yuhs, -RIGH
   uhs
Saramel   SAR uh mel, SER-
saraph   SAY raf, SAH-
Sarchedonus   sahr KED uh
   nuhs
sarcophagus   sahr KAHF uh
   guhs
Sardeus   sahr DEE uhs
sardin, sardine   SAHR din,
   -dighn
Sardis   SAHR dis
Sardite   SAHR dight
Sardius   SAHR di uhs
sardonyx   SAHR do niks
Sarea   suh REE uh

Sarepta   suh REP tuh
Sargon   SAHR gahn
Sarid   SAY rid
Saron   SAY rahn
Sarothie   suh RO thi ee
Sarpi   SAHR pi
Sarsechim   SAHR si kim, sahr
   SEE kim
Sarto, del   del SAHR to
Sartorius   sahr TO ri uhs,
   -TAWR i uhs
Sartre   SAHRTR'
Saruch   SAY ruhk, SER uhk
Sarum   SER uhm
Satan   SAY tuhn, -t'n
Satanael   suh TAN ay uhl
Sathrabuzanes   *sath* ruh BYOO
   zuh neez, -byu ZAY neez
satrap   SAY trap, SAT rap
Saturnian   sa TUR ni uhn, suh-
Saturninus   *sat* ur NIGHN uhs
satyr   SAY tur, SAT ur
Saul   SAWL
Savanarola   suh *vahn* uh RO
   luh, *sav* uhn-
Savaran   SAV uh ran
Savias   suh VIGH uhs
Savigny   sah veen YEE
Savior, Saviour   SAYV yur
Savonarola   suh *vahn* uh RO
   luh, *sav* uhn-
savor, savour   SAY vur
Savoy   suh VOY
Saxa Rubra   SAK suh   ROO
   bruh
Saxon   SAK s'n

KEY: b*ee*, b*i*t, b*e*t, b*ay*, b*a*t, b*oo*t, b*u*tcher, b*o*ne, s*aw*, *ah*, t*ur*n, *uh* h*uh*, s*igh*,
c*ow*, b*oy*, *th*in, *th* in *th*en, *sh*oe, *zh* in a*zh*ure, *ch*op, si*ng*, *hw* in *wh*en.

Saybrook SAY *brook*
Sayce SAYS
Scala Sancta SKAH luh
 SANGK tuh
Scaliger SKAL i jur
scall SKAWL
scape-goat SKAYP *got*
scapular SKAP yu lur
scapulary SKAP yu *ler* i,
 -lur i
scepter SEP tur
sceptic SKEP tik
scepticism SKEP tuh siz 'm
sceptre SEP tur
Sceva SEE vuh
Schaff SHAHF
Schamyl SHAH mil
Scheler SHAY lur, SHEL ur
Schelling SHEL ing
schema SKEE muh
Schenck SHENGK
scherzo SKER tso
Schiller SHIL ur
schism SIZ 'm
Schlegel SHLAY guhl
Schleiermacher SHLIGH ur
 mahk ur, SLIGH-
Schmalkald SHMAHL kahld
Schneckenburger SHNEK uhn
 burg ur
schola cantorum SKO luh kan
 TO ruhm
scholasticism sko LAS tuh siz
 'm
scholiast SKO li ast
scholium SKO li uhm

Schopenhauer SHO puhn *how*
 ur
Schröckh, Schroeckh SHREK
Schubert SHOO burt
Schulz SHOOLTS
Schumann SHOO mahn
schwa SHWAH, SHVAH
Schwabach SHVAH bahk
Schwarzenberg SHVAHRT
 suhn berg, -burg
Schweitzer SHWIGHT sur,
 SWIGHT-
Schwenkfeld SHWENGK felt,
 SHVENGK-
Schwenkfelder SHWENGK
 fel dur, SHVENGK-
Schwenkfeldian shwengk FEL
 di uhn, shvengk-
scillitan SIL uh tuhn
scimitar SIM uh tur
sciomancy SIGH o *man* si
Scone SCOON
Scopus SKO puhs
Scotia SKO shi uh, -shuh
Scotism SKO tiz 'm
Scotus, Duns SKO tuhs, duhnz
scourge SKURJ
scrabble SKRAB 'l
scribe SKRIGHB
scrip SKRIP
scriptorium skrip TO ri uhm,
 -TAWR i uhm
Scripture SKRIP chur
scroll SKROL
Scrope SKROP
Scudder SKUHD ur

KEY: *bee, bit, bet, bay, bat, boot, butcher, bone, saw, ah, turn, uh* huh, *sigh,
cow, boy, thin,* th in *then, shoe, zh* in a*z*ure, *ch*op, sing, *hw* in *wh*en.

scurvy SKUR vi
scutcheon SKUCH uhn
Scythian SITH i uhn, SITH
Scythopolis sigh THAHP o
  lis, -uh luhs, si-
Seah SEE ah
sea-mew SEE *myoo*
Seba SEE buh ,
Sebam SEE bam
se-baptist SEE *bap* tist
Sebaste si BAS ti
Sebastian suh BAS chuhn
Sebat si BAHT, SEE bat
Secacah si KAY kuh, SEK uh
  kah
seceder, seceeder si SEED ur
Sechenias *sek* uh NIGH uhs
Sechu SEE kyoo
Sechuana si CHWAH nah
Secretan sek ray TAN
secretarium *sek* ri TER i uhm
secretum si KREE tuhm
sect SEKT
sectarian sek TER i uhn
sectary SEK tuh ri
Secu SEE kyoo
secular SEK yu lur
Secundus si KUHN duhs
Sedecias *sed* uh SIGH uhs
Sedekias *sed* i KIGH uhs
Seder SAY dur
sede vacante SEE di vuh
  KAN ti
sedes SEE deez
sedes vacans SEE deez VAY
  kanz

sedile si DIGH li
sedilia si DIL i uh
sedition si DISH uhn
seduce si DYOOS, -DOOS
Sedulius si DYOO li uhs
seer SEE ur
seethe SEETH
Sefer SAY fur
Segub SEE guhb
Seir SEE ir, -ur
Seirah si IGH ruh, SEE uh ruh
Seirath si IGH rath, SEE uh
  rath
Sela SEE luh
selah SEE luh
Sela-Hammahlekoth *see* luh
  huh MAH li kahth, -koth
Seled SEE led
Selemia *sel* uh MIGH uh
Selemias *sel* uh MIGH uhs
Seleucia si LYOO shi uh, si
  LOO-
Seleucidae si LYOO si dee, si
  LOO-
Seleucus si LYOO kuhs, si
  LOO-
Selvedge SEL vij
Selwyn SEL win
Sem SEM
Semachiah *sem* uh KIGH uh
semantron si MAN trahn
semasiology si *may* si AHL o ji,
  -uh ji
Semei SEM i igh
Semeias *see* mi IGH uhs
Semein si MEE in, -uhn

KEY: bee, bit, bet, bay, bat, boot, butcher, bone, saw, ah, turn, uh huh, sigh,
cow, boy, thin, th in then, shoe, zh in azure, chop, sing, hw in when.

Semeis   SEM i uhs
Semellius   si MEL i uhs
semi-Arian   *sem* i ER i uhn
seminarist   SEM i *ner* ist, SEM uh-
seminary   SEM uh *ner* i
semiotic   *see* mi AHT ik
semi-Pelagian   *sem* i pi LAY ji uhn
semi-quietism   *sem* i KWIGH uht iz 'm
Semis   SEE mis
Semite   SEM ight, SEE might
Semitic   si MIT ik, se-
Semler   ZEM lur
sempiternity   *sem* pi TUR ni ti
Senaah   si NAY uh, SEN ay uh
senatorium   *sen* uh TO ri uhm, -TAWR i uhm
Seneca   SEN i kuh
Seneh   SEE ne
seneschal   SEN uh shuhl
Senir   SEE nir
Senlis   sahn LEES, -LEE
Sennacherib   suh NAK ur ib
Sens   SAHNS
sensum   SEN suhm
sentential   sen TEN shuhl
sentience   SEN shi uhns, -shuhns
Senua, Senuah   si NYOO uh, SEN yu uh
Seorim   si O rim
separatism   SEP uh ruht iz 'm
Sephar   SEE fahr

Sepharad   si FAY rad, SEF uh rad
Sephardim   si FAHR dim
Sepharvaim   *sef* ahr VAY im, *see* fahr-
Sepharvite   SEE fahr vight, si FAHR-
Sephela   si FEE luh
Sepher Torah   SAY fur TO rah
Sephiroth   SEF uh roth
Sepphoris   SEF o ris, -ruhs
septimanarian   sep ti muh NER i uhn
Septuagesima   *sep* tyu uh JES i muh
Septuagint   SEP tu uh jint, -juhnt, sep TOO-
septum   SEP tuhm
sepulchre   SEP uhl kur
Sepúlveda   say POOL vay dah
sequester   si KWES tur
sequestration   *see* kwes TRAY shuhn, *sek* wes-
Serah   SEE ruh
Seraiah   si RAY yuh, -RIGH uh
seraph   SER uhf
seraphic   si RAF ik
seraphim   SER uh fim
Serar   SEE rahr
Sered   SEE red
Seredite   SER uh dight
Sergius   SUR ji uhs
Sergius Paulus   SUR ji uhs PAWL uhs
serjeant   SAHR juhnt

KEY: b*ee*, b*i*t, b*e*t, b*ay*, b*a*t, b*oo*t, b*u*tcher, b*o*ne, s*aw*, *ah*, t*ur*n, *uh* h*uh*, s*igh*, c*ow*, b*oy*, *th*in, ŧħ in *th*en, *sh*oe, *zh* in a*z*ure, *ch*op, si*ng*, *hw* in *wh*en.

sermo generalis SUR mo *jen*
ur AY lis, -AL uhs
sermon SUR muhn
Seron SEE rahn
serpent SUR puhnt
Serpentinian *sur* puhn TIN i
uhn
Serug SEE ruhg
Servetus sur VEE tuhs
Servite SUR vight
servitor SUR vi tur
Sesis SEE sis
Sesthel SES thel
Sesuto si SOO to
Seth SETH
Sethian SETH i uhn
Sethur SEE thur
Seveneh si VEN e, si
VEEN e
Severian si VIR i uhn, si
VEER-
Severinus *sev* ur IGH nuhs
Severus si VEE ruhs, suh VIR
uhs
Seville suh VIL
Sewall SYOO uhl, SOO uhl
Sexagesima *sek* suh JES uh
muh
Sext SEKST
sexton SEKS tuhn
sextry SEKS tri
Sextus SEKS tuhs
Shaalabbin *shay* uh LAB in
Shaalbim shay AL bim
Shaalbin shay AL bin
Shaalbon shay AL bahn, -bon

Shaalbonite *shay* al BO night,
shay AL bo night
Shaalim SHAY uh lim
Shaaph SHAY af
Shaaraim *shay* uh RAY im
Shaashgaz shay ASH gaz
Shabbethai SHAB i thigh
Shabuoth shah VOO oth
Shachia shuh KIGH uh, SHAK
i uh
Shaddai SHAD ay igh, SHAD
igh
Shadrach SHAD rak, SHAY
drak
Shage, Shagee SHAY gi
Shaharaim *shay* huh RAY im
Shahazimah *shay* huh ZIGH
muh, shuh HAZ i muh
Shahazimath *shay* huh ZIGH
math, shuh HAZ i math
Shahazumah *shay* huh ZOO
muh, shuh HAZ u muh
Shaker SHAYK ur
Shalem SHAY lem, -luhm
Shalim SHAY lim, -luhm
Shalisha, Shalishah shuh LIGH
shuh, SHAL i shah, -uh shah
Shallecheth SHAL i keth, -uh
keth
Shallum SHAL uhm
Shallun SHAL uhn
Shalmai SHAL migh, -may igh
Shalman SHAL man, -muhn
Shalmaneser *shal* muhn EE zur
Shama SHAY muh
Shamai SHAM ay igh

KEY: b*ee*, b*it*, b*et*, b*ay*, b*at*, b*oo*t, b*u*tcher, b*o*ne, s*aw*, *ah*, t*ur*n, *uh* h*uh*, s*igh*,
c*ow*, b*oy*, *th*in, *th* in *th*en, *sh*oe, *zh* in a*z*ure, *ch*op, si*ng*, *hw* in *wh*en.

Shamariah   *sham* uh RIGH uh
Shamash   SHAH mahsh
Shamed   SHAY med
shamefastness   SHAYM *fast*
   nuhs
Shamer   SHAY mur
Shamgar   SHAM gahr
Shamhuth   SHAM huhth
Shamir   SHAY mur
Shamlai   SHAM lay igh, -ligh
Shamma   SHAM uh
Shammah   SHAM uh
Shammai   SHAM ay igh,
   SHAM igh
Shammoth   SHAM ahth, -oth
Shammua, Shammuah   sha
   MYOO uh, SHAM yu uh
Shamsherai   SHAM shuh righ,
   sham shi RAY igh
Shamyl   SHAH mil
Shapham   SHAY fam, -fuhm
Shaphan   SHAY fan, -fuhn
Shaphat   SHAY fat
Shapher   SHAY fur
Shaphir   SHAY fur
Sharai   shuh RAY igh, SHAY
   righ
Sharaim   shuh RAY im
Sharar   SHAY rur
Sharezer   shuh REE zur
Sharon   SHER uhn
Sharonite   SHER uhn ight
Sharuhen   shuh ROO hen
Shashai   SHAY shigh
Shashak   SHAY shak
Shaul   SHAY uhl

Shaulite   SHAY uhl ight
Shaveh   SHAY ve
Shaveh-Kiriathaim   SHAY ve
   kir yuh THAY im
Shavsha   SHAV shuh
shawm   SHAWM
Sheal   SHEE al, -uhl
Shealtiel   shi AL ti el
Sheariah   *shee* uh RIGH uh, shi
   AHR yuh
Shear-Jashub   *shee* ahr JAY
   shuhb
Sheba, Shebah   SHEE buh
Shebam   SHEE bam
Shebaniah   *sheb* uh NIGH uh,
   shi BAN yuh
Shebarim   SHEB uh rim, shi
   BAY rim
Shebat   shi BAHT
Sheber   SHEE bur
Shebna, Shebnah   SHEB
   nuh
Shebuel   shi BYOO uhl, SHEB
   yu el, -uhl
Shecaniah, Shechaniah   *shek* uh
   NIGH uh, shi KAN yuh
Shechem   SHEK uhm, SHEE
   kem, -kuhm
Shechemite   SHEK uhm ight,
   SHEE kuhm ight
Shechina, Shechinah   shi KIGH
   nuh, shuh-
Shedeur   SHED i ur, shi DEE
   ur
sheepcote   SHEEP *kot*, -*kaht*
Sheerah   SHEE uh ruh

KEY: b*ee*, b*i*t, b*e*t, b*a*y, b*a*t, b*oo*t, b*u*tcher, b*o*ne, s*aw*, *ah*, t*ur*n, *uh* h*uh*, s*igh*,
c*ow*, b*oy*, *th*in, t̶h̶ in *th*en, *sh*oe, *zh* in a*z*ure, *ch*op, si*ng*, *hw* in *wh*en.

Sheer (Thursday) SHEER,
  SHIR
Shehariah *shee* huh RIGH uh
shekel SHEK uhl, -'l
Shekinah shi KIGH nuh, shuh-
Shelah SHEE luh
Shelanite SHEE luhn ight, shi
  LAYN ight
Shelemiah *shel* uh MIGH uh,
  shi LEM yuh
Sheleph SHEE lef
Shelesh SHEE lesh
Shelomi shi LO migh, SHEL o
  migh
Shelomith shi LO mith, SHEL
  o mith
Shelomoth shi LO mahth,
  -moth, SHEL o mahth, -moth
Shelumiel shi LYOO mi el, shi
  LOO-
Shem SHEM
Shema shuh MAH
Shemaah shi MAY uh, SHEM
  ay uh
Shemaiah shi MAY yuh,
  -MIGH uh
Shemariah *shem* uh RIGH uh,
  shi MAHR yuh
Shemeber shem EE bur
Shemed SHEE med
Shemer SHEE mur
Shemida, Shemidah shi MIGH
  duh
Shemidaite shi MIGH duh
  ight
Sheminith SHEM uh nith

Shemiramoth shi MIR uh
  mahth, shi MIGH ruh moth,
  shem uh RAY moth
Shemite SHEM ight
Shemitic shem IT ik
Shemone Esre, Shemoneh Esreh
  shuh MO ne ES re
Shem-Tob *shem* TOV
Shemuel shi MYOO el, -uhl,
  SHEM yu el, -uhl
Shen SHEN
Shenazar shi NAY zahr
Shenazzar shi NAZ ahr
Shenir SHEE nur
Sheol SHEE ol, shuh OL
Shepham SHEE fam
Shephathiah *shef* uh THIGH
  uh, shi FATH yuh
Shephatiah *shef* uh TIGH uh,
  shi FAT yuh
Shephelah shef EE lah
Shepher SHEE fur
Shephi SHEE figh
Shepho SHEE fo
Shephupham shi FYOO fam
Shephuphan shi FYOO fan
Sherah SHEE ruh
sherd SHURD
Sherebiah sher uh BIGH uh,
  shi REB yuh
Sheresh SHEE resh
Sherezer shi REE zur
Sherghat SHUR gat, SHER-
Sheshach SHEE shak
Sheshai SHEE shigh
Sheshan SHEE shan

KEY: bee, bit, bet, bay, bat, boot, butcher, bone, saw, ah, turn, uh huh, sigh,
cow, boy, thin, th in then, shoe, zh in azure, chop, sing, hw in when.

Sheshbazzar   shesh BAZ ur
Sheth   SHETH
Shethar   SHEE thahr
Shethar-Bozenai   SHEE thahr
  BAHZ uh nigh
Shethar-Boznai   -BAHZ nigh
Sheva (Biblical name)   SHEE
  vuh
sheva   shuh VAH
shew   SHO
shewa   shuh WAH
shewbread   SHO *bred*
Shibah   SHIV ah
shibboleth   SHIB o luhth
Shibmah   SHIB muh
Shicron   SHIK rahn
Shier   SHEER, SHIR
Shiggaion   shi GAY yahn,
  -GIGH yahn
Shigionoth   *shig* i AHN oth,
  -O noth
Shihon   SHIGH hahn
Shihor   SHIGH hawr
Shihor-Libnath   SHIGH hawr
  LIB nath
Shikkeron   SHIK ur ahn
Shilhi   SHIL high
Shilhim   SHIL him
Shillem   SHIL em, -uhm
Shillemite   SHIL em ight, -uhm
  ight
Shilo   SHIGH lo
Shiloah   shi LO uh
Shiloh   SHIGH lo
Shiloni   shi LO nigh
Shilonite   SHIGH lo night

Shilshah   SHIL shah
Shimea, Shimeah   SHIM i uh
Shimeam   SHIM i am
Shimeath   SHIM i ath
Shimeathite   SHIM i uhth
  ight
Shimei   SHIM i igh
Shimeite   SHIM i ight
Shimeon   SHIM i uhn
Shimhi   SHIM high
Shimi   SHIM igh, SHIGH
  migh
Shimite   SHIM ight
Shimma   SHIM uh
Shimon   SHIGH mahn
Shimrath   SHIM rath
Shimri   SHIM righ
Shimrith   SHIM rith
Shimrom   SHRIM rahm
Shimron   SHIM rahn
Shimronite   SHIM rahn ight
Shimron-Meron   *shim* rahn
  MEE rahn
Shimshai   SHIM shigh, SHIM
  shay igh
shin   SHEEN, SHIN
Shinab   SHIGH nab
Shinar   SHIGH nahr
Shinto   SHIN to
Shion   SHIGH ahn
Shiphi   SHIGH figh
Shiphmite   SHIF might
Shiphrah   SHIF ruh
Shiphtan   SHIF tan, -tuhn
shire-mote   SHIGHR *mot*
Shisha   SHIGH shuh

Shishak   SHIGH shak
Shitrai   SHIT righ, shit RAY
    igh, SHIT ray igh
shittah   SHIT uh
Shittim   SHIT im, -uhm
Shiza   SHIGH zuh
Shoa   SHO uh
Shobab   SHO bab
Shobach   SHO bak
Shobai   SHO bigh, -bay igh
Shobal   SHO bal, -buhl
Shobek   SHO bek
Shobi   SHO bigh
Shocho, Shochoh   SHO ko
Shoham   SHO ham
Shomer   SHO mur
Shophach   SHO fak
Shophan   SHO fan
Shoshannim   sho SHAN im
Shoshannim Eduth   sho SHAN
    im   EE duhth
showbread   SHOW *bred*
shrift   SHRIFT
shrine   SHRIGHN
shrive   SHRIGHV
shriving-pew   SHRIGHV ing
    pyoo
shroud   SHROWD
Shrove   SHROV
Shrovetide   SHROV *tighd*
Shua, Shuah   SHOO uh
Shual   SHOO al, -uhl
Shubael   SHOO bay el, shu
    BAY uhl
Shuhah   SHOO ha
Shuham   SHOO ham

Shuhamite   SHOO ham ight,
    -huhm ight
Shuhite   SHOO hight
Shulamite, Shulammite   SHOO
    luhm ight
Shulem   SHOO lem
Shumathite   SHOO math ight,
    -muhth ight
Shunammite   SHOO nuhm ight
Shunem   SHOO nem
Shuni   SHOO nigh
Shunite   SHOO night
Shupham   SHOO fam
Shuphamite   SHOO fam ight,
    -fuhm ight
Shuppim   SHUHP im
Shur   SHOOR
Shushan   SHOO shan
Shushanchite   shu SHAN kight
Shushan Eduth   SHOO shan
    EE duhth
Shuthalhite   shu THAL hight
Shuthelah   shu THEE luh,
    SHOO thi lah
Shuthelahite   shu THEE luh
    hight
Sia   SIGH uh
Siaha   SIGH uh huh
Siamese   sigh uh MEEZ,
    -MEES
Sibbecai, Sibbechai   SIB uh
    kigh, *sib* uh KAY igh
sibboleth   SIB o luhth
Sibmah   SIB muh
Sibraim   sib RAY im, SIB ray
    im

KEY: b*ee*, b*i*t, b*e*t, b*ay*, b*a*t, b*oo*t, b*u*tcher, b*o*ne, s*aw*, *ah*, t*ur*n, *uh* huh, s*igh*,
c*ow*, b*oy*, *th*in, *th* in *th*en, *sh*oe, *zh* in a*z*ure, *ch*op, si*ng*, *hw* in *wh*en.

Sibylline   SIB uh lighn, -lin
sibyllist   SIB uh list
Sicard   si KAHR
Sicarius   si KAY ri uhs
Sichem   SIGH kem
Sickingen   ZIK ing uhn
Sicyon   SISH i ahn
Siddim   SID im
sideromancy   SID ur o *man* si
Sidon   SIGH duhn, -d'n
Sidonian   si DO ni uhn
Sidonius Apollinaris   si DO ni
   uhs uh *pahl* uh NAY ris,
   -NER uhs
Sienna   si EN uh
Sigebert   SIJ u burt, seezh
   BER
Sigismund   SIJ is muhnd, ZEE
   gis *moont*
siglos   SIG lahs
signate   SIG nayt
Sihon   SIGH hahn
Sihor   SIGH hawr
Sihor-Libnath   -LIB nath
Sikh   SEEK
Silas   SIGH luhs
silentiary   sigh LEN shi *er* i,
   -ur i
Silesius   si LEE shi uhs, -shuhs
Silla   SIL uh
Siloah   si LO uh, sigh-
Siloam   si LO uhm, sigh-
Silva   SEEL vah, SIL vuh
Silvanus   sil VAY nuhs
Simalcue   *sigh* muhl KYOO i
Simeon   SIM i uhn

Simeonite   SIM i uhn ight
Simeon Stylites   SIM i uhn
   stigh LIGH teez
similitude   si MIL uh tyood,
   -tood
Simon   SIGH muhn
Simonian   sigh MO ni uhn
Simon Magus   SIGH muhn
   MAY guhs
simony   SIM uh ni, SIGH
   muh ni
Simplicianus   sim *plis* i AY
   nuhs
Simplicius   sim PLISH i uhs
Simri   SIM righ
simulacrum   sim yu LAY
   kruhm
simultaneum   sigh muhl TAY
   ni uhm
sin   SIN
Sina   SIGH nuh
Sinai   SIGH nigh, -nay igh
Sinaic   sigh NAY ik
Sinaitic   *sigh* nay IT ik
Sinaiticus   *sigh* nay IT i kuhs
Sindon   SIN duhn
sinecure   SIGH ni kyoor, SIN i-
Singhalese   *sing* guh LEEZ
Sinim   SIGH nim
Sinite   SIGH night
Sion   SIGH uhn
Sionite   SIGH uhn ight
Siphmoth   SIF mahth, -moth
Sippai   SIP igh, si PAY igh
si quis   SIGH kwis
Sirach   SIGH rak

KEY: bee, bit, bet, bay, bat, boot, butcher, bone, saw, ah, turn, uh huh, sigh,
cow, boy, thin, th in then, shoe, zh in azure, chop, sing, hw in when.

Sirah   SIGH ruh
Siricius   si RISH i uhs,
  -RISH uhs
Sirion   SIR i ahn
Sirmium   SUR mi uhm
sirocco   si RAHK o
Sisamai   SIS uh migh
Sisera   SIS ur uh
Sisinnes   si SIN eez
Sismai   SIS migh
Sistine   SIS teen, -tin, -tighn
Sith   SITH
Sithri   SITH righ
Sitnah   SIT nuh
Sivan   see VAHN
Sixtus   SIKS tuhs
skeptic   SKEP tik
skepticism   SKEP tuh siz 'm
Slavonic   sluh VAHN ik
Sloane   SLON
Slovenian   slo VEE ni uhn
sluggard   SLUHG urd
Smalcald, Smalkald   SMAWL
  kawld
Smaragdus   sma RAG duhs,
  smuh-
Smectymnuus   smek TIM nyu
  uhs, -nu uhs
smite   SMIGHT
Smyrna   SMUR nuh
snuffer   SNUHF ur
sobriety   so BRIGH uh ti
Socho, Sochoh   SO ko
socialism   SO shul iz 'm
Socinianism   so SIN i uhn iz 'm
Socinus   so SIGH nuhs

sociology   so si AHL o ji, -uh ji
Soco, Socoh   SO ko
Socrates   SAHK ruh teez
sodality   so DAL i ti, -uh ti
Sodi   SO digh
Sodom   SAHD uhm
Sodoma   SAHD o muh
Sodomite   SAHD uhm ight
Sodomitish   SAHD uhm *it* ish
sodomy   SAHD uhm i
Sodor and Man   SO dur   and
  man
Soissons   swah SAWN, -SON
solace   SAHL is, -uhs
solea   SO li uh
Solesmes   so LAYM
solicitant   so LIS uh tuhnt
solifidianism   *sahl* uh FID i
  uhn iz 'm
solipsism   SAHL ip siz 'm
Solomon   SAHL o muhn, -uh
  muhn
Somaschian   so MAS ki uhn
somatic   so MAT ik
somatist   SO muh tist
Somcis   SO mi uhs
sonata   so NAH tuh
soothsayer   SOOTH *say* ur
sop   SAHP
Sopater   SO puh tur, SAHP uh
  tur
Sophereth   so FEE reth, -ruhth,
  SAHF uh reth, SO fi reth
Sopherim   SO fur im
Sophia   so FEE uh
Sophist   SAHF ist

KEY: b*ee*, b*i*t, b*e*t, b*a*y, b*a*t, b*oo*t, b*u*tcher, b*o*ne, s*aw*, *ah*, t*ur*n, *uh* h*uh*, s*igh*,
c*ow*, b*oy*, *th*in, *th* in *th*en, *sh*oe, *zh* in a*z*ure, *ch*op, si*ng*, *hw* in *wh*en.

Sophonias   *sahf* o NIGH uhs,
    sahf uh-
Sora   SO rah
Sorbonne   sawr BAHN,
    -BUHN
sorcery   SAWR sur i
Sorek   SO rek
Sorokin   sawr O kin
sorrel   SAHR uhl, SAWR uhl
Sosipater   so SIP uh tur
sostenuto   *sahs* tay NOO to
Sosthenes   SAHS thi neez
Sostratus   SAHS truh tuhs
Sotai   SO tigh, -tay igh, so TAY
    igh
Soter   SO tur
soteriology   *so* tir i AHL o ji,
    -uh ji
Soto, de   duh SO to
sottish   SAHT ish
sotto voce   SOT o VO chay
soul   SOL
Southcott   SOWTH kaht,
    -kuht
Southcottian   sowth KAHT i
    uhn
sovereignty   SAHV ur uhn ti,
    SAHV rin ti, -ruhn ti
Sozomen   SAHZ o men
Spalatin   spah lah TEEN
Spangenberg   SPAHNG uhn
    berg, -burg
Sparta   SPAHR tuh
sparver   SPAHR vur
spat   SPAT
specter, spectre   SPEK tur

Spener   SPAY nur
Spengler   SPENG glur
sperver   SPUR vur
Speyer, Speier   SPIGH ur
sphinx   SFINGKS
sphragis   SFRAJ is, -uhs
spikenard   SPIGHK nurd,
    -nahrd
Spinoza   spi NO zuh
spire   SPIGHR
Spiridion   spi RID i uhn
spirit   SPIR it, -uht
spiritual   SPIR it chu uhl
sprituality   *spir* it chu AL i ti,
    -uh ti
spital   SPIT uhl, -'l
sponsalia   spahn SAY li uh
sportula   SPAWR chu luh
Spottiswoode   SPAHT is wud
spouse   SPOWS, SPOWZ
Springer   SPRING ur
Spurgeon   SPUR juhn
Squier   SKWIGH ur
squillery   SKWIL ur i
squinch   SKWINCH
Stabat Mater   STAH baht
    MAH tur, STAY bat MAY
    tur
staccato   stuh KAH to
Stachys   STAY kis
stacte   STAK ti
stade   STAYD
stadia   STAY di uh
Stainer   STAY nur
St. Alban   saynt AWL buhn
Standish   STAN dish

KEY: b*ee*, b*i*t, b*e*t, b*ay*, b*a*t, b*oo*t, b*u*tcher, b*o*ne, s*aw*, *ah*, t*ur*n, *uh* h*uh*, s*igh*,
c*ow*, b*oy*, *th*in, *th* in *th*en, *sh*oe, *zh* in a*zh*ure, *ch*op, si*ng*, *hw* in *wh*en.

Stanislas, Stanislaus   STAN uhs lahs
Starets, Staretz   STAH rets
St. Asaph   saynt AZ uhf
stater   STAY tur
stauroanastasima   *stawr o an* uhs TAS i muh
staurolatry   staw RAHL o tri, -uh tri
stauropegion   *staw* ro PEE ji ahn
St. Denis   san di NEE
steeple   STEE p'l
Steiner   STIGH nur
stele   STEE li
stellionatus   *stel* yuhn AYT uhs
Stephanas   STEF uh nuhs
Stephanist   STEF uhn ist
Stephanos   STEF uh nahs
Stephen   STEE ven, -vin, -vuhn
Stercoranist   STUR *ko* ruh nist
Sternhold   STURN *hold*
steward   STYOO urd, STOO-
St. Germain des Prés   san zher *man* day PRAY
sthenic   STHEN ik
sticharion   sti KAY ri ahn
stichometry   sti KAHM uh tri
Stigand   STIG uhnd
stigmatization   *stig* muh ti ZAY shuhn, *stig* muh tigh-
stipend   STIGH pend
stipendiary   stigh PEN di *er* i, -ur i

stoa   STO uh
Stoic   STO ik
Stoicism   STO uh siz 'm
Stolberg   STOL berg, -burg
stole   STOL
stomacher   STUHM uhk ur
St. Omer   san to MER
Stonehenge   STON *henj*
storax   STO raks
stoup   STOOP
Strabo   STRAY bo
strake   STRAYK
stratigraphy   stra TIG ruh fi
Strauss   STROWS
strawed   STRAWD
strew   STROO
stromata   STRO muh tuh
Struensee   STROO uhn zay
Strype   STRIGHP
Stundist   SHTOON dist, STOON-
Sturm   STOORM
Sturm und Drang   SHTOORM unt DRAHNG
Stuttgart   STUT gahrt
stylite   STIGH light
Stylites   stigh LIGH teez
Sua   SYOO uh, SOO-
Suah   SYOO uh, SOO-
Suarez   SWAH rays, -rez
Suba   SYOO buh, SOO-
Subai   SYOO bay igh, SOO-, -bigh
subarrhation   *sub* uh RAY shuhn
subas   SYOO buhs, SOO-

KEY: b*ee*, b*i*t, b*e*t, b*ay*, b*a*t, b*oo*t, b*u*tcher, b*o*ne, s*aw*, *ah*, t*ur*n, *uh* huh, s*igh*, c*ow*, b*oy*, *th*in, *th* in *th*en, *sh*oe, *zh* in a*zh*ure, *ch*op, si*ng*, *hw* in *wh*en.

subcinctorium   *sub* singk TO
ri uhm, -TAWR i uhm
subjectivism   suhb JEK tiv iz 'm
sublapsarian   *suhb* lap SER i
uhn
sublimation   *suhb* li MAY
shuhn, *suhb* luh-
subliminal   *suhb* LIM uh n'l,
suhb LIGH mi n'l, -muh n'l
suborn   suhb AWRN
subsellium   suhb SEL i uhm
substantialist   suhb STAN
shuhl ist
substantive   SUHB stuhn tiv
subtil   SUHB til, SUHT 'l
suburbicarian   suhb *urb* uh
KER i uhn
subvert   suhb VURT
Sucathite   SYOO kuhth ight,
SOO-
succentor   suhk SEN tur
succinctorium   *suhk* singk TO
ri uhm, -TAWR i uhm
succor   SUHK ur
Succoth   SUHK ahth, -oth
Succoth-Benoth   SUHK ahth
BEE nahth, SUHK oth BEE
noth
Suchathite   SYOO kath ight,
SOO kuh thight
Sud   SUHD
Sudarium   syu DER i uhm, su-
Sudias   SYOO di uhs, SOO-
Suetonius   swi TO ni uhs
suffragan   SUHF ruh gan
Suidas   SYOO i duhs, SOO-

Sukkiim   SUHK i im
Sulpician, Sulpitian   suhl PISH
uhn
Sulpicius Severus   suhl PISH i
uhs   si VEE ruhs, -VIR uhs
Sulzer   ZOOLTS ur
Sumerian   syu MIR i uhn, su
MER-
summa   SUHM uh
summist   SUHM ist
summum bonum   SUHM uhm
BO nuhm
sumptuary   SUHMP chu *er* i,
-ur i
Sundanese   *suhn* duh NEEZ,
-NEES
Sundar Singh   *suhn* dahr SING
sup   SUHP
supererogation   *syoo* pur *er* o
GAY shuhn, *soo-*
superfrontal   *syoo* pur FRUHN
t'l, *soo-*
superhumeral   *syoo* pur
HYOO mur uhl, *soo-*
superstition   *syoo* pur STISH
uhn, *soo-*
Suph   SOOF
Suphah   SOO fah
supplication   *suhp* li KAY
shuhn, *suhp* luh-
supralapsarian   *syoo* pruh lap
SER i uhn, *soo-*
Sur   SUR
surcingle   SUR *sing* g'l
surety   SHUR uh ti
surfeit   SUR fit

KEY: b*ee*, b*i*t, b*e*t, b*a*y, b*a*t, b*oo*t, b*u*tcher, b*o*ne, s*aw*, *ah*, t*ur*n, *uh* h*uh*, s*igh*,
c*ow*, b*oy*, *th*in, **th** in *th*en, *sh*oe, *zh* in a*z*ure, *ch*op, si*ng*, *hw* in *wh*en.

Surinam   SOO ri nahm
surplice   SUR plis, -pluhs
surrealism   sur REE uhl iz 'm,
   syu-
surrogate   SUR o gayt
sursum corda   SUR suhm
   KAWR duh
Susa   SYOO suh, SOO-
Susanchite   syu SAN kight, su-
Susanna, Susannah   su ZAN uh
Susi   SYOO sigh, SOO-
sustentation   *suhs* ten TAY
   shuhn
Sutri   SOO tri
swaddle   SWAHD 'l
swaddler   SWAHD lur
swaddling   SWAHD ling
Swahili   swah HEE li
swastika   SWAHS ti kuh
Swedenborg   SWEE d'n bawrg
Swithin   SWITH in, -uhn
sycamine   SIK uh min,
   -mighn
sycamore   SIK uh mor, -mawr
Sychar   SIGH kar
Sychem   SIGH kem
Sychemite   SIGH kem ight
sycomore   SIK uh mor, -mawr
Syelus   sigh EE luhs
Syene   sigh EE ni
syllogism   SIL o jiz 'm, SIL uh-
Sylvester   sil VES tur
sylvestrian   sil VES tri uhn
symbiosis   *sim* bi O sis, -suhs
symbol   SIM buhl, -b'l
symbolism   SIM b'l iz 'm

symbolum   SIM bo luhm
Symbolum Quicunque   SIM bo
   luhm   qwi KUHNG kwi
Symeon   SIM i uhn
Symmachus   SIM uh kuhs
synagogue   SIN uh gahg, -gawg
synapte   si NAP ti
synaxarion   *sin* aks AY ri ahn,
   -ER i ahn
synaxis   si NAK sis
syncretism   SING kri tiz 'm,
   SIN-
syndic   SIN dik
syndicalism   SIN di k'l iz 'm
synedrian   si NED ri uhn
synergism   SIN ur jiz 'm, si
   NUR-
Synesius   si NEE shi uhs,
   -shuhs
Synnada   SIN uh dah
synod   SIN uhd
synodal   SIN uhd uhl
synodical   si NAHD i k'l
synodicon   si NAHD i kahn
synoptic   si NAHP tik
syntercsis   *sin* tur EE sis, suhs
synthesis   SIN thuh sis, -suhs
synthronus   SIN thro nuhs
Syntiche, Syntyche   SIN ti *kee*
synusiast   si NYOO zi ast
Synzygus   SIN zuh guhs
Syracuse   SIR uh *kyoos*, -*kyooz*
Syria   SIR i uh
Syriac   SIR i ak
Syriadamascus   *sir* i uh duh
   MAS kuhs

KEY: bee, bit, bet, bay, bat, boot, butcher, bone, saw, ah, turn, uh huh, sigh,
cow, boy, thin, th in then, shoe, zh in azure, chop. sing, hw in when.

Syria-Maachah   *sir* i uh MAY uh kuh
Syrian   SIR i uhn
Syro-Chaldaean   SIGH ro kal DEE uhn, SIR o-
Syrophenician, Syrophoenician   *sigh* ro fi NISH uhn, *sir* o-
Syrtis   SUR tis, -tuhs
syzygus, Syzygus   SIZ uh guhs
syzygy   SIZ uh ji

Taanach   TAY uh nak
Taanath-Shiloh   TAY uh nath SHIGH lo
Tabbaoth, Tabaoth   tuh BAY ahth, TAB ay oth
Tabbath   TAB uhht
Tabeal   TAY bi uhl
Tabeel   TAY bi el, -uhl
Tabellius   tuh BEL i uhs
Taber   TAY bur
Taberah   TAB uh ruh, ta BEE ruh, tuh-
tabernacle   TAB ur *nak* 'l
Tabitha   TAB uh thuh
taboo   ta BOO, tuh-
Tabor   TAY bur
Taborite   TAY bur ight
Tabret   TAB ret, -rit, -ruht
Tabrimmon   TAB ri mahn, tab RIM uhn
tabula   TAB yu luh
tabula rasa   TAB yu luh RAY suh
tache   TACH
Taché   tah SHAY

Tachmonite   TAK mo night, -muh night
Tadmor   TAD mawr, -mor
Tahan   TAY han
Tahanite   TAY huhn ight
Tahapanes   tuh HAP uh neez
Tahash   TAY hash
Tahath   TAY hath
Tahchemonite   ta KEE muh night, TAH ki mahn ight
Tahpanhes   TAH puhn heez, tah PAN heez
Tahpenes   TAH pi neez, tah PEE neez
Tahrea   TAH ri uh
Tahtim-Hodshi   *tah* tim HAHD shi
Tait   TAYT
talent   TAL ent, -uhnt
talitha cumi   TAL i thuh KOO mi
Talleyrand-Perigord   TAL i rand PER i gawrd, -gord
Tallis, Tally, Talys   TAL is
Talmai   TAL migh, -may igh
Talmage   TAL mayj, maj
Talmon   TAL mahn
Talmud   TAL muhd
Talmudic   tal MUHD ik
Talmudist   TAL muhd ist
Talsas   TAL sas
Tamah   TAY muh
Tamar   TAY mur, -mahr
tamarisk   TAM uh risk
Tamil   TAM il, -uhl
Tammuz   TAM uhz, TA mooz

KEY: b*ee*, b*i*t, b*e*t, b*ay*, b*a*t, b*oo*t, b*u*tcher, b*o*ne, s*aw*, *ah*, t*ur*n, *uh* h*uh*, s*igh*, c*ow*, b*oy*, *th*in, *th* in *th*en, *sh*oe, *zh* in a*z*ure, *ch*op, si*ng*, *hw* in *wh*en.

Tanach (Biblical)   TAY nak
tanach, tanak (Hebrew acrostic)
  tah NAHK
Tanchelmian   tang KEL mi
  uhn
Tancred   TANG kred, -krid
Tanhumeth   tan HYOO meth,
  -muhth
Tannenbaum   TAN uhn bahm,
  -bowm
Tanquelmian   tang KEL mi
  uhn
tanto   TAHN to
Tantum Ergo   TAN tuhm UR
  go
Taoism   DOW iz 'm, TOW-
tapestry   TAP uhs tri
Taphath   TAY fath
Taphnes   TAF neez
Taphon   TAY fahn
Tappuah   ta PYOO uh, TAP
  yu uh
Tarah   TAY ruh, TER uh
Taralah   TAR uh lah
tardo   TAHR do
Tarea   TAY ri uh, tuh REE uh
tares   TERZ
Targum   TAHR guhm, tahr
  GOOM
Tarpelite   TAHR puh light
Tarragona   tah rah GO nuh
Tarshish   TAHR shish
Tarsus   TAHR suhs
Tartak   TAHR tak
Tartan   TAHR tan, -tuhn
Tasso   TAS o

Tatian   TAY shi uhn, -shuhn
Tatianist   TAY shuhn ist, -uhst
Tatnai   TAT nigh, -nay igh
Tattam   TAT uhm
Tattenai   TAT uh nigh
tau   TAW, TOW
Tauler   TOW lur
taurobolium   *taw* ro BO li uhm
tautology   taw TAHL o ji, -uh
  ji
tav   TAHV
taw   TOW
Tchaikovsky   chigh KAHF ski
teat   TEET
Tebah   TEE buh
Tebaliah   *teb* uh LIGH uh, ti
  BAL yuh
Tebeth   tay VAYTH
Te Deum   tee DEE uhm, tay
  DAY oom
Tehaphnehes   ti HAF nuh
  heez, tuh-
Tehinnah   ti HIN uh, tuh-
te igitur   tee IJ uh tur, tay IG
  i toor
Teil   TEEL
Teind   TEEND
tekel   TEE kuhl
Tekoa   ti KO uh
Tekoite   ti KO ight
Tel-Abib (Biblical)   tel AY bib
Tel-Abib, Tel-Aviv (Modern)
  tel uh VEEV
Telah   TEE luh
Telaim   ti LAY im, tuh-
Telassar   ti LAS ur

KEY: b*ee*, b*i*t, b*e*t, b*ay*, b*a*t, b*oo*t, b*u*tcher, b*o*ne, s*aw*, *ah*, t*ur*n, *uh* h*uh*, s*igh*,
c*ow*, b*oy*, *th*in, *th* in *th*en, *sh*oe, *zh* in a*z*ure, *ch*op, si*ng*, *hw* in *wh*en.

telegnosis *tel* eg NO sis, -suhs
Telem TEE lem, -luhm
Telemachus ti LEM uh kuhs,
  tuh-
teleology *tel* i AHL o ji, -uh ji,
  tee li-
telepathy tuh LEP uh thi
Tel-Haresha *tel* huh REE
  shuh
Tel-Harsa *tel* HAHR suh
Tel-Harsha *tel* HAHR shuh
Telinga te LING guh, tuh-
Tell el-Amarna *tel el* uh
  MAHR nuh
Tel-Melah *tel* MEE luh
Telos TEE lahs
tema TEE muh
Temah TEE muh
Teman TEE muhn
Temani TEM uh ni, TEE muh
  ni
Temanite TEE muhn ight
Temeni TEM uh ni, TEE
  muh ni
temperance TEM pur uhns,
  -pruhns
Templar TEM plur
temple TEM p'l
tempo TEM po
temporale *tem* po RAY li
temptation temp TAY shuhn
Tenebrae TEN uh *bree*
Tenison TEN i suhn, -uh suhn
Tennent TEN uhnt
Tenney TEN i
tenon TEN uhn

Teocalli *tee* o KAL i, *tay* o
  KAHL yi
Tephillin te FIL in
Tephon TEE fahn
Terah TEE ruh, -rah
teraphim TER uh fim
terce TURS
terebinth TER uh binth
Teresa tuh REE suh
Teresh TEE resh
Teresian tuh REE shuhn,
  -zhuhn
terminism TUR muhn iz 'm
Tersanctus tur SANGK tuhs
Tersteegen ter STAY guhn
tertia TUR shi uh
tertiary TUR shi *er* i, -shuh ri
Tertius TUR shi uhs
Tertullian tur TUHL i uhn
Tertullus tur TUHL uhs
Testament TES tuh ment,
  -muhnt
Teta TEE tuh
teth TETH, TAYTH
Tetragrammaton *tet* ruh
  GRAM uh tahn
tetrapolitan *tet* ruh PAHL uh
  tuhn
tetrarch TEE trahrk, TET
  rahrk
tetrastyle TET ruh stighl
tetter TET ur
Tetzel TET suhl
Tewkesbury TYOOKS bur i
text TEKST
textual TEKS chu uhl, -tyu uhl

KEY: b*ee*, b*i*t, b*e*t, b*ay*, b*a*t, b*oo*t, b*u*tcher, b*o*ne, s*aw*, *ah*, t*ur*n, *uh* h*uh*, s*igh*,
c*ow*, b*oy*, *th*in, ŧħ in *th*en, *sh*oe, *zh* in a*z*ure, *ch*op, si*ng*, *hw* in *wh*en.

textus TEKS tuhs
textus receptus -ri SEP tuhs
Tezel TET suhl
Thacher THACH ur
Thaddaeus THAD i uhs
Thahash THAY hash
Thales THAY leez
Thamah THAY muh
Thamar THAY mahr
Thammuz THAM uhz
Thamnatha THAM nuh thuh
thanatism THAN uh tiz 'm
Thanksgiving *thangks* GIV ing
Thara THAY ruh, THAR uh
Tharra THAR uh
Tharshish THAHR shish
Thassi THAS igh
thaumaturgy THAW muh *tur* ji
theandric thi AN drik
Theatine THEE uh tin, -tuhn
Thebes THEEBZ
Thebez THEE beez
Theca THEE kuh
Thecla THEK luh
Thecoe thi KO i
Theiner TIGH nur
theism THEE iz 'm
theistic thi IS tik
Thelasar thi LAY sur, thu-
Thelersas thi LUR sas, thuh LUR suhs
Theman THEE man
Themistian thi MIS ti uhn
Theobald THEE o bawld
Theocanus thi AHK uh nuhs

theocracy thi AHK ruh si
theocratic *thee* o KRAT ik
theodicy thi AHD uh si
Theodora *thee* o DO ruh, -DAWR uh
Theodore THEE o dor, -dawr
Theodoret thi AHD uh ret
Theodoric thi AHD uh rik
Theodosian *thee* o DO shuhn
Theodosius *thee* o DO shuhs, -shi uhs
Theodotian *thee* o DO shuhn
Theodotion *thee* o DO shuhn, -shi uhn
Theodotus thi AHD uh tuhs
theogony thi AHG uh ni
Theologal thi AHL o gal
theologian *thee* o LO juhn
theological *thee* o LAHJ i kuhl
theology thi AHL o ji, -uh ji
theomancy THEE o *man* si
Theon THEE ahn
Theopaschite *thee* o PAS kight
theopathetic *thee* o puh THET ik
theopathy thi AHP uh thi
theophany thi AHF uh ni
theophilanthropist *thee* o fi LAN thro pist
Theophilus thi AHF uh luhs
theorem THEE o ruhm, THIR uhm
theosophy thi AHS o fi, -uh fi
Theotocos, Theotokos thi AHT o kahs
Theras THEE ras

KEY: b*ee*, b*i*t, b*e*t, b*a*y, b*a*t, b*oo*t, b*u*tcher, b*o*ne, s*aw*, *ah*, t*ur*n, *uh* h*u*h, s*igh*,
c*ow*, b*oy*, *th*in, ŧħ in *th*en, *sh*oe, *zh* in a*z*ure, *ch*op, si*ng*, *hw* in *wh*en.

Theresa   tuh REE suh
Thermeleth   THUR mi leth,
  -muh leth
Thessalonians   *thes* uh LO ni
  uhns
Thessalonica   *thes* uh lo NIGH
  kuh
thetics   THET iks
Theudas   THYOO duhs
theurgy   thi UR ji
Thierry   ti ER i, tyay REE
Thiers   TYER, ti ER
Thimnathah   THIM nuh thah
Thionville   tyawn VEEL
Thirlwall   THURL wawl
Thisbe   THIZ bi
Thocanus   tho KAY nuhs
Tholuck   TO luk
Thomas   TAHM uhs
Thomei   THAHM i igh
Thomist   TO mist
Thomoi   THAHM o igh
Thondracian   thahn DRAY
  shuhn
Thondraki   thahn DRAK i
Thondrakian   thahn DRAK i
  uhn
Thracia   THRAY shi uh, -shuh
Thracian   THRAY shuhn
Thrasaeus, Thraseus   thray SEE
  uhs
thresh   THRESH
thrum   THRUHM
thumbstall   THUHM *stawl,*
  -stahl
Thummim   THUHM im

thurible   THYOO ruh b'l
thurifer   THYOO ruh fur
Thuringia   thyu RIN ji uh, thu-
Thyatira   *thigh* uh TIGH ruh
thyine   THIGH in
tiara   tigh ER uh, ti AHR uh
Tiberias   tigh BIR i uhs
Tiberius   tigh BIR i uhs
Tibhath   TIB hath
tibia   TIB i uh
Tibni   TIB nigh
tidal   TIGH dal, -duhl
tierce   TIRS, TEERS
Tiglath-Pileser   *tig* lath puh
  LEE zur
Tigré   tee GRAY
Tigris   TIGH gris
Tikvah   TIK vah
Tikvath   TIK vath
Tilgath-Pilneser   *til* gath pil
  NEE zur
Tillemont   tee MAWN, -MON
Tillich   TIL ik
Tillotson   TIL uht suhn
Tilon   TIGH lahn
Timaeus   ti MEE uhs
timbre   TIM bur
timbrel   TIM bruhl
Timna, Timnah   TIM nuh
Timnath   TIM nath
Timnathah   TIM nuh thah
Timnath-Heres   *tim* nath HEE
  reez, -rez
Timnath-Serah   *tim* nath SEE
  ruh
Timnite   TIM night

KEY: b*ee*, b*i*t, b*e*t, b*a*y, b*a*t, b*oo*t, b*u*tcher, b*o*ne, s*aw*, *ah*, t*ur*n, *uh* h*uh*, s*igh*,
c*ow*, b*oy*, *th*in, *th* in *th*en, *sh*oe, *zh* in a*z*ure, *ch*op, si*ng*, *hw* in *wh*en.

Timon TIGH mahn
Timothean ti MO thi uhn
Timotheus ti MO thi uhs
Timothy TIM uh thi
tinction TINGK shuhn
Tindal, Tindall TIN duhl
Tintern TIN turn
Tiphsah TIF suh
tippet TIP et, -uht
tipstaff TIP staf
Tiras TIGH ras, -ruhs
Tirathite TIGH ruhth ight
Tirhakah TUR huh kah, tur
  HAY
Tirhana, Tirhanah TUR huh
  nah, tur HAY-
Tiria TIR i uh, TIGH ri uh
Tirshatha tur SHAY thuh,
  TUR shuh thuh
Tirzah TUR zuh
Tischendorf TISH uhn dorf,
  -dawrf
Tishbe TISH bi
Tishbite TISH bight
Tishri TISH ri
Tisri TIZ ri
Titan TIGH t'n
tithe TIGHTH
Titius Justus TISH uhs JUHS
  tuhs
tittle TIT'l
titular TIT chu lur, -tyu lur
titulus TIT chu luhs, -tyu luhs
Titus TIGH tuhs
Titus Justus TIGH tuhs
  JUHS tuhs

Titus Manius TIGH tuhs
  MAY ni uhs
Tizite TIGH zight
Toah TO uh
Tob TAHB, TOB
Tob-Adonijah tahb ad uh
  NIGH juh, tob-
Tobiah to BIGH uh
Tobias to BIGH uhs
Tobie TO bi
Tobiel to BIGH uhl, TO bi
  el
Tobijah to BIGH juh
Tobit TO bit, -buht
Tochen TO ken
Togarmah to GAHR muh
Toggenburg TAWG uhn
  boork
Tohoroth to ho ROTH
Tohu TO hyoo
Toi TO igh, -i
Tokhath TAHK hath
Tola TO luh
Tolad TO lad
Tolaite TO lay ight
Toland TO luhnd
Tolbanes TAHL buh neez,
  tahl BAY neez
Toledo to LEE do
Tolstoy TOL stoy
tomb TOOM
tome TOM
Tongan TAHN guhn
tongs TAHNGZ, TAWNGZ
tonsure TAHN shur
Tooke TOOK

KEY: bee, bit, bet, bay, bat, boot, butcher, bone, saw, ah, turn, uh huh, sigh,
cow, boy, thin, th in then, shoe, zh in azure, chop, sing, hw in when.

toparchy   TO pahr ki, TAHP ahr ki

topaz   TO paz

Tophel   TO fel

Tophet, Topheth   TO fet

Torah   TO ruh, TAWR uh

Tordesillas   tor de SEEL yahs, tawr-

Torgau   TOR gow, TAWR-

Tormah   TAWR muh

torment   TAWR ment (n.), tawr MENT (v.)

Torquemada   tor kuh MAH duh, tawr-

Tortosa   tor TO suh, tawr-

Tosefta, Tosephta   to SEF tuh

totemism   TO tuhm iz 'm

Tou   TO oo

Toulouse   too LOOZ

Tours   TOOR

Toynbee   TOYN bi

trachonitis   trak o NIGH tuhs, trak uh-

Tractarianism   trak TER i uhn iz 'm

tractator   trak TAY tur

tradition   truh DISH uhn

traditor   TRAD i tor, -tawr

traducianism   tra DYOO shuhn iz 'm, truh DOO-

tragacanth   TRAG uh kanth

Trajan   TRAY juhn

Trani   TRAH ni

transcendent   tran SEN dent, -duhnt

transcendentalism   tran sen DEN tuhl iz 'm, tran suhn-

transenna   tran SEN uh

transfiguration   trans fig yu RAY shuhn

transgression   trans GRESH uhn, tranz-

translation   trans LAY shuhn, tranz-

transmigration   trans migh GRAY shuhn, tranz-

transubstantiation   tran suhb stan shi AY shuhn

Trappist   TRAP ist, -uhst

travail   TRAV ayl, -'l

Treacle   TREE k'l

treble   TREB 'l

Tregelles   tre GEL uhs

Trelawney   tre LAW ni

tremolo   TREM uh lo

Trendelenburg   TREN duhl uhn burg

Trent   TRENT

trental   TREN tuhl, -t'l

trephine   tri FIGHN, -FEEN

trespass   TRES puhs, -pas

Trèves   TREEVZ

tribulation   trib yu LAY shuhn

Tribur   TREE bur

tricerion   trigh SEE ri ahn

trichotomy   trigh KAHT uh mi

triclinium   trigh KLIN i uhm

Tridentine   trigh DEN tin, -tighn

Trier   TRIGH ur

trigon   TRIGH gahn

trikerion   trigh KEE ri ahn
Trine   TRIGHN
Trinitarian   trin uh TER i uhn
Trinity   TRIN i ti, -uh ti
triodion   trigh O di ahn
Tripolis   TRIP o lis, -uh luhs
triptych   TRIP tik
triquetral   trigh KWEE truhl,
    -KWET ruhl
trisacramentarian   trigh *sak* ruh
    men TER i uhn
Trisagion   tris AG i ahn, tris
    AY gi ahn
tritheist   TRIGH thi ist
trito-   TRIGH to-, TREE-
Triune   TRIGH oon
trivium   TRIV i uhm
Troas   TRO as
Troeltsch   TRELCH
Trogyllium   tro JIL i uhm, tro
    GIL-
troparion   tro PAY ri ahn
trope   TROP
Trophimus   TRAHF i muhs,
    -uh muhs
tropological   *trahp* o LAHJ i
    kuhl, *trahp* uh-
troppo   TRAWP o, TROP o
troth   TRAHTH, TRAWTH
trow   TRO
Troyes   TRWAH, TROYZ
Trullan   TRUHL uhn
trump   TRUHMP
Truro   TROO ro
Tryphaena, Tryphena   trigh
    FEE nuh

Tryphon   TRIGH fahn
Tryphosa   trigh FO suh
Tsadhe   tsah THAY, TSAH
    thay
Tschaikowsky   chigh KAHF ski
Tubal   TYOO buhl, TOO-
Tubal-Cain   TYOO buhl *kayn*,
    TOO-
Tubias   TYOO bi uhs, TOO-
Tubieni   *tyoo* bi EE ni, *too*-
Tübingen   TOO bing uhn,
    TUR-
tuism   TYOO iz 'm, TOO-
Tunstall   TUHN stuhl
Tulchan   TUHL kan, -kuhn
Tulchin   TUHL kin, -kuhn
tumbler   TUHM blur
tunic   TYOO nik, TOO-
tunicle   TYOO ni k'l, TOO-
Tunker   TUHNGK ur
Turin   TYOO rin, tyu RIN
Turlupin   TUR lyu pin, -luh
    pin
Turretini   *toor* et TEE ni
Tutiorism   TYOO shi ur iz 'm,
    TOO
Tyana   TIGH uh nuh
Tychicus   TIK i kuhs
tychism   TIGH kiz 'm
Tyndale   TIN duhl
typicon   TIP i kahn
typicum   TIP i kuhm
typology   tigh PAHL o ji, -uh
    ji
Tyrannus   tigh RAN uhs
Tyre   TIGHR

KEY: b*ee*, b*i*t, b*e*t, b*a*y, b*a*t, b*oo*t, b*u*tcher, b*o*ne, s*aw*, *ah*, t*ur*n, *uh* h*uh*, s*igh*,
c*ow*, b*oy*, *th*in, *th* in *th*en, *sh*oe, *zh* in a*z*ure, *ch*op, si*ng*, *hw* in *wh*en.

Tyrian   TIR i uhn
Tyropoeon   *tigh* ro PEE ahn,
   -uhn
Tyrus   TIGH ruhs
Tzaddi   tsah DEE, TSAH di

Ubbonite   UHB ahn ight
ubiety   yu BIGH uh ti
ubiquitarian   yu *bik* wuh TER i
   uhn
Ucal   YOO kal
Udall   YOO dal, -duhl
Ueberweg   OO bur veg
Uel   YOO el, -uhl
Ugarit   YOO gur it
Ugaritic   *yoo* guh RIT ik
Ugolino della Gherardesca   *oo*
   go LEE no   *del* uh   *gay* rahr
   DES kuh
Uhland   OO lahnt, OO land
Uhlich   OO lik
Uknaz   UHK naz
Ulai   YOO ligh, -lay igh
Ulam   YOO lam, -luhm
Ulfilas   UHL fuh las
Ulla   UHL uh
Ullmann   OOL mahn
Ulphilas   UHL fuh las
Ulrich   UHL rik
Ulrici   ool REET si
Ulster   UHL stur
ultramontanist   *uhl* truh
   MAHN tuh nist
umbraculum   uhm BRAK yu
   luhm
Ummah   UHM uh

Unam Sanctam   YOO nuhm
   SANGK tuhm
unanimism   yu NAN uh miz 'm
uncial   UHN shi uhl, -shuhl
unction   UHNGK shuhn
Uniat   YOO ni at, -uht
Uniate   YOO ni ayt
unicorn   YOO ni kawrn
Unigenitus   *yoo* ni JEN i tuhs,
   -uh tuhs
Unitarianism   *yoo* nuh TER i
   uhn iz 'm
Unitas Fratrum   YOO ni tas
   FRAY truhm, YOO ni tahs
   FRAH truhm
unitive   YOO nuh tiv
Universalism   *yoo* nuh VUR
   suhl iz 'm
Unni   UHN igh
Unno   UHN o
upbraid   uhp BRAYD
Upham   UHP uhm
upharsin   yu FAHR sin, -suhn
Uphaz   YOO faz
Upsala   UHP *sah* luh
Ur   UR
Urban   UR buhn
urbane   ur BAYN
Urbanus   ur BAY nuhs
Urbino   ur BEE no
Urcicinus   *ur* suh SIGH nuhs
Urgel   oor HEL, -GEL
Uri   YOO righ
Uriah   yu RIGH uh
Urias   yu RIGH uhs
Uriel   YOO ri el, -uhl

KEY: b*ee*, b*i*t, b*e*t, b*ay*, b*a*t, b*oo*t, b*u*tcher, b*o*ne, s*aw*, *ah*, t*ur*n, *uh* h*uh*, s*igh*,
c*ow*, b*oy*, *th*in, *th* in *th*en, *sh*oe, *zh* in a*zh*ure, *ch*op, si*ng*, *hw* in *wh*en.

Urijah yu RIGH juh
Urim YOO rim
Urmarcus oor MAHR kuhs, ur-
Ursicinus *ur* suh SIGH nuhs
Ursinus ur SIGH nuhs
Ursula UR syu luh, -suh luh
Ursuline UR syu lin, -suh lin,
 -lighn
Usager YOOZ ij ur
Ushabti yu SHAB ti
Ushebti yu SHEB ti
Ussher UHSH ur
usury YOO zhur i
Uta YOO tuh
Uthai YOO thigh, -thay igh
Uthi YOO thigh
Utica YOO ti kuh
utilitarianism yu *til* uh TER i
 uhn iz 'm
Utopian yu TO pi uhn
Utraquism YOO truh kwiz 'm
Utrecht YOO trekt
Uz UHZ
Uzai YOO zigh, -zay igh
Uzal YOO zal, -zuhl
Uzza UHZ uh
Uzzah UHZ uh
Uzzen-Sheerah UHZ uhn
 SHEE ruh
Uzzi UHZ igh
Uzzia uh ZIGH uh
Uzziah uh ZIGH uh
Uzziel uh ZIGH uhl, UHZ i
 el, -uhl
Uzzielite uh ZIGH uhl ight,
 uhz i EE light

vaccary VAK uh ri
vachery VASH ur i
vade mecum *vay* di MEE
 kuhm
Vagi VAY jigh
Vaheb VAY heb
Vaizatha VIGH zuh thuh, vay
 IZ uh thuh
Vajezatha vuh JEZ uh thuh,
 vaj uh ZAY thuh
Valdes vahl DAYS, VAL dez
Valence vah LONS
Valencia vuh LEN shi uh
Valens VAY luhnz
Valentia vuh LEN shi uh
Valentine VAL uhn tighn
Valentinian *val* uhn TIN i uhn
Valentinus *val* uhn TIGH
 nuhs
Valerian vuh LEE ri uhn, vuh
 LER i uhn
Valla VAHL uh
Valladolid *val* uh do LID
Vallombrosan *val* ahm BRO
 suhn
Vallumbrosan *val* uhm BRO
 suhn
Vandal VAN duhl
Van Dyck, Vandyke van
 DIGHK
Vaniah vuh NIGH uh
Vanini vah NEE ni
Vanist VAN ist, -uhst
Vannes VAHN
Van Rensselaer van REN suh
 lur

Vashni   VASH nigh
Vashti   VASH tigh
vassal   VAS uhl
Vassar   VAS uhr
Vassy   vah SEE
Vatican   VAT i kuhn
Vaughan   VAWN, VAHN
vaunt   VAWNT
vav   VAHV
Vedan   VE dan, -duhn
veneration   *ven* ur AY shuhn
venial   VEE ni uhl
venite   vi NIGH ti, ve NEE
   tay
Vercelli   ver CHEL i
verdigris   VUR di grees, -gris
verdour   VUR door
Verdun   ver DUHN, vur-
verge   VURJ
verger   VUR jur
vernacle   VUR nuh k'l
vernacular   vur NAK yu lur
Verneuil   ver NEY
Verona   vuh RO nuh
Veronica   vuh RAHN i kuh
verset   VUR set, -sit, -suht, vur
   SET
versicle   VUR si k'l
Vespasian   ves PAY zhi uhn,
   -zhuhn
vesper   VES pur
vesperal   VES pur uhl
vesperale   *ves* pur AY li
vestal   VES tuhl, -t'l
vestiarian   *ves* ti ER i uhn
vestibule   VES tuh byool

vestment   VEST ment, -muhnt
vestry   VES tri
Veuillot   vi YO
vexation   veks AY shuhn
Vexilla regis prodeunt   vek SIL
   uh REE jis   PRO di uhnt
vexillum   vek SIL uhm
Vezelay   vayz LAY
Via Dolorosa   VIGH uh *dahl*
   uh RO suh, VEE uh   *do* lo
   RO suh
vial   VIGH uhl
viaticum   vigh AT i kuhm
vicar   VIK ur
vicarious   vigh KER i uhs
Vico   VEE ko
Victoria   vik TO ri uh, vik
   TAWR i uh
Victorine   VIK to *reen*, -tawr
   een
victual   VIT 'l
Vienne   VYEN
vigil   VIJ uhl
Vigilius   vi JIL i uhs
vile   VIGHL
Villanova   vil uh NO vuh
Villars   vee LAHR
Villegaignon   veel gay
   NYAWN, -NYON
Villeneuve   veel NEV
Villiers   VIL yurz
Vincent   VIN suhnt
Vincentian   vin SEN shuhn
Vinci, da   duh VIN chi
Vinet   vee NAY
viper   VIGH pur

KEY: bee, bit, bet, bay, bat, boot, butcher, bone, saw, ah, turn, uh huh, sigh,
cow, boy, thin, th in then, shoe, zh in azure, chop, sing, hw in when.

virgin   VUR jin, -juhn
virtualism   VUR chu uhl iz 'm,
   VUR tyu-
virtuoso   *vur* chu O so, *vur* tyu-
Visconti   vis KAHN ti
visitant   VIZ uh tuhnt
Visser 't Hooft   VIS ur *tuft*,
   -*tooft*
Vitalis   vigh TAY lis, -luhs
Vitellius   vi TEL i uhs
Vitus   VIGH tuhs
vivace   vi VAH chay
Vivaldi   vi VAHL di
Vladimir   VLA duh mir, -mur
Vogel   FO guhl, VO-
volition   vo LISH uhn
volo   VO lo
volow   VUL o
Voltaire   vahl TER
voluntary   VAHL un *ter* i, -tur i
Vophsi   VAHF sigh
Voss   FAHS
Vossius   VAHS i uhs
vota   VO tuh
votive   VO tiv
vox humana   VAHKS hyu
   MAY nuh, -MAH nuh
Vulgate   VUHL gayt

Wace   WAHS, WAYS
wadi, wady   WAH di
wafer   WAY fur
Wagner (Wilhelm Richard)
   VAHG nur
Waheb   WAY heb
Waite   WAYT

wake   WAYK
Walafrid Strabo   WAHL uh
   frid STRAY bo
Walburga   wawl BUR guh
Walch   VAHLCH
Waldenses   wahl DEN seez
Waldensian   wahl DEN si uhn,
   -shuhn
Waldo   WAHL do, vahl DO
Wallachian   wah LAY ki uhn
Walloon   wah LOON
Walpurgis   vahl POOR gis
Walther   VAHL tur
Wartburg   VAHRT boorg,
   WAWRT burg
wassail   WAHS 'l, -ayl
waw   WAW, WOW
Weiss   VIGHS, WIGHS
Wellhausen   VEL how zuhn
wen   WEN
Wenceslas, Wenceslaus   WEN
   suhs lahs
Wesley   WES li
Wesleyan   WES li uhn, WEZ-
Wessel   VES uhl
Westcott   WEST kaht
Westeras   VES tur ahs
Westminster   WEST *min* stur
Westphal   WEST fawl
Westphalia   west FAY li uh
Wette   VET uh, WET uh
Wexford   WEKS furd
Weymouth   WAY muhth
Whately   HWAYT li
whelp   HWELP
Whewell   HYOO uhl

KEY: b*ee*, b*i*t, b*e*t, b*ay*, b*a*t, b*oo*t, b*u*tcher, b*o*ne, s*aw*, *ah*, t*ur*n, *uh* h*uh*, s*igh*,
c*ow*, b*oy*, *th*in, *th* in *th*en, *sh*oe, *zh* in a*zh*ure, *ch*op, si*ng*, *hw* in *wh*en.

Whiston HWIS tuhn
Whistonian hwis TO ni uhn
Whitgift HWIT gift
Whitsunday HWIT *suhn* di,
-suhn *day*
Whitsuntide HWIT suhn
tighd
Wicliff WIK lif
Wieman WIGH muhn
Wilbrord WIL brawrd
Wilfrid WIL frid, -fruhd
Willibald WIL i bawld
Willibrord WIL i brawrd
wimple WIM p'l
Winchelsea WIN chuhl si
Windisch VIN dish
Windthorst VINT horst
winebibber WIGHN *bib* ur
Winifred WIN uh fred, -fruhd
winnow WIN o
Wishart WISH ahrt
wist WIST
witch WICH
Wittenberg WIT uhn burg,
VIT uhn berk
Wittgenstein VIT guhn stighn
Wolfenbuttel VOLF uhn *byoo*
tuhl
Wolsey WUL zi
wont WUHNT, WAWNT,
WONT, WAHNT
Worcester WUS tur
Worms WURMZ, VAWRMS
worship WUR ship, -shuhp
wot WAHT
wrath RATH

wrest REST
wroth RAHTH, RAWTH
wrought RAWT
Wulfric WUL frik
Wulfstan WULF stan
Wulstan WUL stan
Wundt VOONT
Wurtemberg VOORT uhm
berk, WURT uhm burg
Wycliffe WIK lif
Wynfrith WIN frith

Xanthicus ZAN thi kuhs
Xavier ZAY vi ur, ZAV i ur
Xenocrates zi NAHK ruh teez
Xenophanes zi NAHF uh neez
Xerxes ZURK seez
Ximenes hi MAY nays

Yah YAH
Yahweh YAH way, -we
Yahwism YAH wiz 'm
Yaveh YAH vay, -ve
yea YAY
Yeomans YO muhnz
yew YOO
Yigdal yig DAHL, YIG dahl
Yiron yi RAHN, -RON
yodh YOTH, YOD
Yom Kippur YAHM KIP ur,
YOM ki POOR
Yom Teruah YAHM TER u
uh, YOM-
Yom Tob YAHM TOB,
YOM TOV
Yule YOOL

KEY: b*ee*, b*i*t, b*e*t, b*ay*, b*a*t, b*oo*t, b*u*tcher, b*o*ne, s*aw*, *ah*, t*ur*n, *uh* h*uh*, s*igh*,
c*ow*, b*oy*, *th*in, *th* in *th*en, *sh*oe, *zh* in a*zh*ure, *ch*op, si*ng*, *hw* in *wh*en.

Yves EEV
Yves d'Evreux eev dayv RUR,
-ROO

Zaanaim *zay* uh NAY im
Zaanan ZAY uh nan
Zaanannim *zay* uh NAN im
Zaavan ZAY uh van
Zabad ZAY bad
Zabadaean, Zabadean *zab* uh
DEE uhn
Zabadaias *zab* uh DAY yuhs
Zabadeas *zab* uh DEE uhs
Zabbai ZAB ay igh, ZAB igh
Zabbud ZAB uhd
Zabdeus zab DEE uhs
Zabdi ZAB digh
Zabdiel ZAB di el, -uhl
Zabud ZAY buhd
Zabulon ZAB yu lahn
Zaccai ZAK ay igh, ZAK igh
Zacchaeus, Zaccheus za KEE
uhs
Zacchur, Zaccur ZAK ur
Zachariah *zak* uh RIGH uh
Zacharias *zak* uh RIGH uhs
Zachary ZAK uh ri
Zacher ZAY kur
Zadok ZAY dahk
Zaham ZAY ham
Zahn TSAHN, ZAHN
Zain ZAH in
Zair ZAY ir, -ur
Zakkur ZAK ur
Zalaph ZAY laf
Zalmon ZAL mahn, -muhn

Zalmonah zal MO nuh
Zalmunna, Zalmunnah zal
MUHN uh
Zambis ZAM bis, -buhs
Zambri ZAM brigh
Zamoth ZAY mahth, -moth
Zamzummim zam ZUHM
im
Zanoah za NO uh, zuh-
Zaphenath-Paneah zaf EE
nath pan EE uh
Zaphnath-Paaneah ZAF nath
pay uh NEE uh
Zaphon ZAY fahn
Zara ZAY ruh
Zaraces ZAR uh seez, ZER-
Zarah ZAY ruh
Zaraias zuh RAY yuhs, -RIGH
uhs
Zarakes ZAR uh keez, ZER-
Zarathustra *zar* uh THOOS
truh, *zar*
Zardeus zahr DEE uhs
Zareah ZAY ri uh, zuh REE uh
Zareathite ZAY ri uhth ight,
zuh REE-
Zared ZAY red
Zarephath ZAR i fath, -uh fath,
ZER-
Zaretan ZAR i tan, -uh tan,
ZER-
Zarethan ZAR i than, ZER uh
than
Zareth-Shahar *zay* reth SHAY
hahr
Zarhite ZAHR hight

KEY: bee, bit, bet, bay, bat, boot, butcher, bone, saw, ah, turn, uh huh, sigh,
cow, boy, thin, th in then, shoe, zh in azure, chop, sing, hw in when.

Zartanah   zahr TAY nuh,
ZAHR tuh nah
Zarthan   ZAHR than
Zathoe   ZATH o i, zuh THO i
Zathui   zuh THYOO i,
-THOO i
Zatthu   ZAT thyu, -thoo
Zatthui   ZAT thyu igh, -thu
igh
Zattu   ZAT yu
Zavan   ZAY van
zayin   ZAH yin
Zaza   ZAY zuh
zealot   ZEL uht
Zebadiah   *zeb* uh DIGH uh
Zebah   ZEE buh
Zebaim   zi BAY im
Zebedee   ZEB uh *dee*
Zebida, Zebidah   zi BIGH duh,
ZEB i duh, -uh duh
Zebina   zi BIGH nuh
Zeboiim   zi BOY im
Zeboim   zi BO im
Zebudah   zi BYOO duh, zi
BOO-
Zebul   ZEE buhl
Zebulonite   ZEB yu luhn ight
Zebulun   ZEB yu luhn
Zebulunite   ZEB yu luhn ight
Zechariah   *zek* uh RIGH uh
Zecher   ZEE kur
Zechrias   zek RIGH uhs
Zedad   ZEE dad
Zedechias   *zed* uh KIGH uhs
Zedekiah   *zed* uh KIGH uh
Zeeb   ZEE eb, ZEEB

Zela, Zelah   ZEE luh
Zelek   ZEE lek
Zelophehad   zi LO fi had, -fuh
had
Zelotes   zi LO teez
Zelzah   ZEL zuh
Zemaraim   *zem* uh RAY im
Zemarite   ZEM uh right
Zemer   ZEM ur
Zemirah   zi MIGH ruh
Zenan   ZEE nan
Zenas   ZEE nuhs
Zeno   ZEE no
Zephaniah   *zef* uh NIGH uh
Zephath   ZEE fath
Zephathah   ZEF uh thuh
Zephi   ZEE figh
Zepho   ZEE fo
Zephon   ZEE fahn
Zephonite   ZEE fahn ight, zi
FO night
Zephyrinus   *zef* uh RIGH nuhs
Zer   ZUR
Zerah   ZEE ruh
Zerahiah   *zer* uh HIGH uh
Zerahite   ZEE ruh hight
Zered   ZEE red
Zereda, Zeredah   ZER i duh,
-uh duh, ze REE duh
Zeredath   ZER uh dath   •
Zeredatha, Zeredathah   *zer* uh
DAY thuh, zi RED uh thuh
Zererah   ZER uh ruh
Zererath   ZER i rath, -uh rath
Zeresh   ZEE resh
Zereth   ZEE reth

KEY: b*ee*, b*i*t, b*e*t, b*ay*, b*a*t, b*oo*t, b*u*tcher, b*o*ne, s*aw*, *ah*, t*ur*n, *uh* h*uh*, s*igh*,
c*ow*, b*oy*, *th*in, *th* in *th*en, *sh*oe, *zh* in a*z*ure, *ch*op, si*ng*, *hw* in *wh*en.

Zereth-Shahar   ZEE reth SHAY
  hahr
Zeri   ZEE righ
Zeror   ZEE rawr
Zeruah   zi ROO uh, zuh-
Zerubbabel   zuh RUHB uh
  buhl
Zeruiah   zer uh IGH uh, zi
  ROO yuh, zuh-
Zetham   ZEE tham, -thuhm
Zethan   ZEE than, -thuhn
Zethar   ZEE thahr
Zeus   ZYOOS, ZOOS
Zia   ZIGH uh
Ziba   ZIGH buh
Zibeon   ZIB i uhn
Zibia, Zibiah   ZIB i uh
Zichri   ZIK righ
Ziddim   ZID im
Zid-Kijah   zid KIGH juh
Zidon   ZIGH duhn, -d'n
Zidonian   zigh DO ni uhn
Zif   ZIF
ziggurat   ZIG u rat, -raht
Ziha   ZIGH huh
Ziklag   ZIK lag
zikurat   ZIK u rat, -raht
Zillah   ZIL uh
Zillerthal   TSIL ur tahl, ZIL ur
  thahl
Zillethai   ZIL i thigh, zil EE
  thay igh
Zilpah   ZIL puh
Zilthai   ZIL thigh, -thay igh
Zimmah   ZIM uh
Zimran   ZIM ran

Zimri   ZIM righ
Zin   ZIN
Zina   ZIGH nuh
Zinzendorf   TSIN tsuhn dorf,
  -dawrf, ZIN zuhn-
Zion   ZIGH uhn
Zior   ZIGH awr
Ziph   ZIF
Ziphah   ZIGH fuh
Ziphim   ZIF im
Ziphion   ZIF i ahn
Ziphite   ZIF ight
Ziphron   ZIF rahn
Zippor   ZIP awr, -ur
Zipporah   zi PO ruh, ZIP o
  ruh, -uh ruh
Zithri   ZITH righ
Ziv   ZIV
Ziz   ZIZ
Ziza, Zizah   ZIGH zuh
Zoan   ZO an
Zoar   ZO ur
Zoba, Zobah   ZO buh
Zobebah   zo BEE buh
Zohar   ZO hahr
Zoheleth   ZO huh leth
Zoheth   ZO heth
Zophah   ZO fuh
Zophai   ZO figh, -fay igh
Zophar   ZO fur
Zophim   ZO fim
Zorah   ZO ruh
Zorathite   ZO rath ight,
  -ruhth ight
Zoreah   ZO ri uh
Zorite   ZO right

KEY: bee, bit, bet, bay, bat, boot, butcher, bone, saw, ah, turn, uh huh, sigh,
cow, boy, thin, th in then, shoe, zh in azure, chop, sing, hw in when.

Zoroastrianism   *zo* ro AS tri uhn
iz 'm, *zawr* o-
Zorababel   zo RAHB uh buhl,
zo RO buh buhl
Zorzelleus   zawr ZEL i uhs
Zosimus   ZAHS i muhs, -uh
muhs
Zuar   ZYOO ur, ZOO ur
zucchetto   tsoo KET o
Zuph   ZUHF

Zur   ZUR
Zurich   ZU rik, TSOO rik
Zuriel   ZYOO ri el, ZOO-
Zurishaddai   *zyoo* ri SHAD ay
igh, *zoo*-, -SHAD igh
Zuzim   ZYOO zim, ZOO-
Zwichau, Zwickau   TSVIK ow,
ZWIK ow
Zwingli   TSVING li, ZWING
li, SWING li

KEY: b*ee*, b*i*t, b*e*t, b*ay*, b*a*t, b*oo*t, b*u*tcher, b*o*ne, s*aw*, *ah*, t*ur*n, *uh* huh, s*igh*,
c*ow*, b*oy*, *th*in, *th* in *th*en, *sh*oe, *zh* in a*z*ure, *ch*op, si*ng*, *hw* in *wh*en.